Germans of Waterloo Region

Village View St. Clements by Peter Etril Snyder 1996 © Cynthia Weber

Edited by

Mathias Schulze
Grit Liebscher
Sebastian Siebel-Achenbach

WATERLOO CENTRE *for*
Germanstudies

Title:
Germans of Waterloo Region / edited by Mathias Schulze, Grit Liebscher, and Sebastian Siebel-Achenbach.

Names:
Schulze, Mathias, 1963- editor. | Liebscher, Grit, 1968- editor. | Siebel-Achenbach, Sebastian, 1958- editor. | Waterloo Centre for German Studies

Description:
Includes bibliographical references.
Text primarily in English with some quotations in German.
Identifiers:
ISBN 9781989048092 (paperback) | ISBN 9781989048108 (hardcover)
ISBN 9781989048115 (ebook) | ISBN 9781989048122 (ebook)

Subjects:
LCSH: Germans--Ontario--Waterloo (Regional Municipality)--History--1938-2011
LCSH: Germans--Ontario--Waterloo (Regional Municipality)--Social conditions--1938-2011
LCSH: Waterloo (Ont. : Regional municipality)--Emigration and immigration--1938-2011
LCGFT: Oral histories

Classification:
FC3100 G3 G47 2022 | LCC F1059 W32 G47 2022 | DDC 971.344

Copyright, 2022:
Waterloo Centre for German Studies (WCGS) wcgs.ca
Department of Germanic and Slavic Studies
University of Waterloo
wcgs@uwaterloo.ca

Editing, design:
Peter Geldart, Danielle Michaud Aubrey
Petra Books | petrabooks.ca
2022

Gill Sans 14, 12, Arial 9, Times New Roman 11/13,
ca. 77,000 words
43 illustrations
206 pages

Front cover: Village View St. Clements by Peter Etril Snyder 1996 © Cynthia Weber.
Back cover: Rosina on the boat from Germany to Montréal Canada in 1960. © Rosina Mühlberghuber.

The best efforts have been made to respect people, organizations and copyright holders. Should you have any questions please contact the publisher. info@petrabooks.ca

Oak leaves.
Artist: Walther Otto Müller, botanist.
In Otto Wilhelm Thomé: *Flora von Deutschland, Österreich und der Schweiz* (1885). http://www.biolib.de

Table of Contents

Preface: Changing Times!

Walter Stechel

In August of 1897 the Toronto-based German Consul came to Berlin/ Ontario (today Kitchener) to assist in unveiling a bust of Kaiser Wilhelm I on top of a peace monument. Today, as Consul General of Germany[1] in Toronto, I am honoured to write a foreword to a collection of essays on the Germans of Waterloo Region. In a way my distant predecessor and I both recognize the German heritage of Waterloo County. But today we commemorate in a different spirit — we do not expect Canadians of German ancestry to put up busts of German personalities and honour German achievements, but we focus on the German-Canadians themselves. We want to understand their motivation for emigration to Canada, their fate in the new homeland, and the way they participate in two cultures — in short, their transnational belonging.

Germans of Waterloo Region provides important help in this understanding. Based on 110 interviews in the Waterloo Centre for German Studies' Oral History Project, we have first-hand experience from a wide range of German-speaking immigrants. Their recollections convey feelings of loss and hope, of determination and achievement, of belonging and the distinction between Heimat (habitat) and Zuhause (home) — the lost but not forgotten, and the new home.

These memories are more important today than ever. Large numbers of ethnic Germans (Volksdeutsche) came to Canada after World War II and in 1951 made Germans the largest group of immigrants to Canada. Seventy years later they are aging, and their recollections may soon be lost. Recollections of their homelands in Hungary, Poland, Romania, or Yugoslavia, of their decision to leave the Heimat, their transition to a new country, learning the language, finding a job, and integrating while maintaining German language, customs, and traditions at home and in clubs. All these aspects are addressed by the interviewees and analyzed carefully in the chapters of this book.

German immigration to Canada did not end in 1951. It continues until today. But whereas the post-World War II migration to Canada was driven by the experience of war and ethnic cleansing, today's German immigrants are driven by curiosity, archetypical wanderlust, and often transcontinental love.

This generational change signals not only a shift in experiences and motivations but also changes in society overall. Whereas Germans in the 1950s sought common language, joint activities, and camaraderie in German clubs, parishes, and festivals, today's German immigrants — and not only they — rely more on social media and prefer spontaneous appointments to regular commitments.

---

1 Preface by Walter Stechel, Generalkonsul der Bundesrepublik Deutschland, Toronto (2013-2016).

We may regret this loss in social capital and social infrastructure, but we would have difficulties in reversing it. We may regret the move from personal interactions in a club house to the virtual interaction on Facebook, but we should not forget the difficulty and cost of a telephone call to Germany in the 1950s and '60s or the scarcity and cost of German newspapers in Canada. Today internet telephony and access to German media through internet or cable channels are ubiquitous. Direct and affordable flights facilitate travel. The Beibehaltungsgenehmigung, a special permit, helps Germans to become Canadian while maintaining their German citizenship.

All these factors contribute to maintaining the transnational belonging that is such an important asset in the German-Canadian friendship. Because, in the end it is not diplomacy and treaties that determine the quality of bilateral relations, but the density of personal relations at all levels and the respect that a community commands in a nation. German-Canadians command this respect and add very visible and idiosyncratic threads to the Canadian fabric. But as they increasingly melt into the Canadian identity it is important to recall and commemorate all those who came to build a new life for themselves and their children in a distant but promising land. *Germans in Waterloo Region* is an appropriate tribute to these builders.

The Oral History Project

Elizabeth Wendy Milne and Mathias Schulze

An Overview

The number of German immigrants who arrived in Canada in the decades immediately after the end of World War II and during the Wirtschaftswunder (economic miracle) years are dwindling, and the risk of losing first-hand accounts of their immigration experience grows greater with each passing year. The idea of collecting and preserving these stories began to percolate throughout Waterloo Region's German-Canadian community. Hoping to systematically gather this information and produce a book in which the stories of German immigrants to Waterloo Region would be recounted, Marga Weigel, the President of the German-Canadian Education Fund, approached the Waterloo Centre for German Studies (the 'Centre') in early 2013.

The Centre was officially founded in June 2004 by the University of Waterloo. Its genesis goes back to the late 1990s when, in conjunction with a major fundraising campaign, the decision was made to establish a research centre at the university to ensure "the contribution of German-speaking Canadians and scholarship on all aspects of German language and culture, past, present and future [be] fostered, studied, preserved and disseminated locally, nationally and internationally."[2] In 2009-2010, the Centre set up five distinct research groups, one to focus specifically on German-Canadian studies. This group aimed to investigate historical, cultural, and linguistic phenomena and processes in German-Canadian communities particularly in the Waterloo Region. Gathering information on and researching the history of the local German community falls within the purview of this research group.

In the spring of 2013, a brain-storming meeting was held with community members and Centre researchers. The outcome of the meeting was the creation of the Oral History Project (OHP), which would become the largest project of its kind for the Centre. A project of this scope requires a dedicated, active, and talented Advisory Group. The OHP was able to recruit and rely on the support and hard work of Kim Bardwell, Emma Betz, Ernst Friedel, David John, Grit Liebscher, Manfred Richter, Helene Schramek, Sebastian Siebel-Achenbach, Lori Straus, Linda Warley, Marga Weigel, and Mat Schulze, the project coordinator.

The scope of the OHP was to collect the life stories of German-speaking immigrants to Canada by conducting biographic interviews with members of the German-Canadian community[3] who have ties to Waterloo Region. The interviews

---

2 "About the Centre", Waterloo Centre for German Studies, accessed December 16, 2015, https://uwaterloo.ca/centre-for-german-studies/about

3 The phrase German-Canadian community includes immigrants from German-speaking central Europe and from regions in countries such as the former Czechoslovakia, Hungary, Lithuania, Poland, Romania, and the former Yugoslavia as well as their descendants.

would be video-recorded, transcribed, and the information gathered presented in two distinct ways. The initial presentation was to be a book which would contain individual community members' recollections of their immigration and settlement experiences. These accounts would be embedded within the larger, historical context. The book chapters would focus on a variety of migration-related topics, such as life before immigration to Canada, the immigration experience, life after arrival in Canada, work experience, language, and maintaining social and cultural heritage.

Secondly, transcripts would be redacted, so that individual interviewees could not be identified, and compiled into an archive (a 'corpus') which would be available to scholars in applied linguistics, cultural studies, and history.

As with any research project in which human participants are involved, the first step for the OHP was to submit a research ethics application, made in accordance with the Government of Canada's Tri-Council Policy Statement, to the University of Waterloo's Ethics Review Board. The application included the proposal to conduct and transcribe the interviews, and information on how the data would be used for this book and the corpus. The application also included information on how the data would be collected, stored, and used during every step of the research process; how interviewees were to be recruited, a sample of the type of questions which would be asked, and samples of the permission forms to be used. In his role as project coordinator, Mat Schulze was responsible for ensuring that everyone working on any aspect of the project adhered to the stated requirements and stipulated guidelines. Once the approval was received, OHP sought volunteers willing to tell their story.

The Interviews

The OHP Committee's initial goal was to collect forty interviews by December 2014, a target of about three interviews per month. Interviewers would be found from within the University of Waterloo community of German Studies graduate students, professors, and Centre staff. Everyone was proficient in both German and English so that interviewees were free to conduct the interview in either language.

The more critical and complex task was to find people willing to spend an hour of their time to talk about their migration experiences and to share their personal stories. The OHP Advisory Group, interested community members, and the Centre began recruiting interviewees through personal connections, flyers, and local radio and TV broadcasts with some success. The first interview took place on October 15, 2013, when interviewers Julia Roitsch and Sam Schirm met with Michael Eckardt. As more people were interviewed, interest in the project grew rapidly through word-of-mouth, and the initial goal of forty interviews was met by April 2014, eight months ahead of schedule.

Through the successful fundraising efforts of advisory group members Ernst Friedel, Manfred Richter, and Marga Weigel, an additional $20,000 in funding had been secured in April 2014. The interview recruitment process could be extended through December 2014, which allowed for significantly more than the originally planned forty interviews to be conducted.[4] By the time the video recorder was turned off at the conclusion of the last interview on March 17, 2015, there were a total of 110 video-recorded interviews.[5] Of those interviews, 19 were with married couples such as Renate and Jörg Stieber or other family pairs such as Barnhild Pfenning and her son Wolfgang Pfenning. A total of 23 interviewers spoke to and gathered the stories of 129 German-speaking immigrants or their family members, of which 57 were women. The interview process allowed the OHP to gather a treasure trove of 124 hours of video and audio footage. The interviewers, in alphabetical order, were: Derek Andrews, Taylor Antoniazzi, Ina Bendig, Sebastian Buchspiess, Stephanie Cooper, Tanya Hagman, Katharina Leuner, Judith Linneweber, Sara Marsh, Elizabeth Milne, Maike Mueller, Alan Nanders, Jennifer Redler, Julia Roitsch, Britta Rumpf, Sam Schirm, Friederike Schlein, Mat Schulze, Sebastian Siebel-Achenbach, Jelena Srdjenovic, Lori Straus, Katharine Unkelbach, and Sara Werthmueller.

The Interviewees

With such a large number of people coming forward to be part of the OHP, the authors of this book were able to gather personal biographical histories from German-speaking immigrants who arrived in Canada between 1938 and 2011. Not surprisingly, the largest number of arrivals came in the 1950s, and almost half of the project participants fall into that demographic. However, each decade between 1938 and 2011 was represented by a least one interview.

Project participants came not only from Germany and Austria but also from former Czechoslovakia, Hungary, Lithuania, Poland, Romania, and former Yugoslavia. Some were born in Canada to immigrant parents. Some arrived as young children. Some moved with their families. Some came alone. Earlier immigrants arrived by boat, later ones by airplane. Some could barely speak English when they arrived. Others were fluently bilingual. Among all the unique and personal stories, some common themes of Heimat[6], acclimatization, and the struggles of adapting to a new culture did recur.

In speaking about the experiences of crossing continents and cultures, sometimes interviewees would suddenly switch between languages. Sometimes it was only a word or two. Often the switch happened when the speaker wanted to recite an aphorism or a line of poetry that was particularly appropriate to the topic being discussed.

Several participants provided additional materials to the OHP: letters, pamphlets, articles, pictures, and other personal items. These were digitized and archived.

---

4 "$20,000 Donation Increases Scope of Oral History Project | Waterloo Centre for German Studies", accessed January 18, 2016, https://uwaterloo.ca/centre-for-german-studies/news/20000-donation-increases-scope-oral-history-project
5 "Oral History Project", Waterloo Centre for German Studies, accessed December 17, 2015, https://uwaterloo.ca/centre-for-german-studies/research-activities/oral-history-project
6 Translation: habitat, homeland.

Transcribing and Coding

During the time the interviews were being conducted, transcription work was already underway. This was the most labour-intensive stage of the project. On average, for each hour of recorded interview, between four and five hours were needed to produce an accurate and complete transcript. The 124 hours of interviews would require almost 600 hours of transcription time. A call went out to students in the University of Waterloo's German programs requesting participation in the project as a paid transcriber. Even with thirty-three transcribers at the University of Waterloo, in order to ensure completion deadlines were met, eighteen transcripts were completed by corporate transcription services Transcript Divas[7] or Transkribisch.[8] The transcription team members, in alphabetical order, were: Taylor Antoniazzi, Richard Barnett, Allison Cattel, Stephanie Cooper, Janna Flaming, Martin Gerhard, Tanya Hagman, Mario Hirstein, Daisy Hu, Misty Jackman, Jeff Lapalme, Jen Lee, Feiran Lei, Wes Lindinger, Judith Linneweber, Elizabeth Milne, Maike Mueller, Ruth Post, Vince Ren, Maike Rocker, Julia Roitsch, Daniela Roth, Britta Rumpf, Nadine Singh, Jelena Srdjenovic, Lori Straus, Stefanie Templin, Katharine Unkelbach, Melanie Weiß, Sara Werthmueller, Roger Wilkinson, Morgan Wood, and Kristin Yaworski.

The transcripts had to be completed to meet both project goals outlined above. The transcripts were initially used for content analysis by authors of the chapters of this book. This meant they had to be made available in a format that was easily accessible and searchable. Secondly, for the data to be included in a corpus for future research, the transcripts had to be compatible with the guidelines from the *Gesprächsanalytisches Transkriptionssystem 2 (GAT 2)* and the CHAT transcription format. [9] These stringent criteria ensure consistency and hence enable future researchers to work with the corpus systematically.

The following excerpt from Helene Schramek's interview is an example of how the data was prepared. Whenever Helene is speaking, the transcript line is marked *HSC. The interview was conducted by Taylor Antoniazzi. She is designated here as *TAN.

*TAN:	so after your parents had been in Canada for a while.
*TAN:	do you know if they used more English?
*TAN:	or German in everyday life?
*HSC:	English in business.
*TAN:	mhm.
*HSC:	but German at home.
*TAN:	okay.
*HSC:	so even when we were there.

---

7 "Transcript Divas Transcription Services Toronto", accessed January 18, 2016, http://transcriptdivas.ca/. Now called "Transcript Heroes" https://transcriptheroes.ca

8 "Transkription von Interviews u.a. | Günstige Preise", accessed January 18, 2016, http://www.transkribisch.de/cgi-bin/transkribisch/index.html

9 For GAT 2, see http://www.gespraechsforschung-ozs.de/heft2009/px-gat2.pdf, accessed July 29, 2019; for CHAT, see https://talkbank.org/manuals/CHAT.pdf

```
*HSC:     it would be speaking German with my parents.
*TAN:     mhm.
*HSC:     but when they went out um like i said.
*HSC:     other than when they were with their friends.
*HSC:     their German speaking friends they always spoke English.
```

As per the corpus transcript guidelines, only proper names are capitalized, even the English "I" is rendered as "i" in this format. Transcribers were required to add in all the small verbal encouragement sounds we tend to make while speaking, things like "mhm" or "okay" or "ahh." Transcribers were not to add punctuation. Instead, each thought or clause, was to be contained on a separate line. Once completed, the transcribers returned the transcripts for proofreading and formatting.

Beyond transcription and formatting, there remained a final step before the transcripts were ready to be used by the authors. Each transcript was read through again and identifying tags were inserted to mark the lines in the transcript where specific topics were addressed. This way authors could search for specific tags and quickly find the topics pertinent to their research such as education, language, or family. The completed transcripts were then tagged and uploaded to a central database to which all authors of this book were given access. These post-transcription assignments were completed by the OHP's eleven research assistants, in alphabetical order: Stephanie Cooper, Isabelle Eberz, Misty Jackman, Feiran Lei, Katharina Leuner, Wes Lindinger, Elizabeth Milne, Julia Roitsch, Daniela Roth, Katharine Unkelbach, and Melanie Weiß.

Editors, Authors, and Writing a Book

Marga Weigel had approached Mat Schulze asking whether the Centre would take on the project of writing a book about the German immigrants of the 1950s and 60s. After some consideration and consulting with other researchers in the Centre, he agreed and started spearheading the OHP. It was thus consequential that he also became the lead editor. Before embarking on this complex endeavour, he recruited Centre members Grit Liebscher, an applied linguist, and Sebastian Siebel-Achenbach, a historian, as co-editors.

The OHP was able to recruit chapter authors through the Centre. The editors planned to have each chapter written by two authors, one a graduate student and the other a university professor. At a meeting held May 7, 2015, the prospective authors gathered around a boardroom table and listened as the writing phase of the project was outlined. Chapter topics and writing partners were assigned and timelines were put forth. Some of the graduate student authors are members of the Intercultural German Studies Program, a joint Master Program run by the University of Waterloo and the University of Mannheim. This meant some authors were in Germany during a portion of the writing and editing process. With today's technology, the geographical divide was not an issue.

In addition to making each of the transcripts available for research, authors were given access to the digitized documents provided by the interviewees, pamphlets, and articles. The University of Waterloo librarians also provided an extensive bibliography of potential resource articles and books.

Each writing team worked with the editors to create their assigned chapter. The goal was to create a book which would be relevant to both the local community and, with the personal stories contextualized, to a broader audience.[10] Each chapter went through at least three draft stages and has been edited and commented upon by the three editors after each stage. In spring of 2017, we selected Petra Books in Ottawa as our publisher. The editors would like to extend their deep gratitude to Petra Books, more specifically to Peter Geldart and Danielle Aubrey, for their diligent and precise work. Their support, patience and, at times, nudging during the production of the book provided a strong basis for completing the publication, despite times of unforeseen delays and set-backs encountered by the editors.

Following this introduction, this book begins by presenting an overview of the history of Waterloo Region paying particular attention to the immigration and acculturation of German speakers over the span of two hundred years. This is followed by four chapters on the places of origin of our interviewees. Since a large group of German speakers in Waterloo Region are Mennonites, we begin with introducing these groups. In this chapter, the authors had to draw on interviews from two other projects at the University of Waterloo. The next three chapters reflect that our interviewees came from different places in Europe: south-eastern Europe, east-central Europe, and Germany and Austria. These chapters comprise the first part of the book, often depicting the childhood and youth of our interviewees. The second part starts with the situation immigrants faced and their first impressions when they arrived in Canada. This part also includes a chapter on an important aspect of life for immigrants — earning a living. Here we focus on the jobs our interviewees found, the businesses they built, and the contributions they made to the economy in Waterloo Region. The subsequent three chapters discuss from various perspectives who exactly the German-Canadian people are: how they reflect on and actively live their German heritage, how they feel about their home in Canada, and how they still connect to German culture and the places from which they came. The German and English languages — and some others — did not only figure prominently in our thinking as researchers and authors but were also mentioned frequently in the interviews; we dedicated the penultimate chapter to this topic. In the last chapter, we return to the topic of childhood by speaking about family life and the next generation, the children and grandchildren of the interviewees.

---

10 "Research Links Personal and Public Histories of German-Canadians | Waterloo News", accessed January 15, 2016, https://uwaterloo.ca/news/news/research-links-personal-and-public-histories-german

The History of Waterloo Region

Elizabeth Wendy Milne and Mathias Schulze

In May 2011, Hendrik Walther left Germany to become a resident of Canada. He is pursuing his graduate studies at the University of Waterloo's Centre for Contact Lens Research and so moved to Waterloo Region. Hendrik is taking the opportunity to conduct research at "das größte Kontaktlinsenforschungsinstitut weltweit."[11] The year before, Christopher Wolff and his family moved to Waterloo Region so that he could pursue his career at Christie Digital Systems, a job opportunity he discovered more than two years earlier while on vacation in Canada with his wife Daniela.

Waterloo Region has been offering opportunities to immigrants and settlers since before the country of Canada was founded. Hendrik, and Christopher and Daniela are but three of the more recent arrivals in a long line of German speakers to settle in this area.

Sir Frederick Haldimand, Governor of Québec, granted the lands destined to become Waterloo County to the Iroquois Confederacy in 1784 to replace the lands lost by the Indigenous people during the American War of Independence. The Iroquois Six Nations, under the leadership of Joseph Brant, made an application to the Legislative Council and Executive Council and to the governors of the day to sell

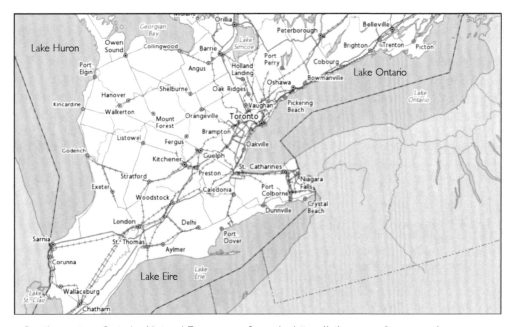

South-western Ontario. Natural Resources Canada. https://atlas.gc.ca/toporama/en
https://open.canada.ca/en/open-government-licence-canada

---

11 Translation: the largest contact lens research institute worldwide.

part of their land. In 1798, they sold the 93,160 acres known as Block 2 to Richard Beasley, John Baptiste Rouseau, and James Wilson. Beasley later secured a mortgage, bought out his partners, and almost immediately began offering parcels of Block 2 land for sale.[12]

The opportunity for land ownership attracted a group of settlers for whom the isolated location was ideal: Mennonite farmers from Pennsylvania. By 1801, twelve families had settled on land in Block 2, including Sam Bricker, who two years after the purchase learned that Beasley had sold the land before retiring the mortgage.[13] The Mennonite settlers, on learning about this situation, were initially quite anxious as the existence of the mortgage meant they did not have clear title to the lands.[14] Sam and John Erb decided to take advantage of the situation by offering to purchase all of the unsettled portion of Beasley's land, some 60,000 acres. The requisite funds were raised from Mennonites in Lancaster County, Pennsylvania, through "an appeal to religious sentiment as well as economic advantage."[15] The Erb brothers, together with twenty-three other farmers, joined together to form the 'German Company'. The newly created association raised the requisite funds, bought the 60,000 acres, and received a clear deed.[16] The land was surveyed and divided into 128 lots of 448 acres and 32 lots of 83 acres, which were then distributed to the shareholders of the German Company by the drawing of lots.[17]

This settlement differed from those of the predominantly Anglo-Saxon enclaves: the land was physically isolated, the settlers were often related by family ties, and they shared a common religion and common language other than English.[18]

Among those who settled in Block 2 were Benjamin Eby and his wife, Mary Brubacher. They came to Upper Canada in 1807. Eby's concern was for "the settlers' spiritual welfare…[and] he was appointed preacher in 1809."[19] He promoted the building of the first Mennonite Versammlungshaus (meeting house), and the 1813 meeting house became the first church in Waterloo County. An annex was added to the church in 1818, in which Bishop Eby opened a school and taught students in German, using the Bible as a textbook.[20] The church and its annex were affectionately called 'Ben Eby's'. The church became the centre of the little community which became known as Ebytown.[21]

---

12 Geoffrey Hayes, Waterloo County: An Illustrated History (Kitchener: Waterloo Historical Society, 1997), 3.
13 John English and Kenneth McLaughlin. Kitchener. An illustrated History. (Waterloo: Wilfrid Laurier University Press, 1983), 17.
14 Marg Rowell, Welcome to Waterloo: An Illustrated History of Waterloo Ontario in Celebration of Its 125th Anniversary 1857-1982, 1st ed. (Waterloo: Waterloo Printing Co, 1982), 8.
15 English, Kitchener, 19.
16 W.V. Uttley, A History of Kitchener, Ontario (Waterloo: Wilfrid Laurier University Press, 1975), 9.
17 Rowell, Welcome to Waterloo, 9.
18 English, Kitchener, 20.
19 Uttley, A History, 21.
20 Uttley, A History, 27.
21 English, Kitchener, 16.

An estimated 1200 to 1500 Pennsylvania-Germans settled in the region between 1800 and 1825.[22] Ebytown, still known as Block 2, or alternately referred to as the German Company Tract, remained an almost exclusively Mennonite settlement until the 1820s.

The little hamlet of Ebytown grew as immigrants continued to settle in the area. An administrative decision in 1816 elevated Block 2 to the status of Waterloo Township. In 1833, Ebytown was renamed Berlin. Traditional lore attributes the name change to Bishop Eby, who renamed the settlement to welcome new arrivals, also German speakers, but no longer predominantly Mennonite.[23]

The next wave of immigrants to Waterloo Township came from Europe. The end of the Napoleonic Wars in 1815 brought a severe economic depression to Germany.[24] Changes in economic policies and landholding practices in the German states pushed many of the small farmers from their lands. Craftsmen and artisans also found their livelihoods threatened by the new wave of industrialization and mechanization. This resulted in an unprecedented migration of Europeans to North America.

> "In 1833…over twenty thousand are said to have emigrated and in the decade of the 1840s it is estimated that between sixty and one hundred thousand people left Germany annually."[25]

The immigrants settling in Waterloo Township came from all parts of central Europe:

> "Baden and Bavaria, from the province of Hesse-Darmstadt, the kingdom of Prussia, the principality of Waldeck, the kingdom of Württemberg, and from Alsace and Lorraine. Others came from the Baltic states, the kingdom of Saxony, and the Grand Duchy of Mecklenburg and the Duchy of Holstein."[26]

These immigrants came from many different religious, social, and economic groups. Their sense of individuality would remain and be reflected in their attitudes toward industrial and commercial development. They were bound, however, by their common language and the pride in their craftsmanship. Amongst the settlers were "weavers, wagonmakers, shoemakers and coopers…builders, masons, carpenters and mechanics, as well as chairmakers, pumpmakers, potters, blacksmiths, metalworkers and general merchants."[27]

The rapid increase in population and land settlement within Upper Canada led to sometimes contentious issues of political governance, in particular the redrawing of township lines and the designation of county seats. The County of Waterloo was

22 Ulrich Frisse, Berlin, Ontario, 1800-1916: Historische Identitäten von "Kanadas deutscher Hauptstadt" (New Dundee: Trans-Atlantic Publishing, 2003), 39.
23 Hayes, Waterloo County, 13.
24 Frisse, Berlin, Ontario, 41.
25 English, Kitchener, 22.
26 English, Kitchener, 25.
27 English, Kitchener, 25.

created in 1853, and Berlin was afforded the honour of becoming the new county seat. County buildings were built, and the following year, Berlin's residents petitioned Queen Victoria to become an incorporated village.[28]

The *Canada Museum und Allgemeine Zeitung*, the first German newspaper in Upper Canada, began publishing in 1833, the same year Bishop Eby opened his new, larger meeting house. A Lutheran congregation was established in 1835 in Berlin and other German congregations followed.[29] The first Berlin band, formed in 1856 by Heinrich Glebe and George Hess, joined with a previously rival musical group established by Wilhelm Kaiser to become the Berlin Musical Society. Two hundred singers from nearby village choirs participated in the first song festival held in 1862. The Concordia Club was founded in 1873 to uphold and further German traditions, thereby also giving young German couples a place to meet.[30] Ontario's first kindergarten class was taught in Berlin in 1882.[31] Berlin became a stop on the Toronto-Sarnia line of the Grand Trunk Railway in 1856, followed by other lines which connected the town to other Ontario communities.[32] Berlin had established itself as the cultural, religious, commercial and social centre for the area. County politics saw fierce competition between the townships, towns, and villages.

> "Preston, Berlin, Hespeler, New Hamburg, and Waterloo village each
> gained council seats as incorporated villages through the 1850s…a
> time of rapid growth; the county's population grew by 45%."[33]

Nine years after the creation of the Dominion of Canada, in February 1876 the village of Waterloo, just north of Berlin, received its town incorporation. Rich farmland surrounded a centre focused on insurance, mill industries, small-business manufacturing, and merchants. The town, and later city, shared with the rest of the country, in the economic downturn of the late 19th century.[34]

As the 19th century came to a close, Waterloo County continued to embrace and enthusiastically celebrate its German heritage. A bust of Kaiser Wilhelm I sitting atop the Friedensdenkmal (peace memorial) was unveiled in Victoria Park in August 1897. In attendance at the ceremony were singers, bands, county residents, the mayor of Berlin, and the Toronto-based German consul. A scant three years later, in January 1900, the Concordia Club hosted the first birthday celebration for Kaiser Wilhelm II. Since Germany had not been involved in any wars from the time he ascended the throne in 1888, Kaiser Wilhelm II was honoured as Friedenskaiser (Emperor of Peace). These celebrations provided Canadian-born descendants of German-speaking immigrants a festive tie to the homeland of their parents and grandparents. Although 70% of Berlin's population was German by ethnic origin, by 1912 only 8.3% of the

---

28 English, Kitchener, 28.
29 English, Kitchener, 26.
30 English, Kitchener, 62.
31 Neil Ballantyne, Century Celebration: 1912-2012: Kitchener Marks 100 Years as a City (Kitchener: Metroland Media Group, 2012), 63.
32 Rowell, Welcome to Waterloo, 18.
33 Hayes, Waterloo County, 34.
34 Rowell, Welcome to Waterloo, 35.

city's residents had been born in Germany. As a popular social link to a shared history, the birthday celebrations continued to be held until a mere six months prior to the outbreak of World War I in 1914.[35]

Britain declared war against Germany on August 4, 1914, and given Canada's status as a British dominion, it was automatically at war with Germany as well. In the overnight hours of Saturday, August 22, 1914, the bust of Kaiser Wilhelm I was pulled off the memorial and tossed into Victoria Park Lake. The bust was found the next morning and placed in the Concordia Club for safekeeping.

As the war progressed, anti-German sentiment increased and loyalty to Britain by German-speaking descendants was questioned with ever greater fervour. The bust of Kaiser Wilhelm I was once again the focus of vandalism, and on February 15, 1916, soldiers from the 118th Battalion together with members of the public broke into the Concordia Club, wrecked the building and stole the bust. Paraded around town, the bust was spit upon, beaten with sticks, and eventually taken to the battalion barracks on Queen Street to be used for target practice. The bust then disappeared and was not recovered, and while mystery does surround its fate, the prevailing theory is that the bust was melted down, and the bronze was used to make napkin rings bearing the crest of the 118th battalion.[36]

The stamp "Made in Berlin," previously a mark of fine craftsmanship and community pride, was now seen to be a hindrance to business. The primary concern for Berlin's economic security, likely spurred on by the overt display of anti-German feeling earlier in the month, saw city council passing a resolution on February 21, 1916, "imploring the provincial legislature to change the city's name."[37] Civil peace concerns delayed the request, but a private member's bill was passed allowing the city to hold its name-change plebiscite. On May 19, 1916, a vote asking whether the name should be changed was held. The yes-side narrowly carried the day, and the difficult process of determining a new name began.[38]

From the 114 name suggestions, voters were asked to choose from only six during the second name-change plebiscite which was held from June 24 to 27, 1916. The ballot, written in both English and German, gave Adanac, Benton, Brock, Corona, Keowana, and Kitchener as the choices. Despite many ballots spoiled by being marked Berlin or Waterloo, Kitchener was "the favourite choice of an unpopular decision."[39] The name change was made official on September 1, 1916, a scant six and a half months after the passing of the initial city council resolution.

On November 7, 1918, having heard rumours the fighting had stopped in Europe, thousands took to the streets in Kitchener and Waterloo waving the Union Jack, and banging pots and pans.[40] The Armistice was signed on November 11, 1918, and in

---

35 Frisse, Berlin, Ontario, 158.
36 Frisse, Berlin, Ontario, 158.
37 English, Kitchener, 120.
38 English, Kitchener, 124.
39 Ballantyne, Century, 21.
40 Ballantyne, Century, 22.

1919, the *Daily Telegraph* printed the names of the 3,763 Waterloo County men and women who had enlisted during the war. Photographs of most of the county's 486 fatalities made up eleven pages of that edition.[41]

The post-war years saw municipal budgets expand to meet increasing expectations. There was a boom in school building, in particular for vocational training and high schools. In 1924, the Kitchener-Waterloo Collegiate Institute and Vocational School opened, and Waterloo College, which emerged from Waterloo Lutheran Seminary that same year, received support from Waterloo County Council. The building of new roads comprised the largest expenditures through the 1920s and 30s. S.S. Kresge, the predecessor of KMart Corporation, located its first Canadian store in downtown Kitchener in 1928. Kitchener native, Walter Zeller, followed suit, opening his first store on King Street four years later.[42] The twenties brought a higher standard of living to residents of Waterloo County, with most benefitting from the general prosperity. Despite the average work week dropping to forty-two hours by 1928, higher hourly wages made up the difference in take-home pay. "This prosperity began to seem normal, as each year its symbols — new factories, grander homes, paved roads, and manicured lawns — multiplied in all city wards."[43]

In the 1920s and 30s, the influence of the German population on Waterloo County dwindled. Before World War I, Kitchener was overwhelmingly German. With little German immigration between 1911 and 1914, none during World War I, and a 1919 order-in-council which allowed the government to prohibit immigration based on race and nationality, the percentage of the population who were ethnically German dropped to 55.6% in 1921 and 53% in 1931. After World War I, immigration policies remained restrictive as the return of Canadian veterans, together with the termination of war activities, resulted in a surplus of labour in local markets.[44] It was not until 1923 that the restrictions were lifted, and many so-called Volksdeutsche[45] (ethnic Germans) from southern and eastern Europe began to arrive. German cinema and theatre, cultural events and schools were revived.[46]

Kitchener was still Canada's German Capital when Adolf Hitler took power in Germany in 1933. After witnessing the disintegration of the Weimar Republic, many people in Waterloo Region, as elsewhere, feared that Germany would become a communist state. Thus, the *Daily Record's* editor, W.J. Motz, like many others,

---

41 Hayes, Waterloo County, 130.
42 Hayes, Waterloo County, 139–140.
43 English, Kitchener, 143.
44 Robert J.C. Stead, "Canada's Immigration Policy", Annals of the American Academy of Political and Social Science 107 (May 1, 1923): 59.
45 The term Volksdeutsche is problematic, having its origin in Nazi Germany and being used in contrast to Reichsdeutsche (Germans from within the borders of Germany at that time). However, many interviewees use it without any ideological overtones because such labels played a significant role in their migration history. For a discussion of the terminology, see p. 18 in: Dailey-O'Cain, Jennifer and Grit Liebscher. 2011. Germans from different places: constructing a German space in urban Canada. Journal of Germanic Linguistics 23/4 (special issue on Germanic languages and migration in North America, ed. by Kristine Horner), 315-345.
46 English, Kitchener, 161.

originally welcomed Hitler's arrival on the world stage.[47] However, by 1936, "the *Record* had ceased to extend 'sympathetic understanding' to Hitler and tended to emphasize the distinction between Hitler and the German people."[48] In 1939, the Concordia Club suspended its activities[49], and other German social clubs in Waterloo County followed suit. Community leaders did everything possible to reinforce the idea of the German speakers' loyalty to Canada. Whereas some six months prior to World War I, the Kaiser's birthday was celebrated, Hitler did not receive a similar honour.[50] Indeed, hoping to catch a glimpse of the royal couple, thousands lined the rail tracks on June 6, 1939, when King George VI and Queen Elizabeth came to Waterloo County.[51] On September 10, 1939, one week after Britain declared war on Germany, Canada followed suit with its own declaration. World War II had begun.

Not surprisingly, immigration to Canada was restricted during the war years, with levels dropping to rates below those seen during the Great Depression years.[52] After World War II, the *Canadian Citizenship Act* came into force on January 1, 1947, and with that, Canada became the first Commonwealth country to create its own class of citizenship separate from Great Britain. The year 1947 also saw the first wave of Displaced Persons, including ethnic Germans arriving in Canada, many of whom came to Waterloo County.[53] "Between 1946 and 1950, the county welcomed 5,380 immigrants."[54]

Many of the people interviewed for this book were among these immigrants. For example, Waldemar Reinhardt was eleven when he landed in Halifax on January 14, 1949. Like many others, he travelled aboard the MV Beaverbrae, a ship that, in collaboration with the Canadian Christian Council for the Resettlement of Refugees and the Canadian government, sailed about every 28 days with approximately 773 passengers between Bremen, Amsterdam, and Antwerp to Halifax, Saint John, or Québec City. She carried a total of 33,259 passengers during her service between 1948 and 1954.[55] From Halifax, Waldemar's family embarked on a two-day train journey to Toronto, where they lived for about a year before moving to the Kitchener

---

47 English, Kitchener, 161.
48 English, Kitchener, 163.
49 "Concordia Club History", accessed January 20, 2016, https://www.concordiaclub.ca/index.php?option=com_content&view=article&id=2&Itemid=2
50 English, Kitchener, 164.
51 Hayes, Waterloo County, 164.
52 "Stats Canada Download of Table A350.xlsx", as referenced in The Pier Goes To War: Halifax's Pier 21 and the Second World War | CMIP 21 Web: https://www.pier21.ca/blog/steve-schwinghamer/the-pier-goes-to-war-halifax-s-pier-21-and-the-second-world-war
53 Bastian Bryan Lovasz, "Animosity, Ambivalence and Co-Operation Manifestations of Heterogeneous German Identities in the Kitchener-Waterloo Area during and after WWII." (Library and Archives Canada - Bibliothèque et Archives Canada, 2010), 39.
54 Ballantyne, Century, 56.
55 "Beaverbrae", accessed May 21, 2019, https://www.theshipslist.com/ships/descriptions/ShipsB.shtml#beav

area because it was "basically the more German community."[56] His father had been a flour miller, but unable to find employment in his trade, he worked initially in furniture factories and later in construction.

Waterloo County was one of Ontario's manufacturing hubs. B.F. Goodrich and Dominion Tire both had major operations in Kitchener, prompting the city to be nicknamed 'the rubber capital of Canada'. Cluett, Peabody & Co (the Arrow Shirt Company), Dominion Button, J.M. Schneider, and Kuntz Electroplating, among others, offered employment opportunities to the steady stream of immigrants. "The new dream was to own a home in the suburbs with a swing set in the large yard out back." [57]

In 1950, the same year that George Emory Zehr opened his first supermarket in Kitchener, Canada's minister of citizenship and immigration, Walter Harris, proclaimed at a local citizenship ceremony that "[s]ome of our best citizens come from Germany."[58] This was also the year the immigration restrictions on so-called Reichsdeutsche (Germans from the former German Reich) were lifted, and the Department of Citizenship & Immigration actively began recruiting German immigrants.[59] This change in focus resulted in 32,395 Germans immigrating to Canada in 1951, an increase of 456% over the previous year.[60]

Elisabeth O'Reilly's parents arrived in 1950 with no English-speaking skills but a strong desire to work hard, buy land, and build themselves a home. In the fall of 1951, her industrious parents purchased the land, and by the winter of 1952, with a newborn Elisabeth, they were already building their house. Her mother worked dayshift, her father nightshift, and the language spoken in the home was German.

By the time Dorothea Snell came to Canada in 1955, the Concordia Club had resumed activities; Kitchener's former mayor and head of Breithaupt Leather Company, Louis Orville Breithaupt, was Lieutenant Governor of Ontario (1952-1957). Kitchener had celebrated its centenary of incorporation as the Village of Berlin (June 27-July 3, 1953), and Hurricane Hazel had violently blown through southern Ontario in October of 1954 forcing 200 people to leave their Bridgeport homes.[61] Dorothea estimates that on her trans-Atlantic voyage, only 10% of the ship's passengers were immigrants, the rest were Canadian soldiers returning home. She took the opportunity to practise her English-speaking skills and remembers a conversation with one young soldier originally from London, Ontario, who taught her some of the finer points of polite conversation. Dorothea learned that when you entertain a guest, you don't just say "sit down," you say "please, have a seat."

---

56 Quotes, such as this by Waldemar Reinhardt, are from the interviews with participants in the Oral History Project. Future quotes throughout the book will be without footnotes, unless the name of the participant is not clear from the context.
57 Ballantyne, Century, 51.
58 Ballantyne, Century, 57.
59 Ronald Schmalz, "Former Enemies Come to Canada: Ottawa and the Post-war German Immigration Boom, 1951-57" (Ph.D. diss., University of Ottawa, 2000), 79.
60 Schmalz, "Former Enemies Come to Canada," 95.
61 Ballantyne, Century, 57.

Ingo Schoppel was one of the very few landed immigrants who came into Canada via Windsor. His father worked for Pan American Airlines, and in 1957 Pan Am did not land in Toronto. So, Ingo disembarked in Detroit, Michigan, and at twenty years of age, headed to the Detroit River and crossed into Canada on his own. Ingo's first home was on King Street West, right across from the Kitchener Collegiate & Vocational School. KCI, as the school is commonly known, had begun as the Berlin Grammar School in 1855.[62] Ingo arrived in Canada at a time of great innovation and discovery. While the term Wirtschaftswunder (economic miracle) itself would not be coined for another two years, a global economic and scientific boom was underway. Not wanting to be left behind, and

> "eager to move to improve research and development capacity,
> Kitchener business leaders…took the lead in 1957 in creating a new
> engineering school, the University of Waterloo."[63]

Under the direction of Reverend Cornelius Siegfried, one of the University of Waterloo's founders, St. Jerome's College was federated with the University from its inception. St. Jerome's had a long-established relationship with the German community in the region. Back in 1857, approximately 12,000 German-speaking Catholics in Waterloo County lived in an organized but priest-less community. Father Eugene Funcken was sent to lead the Congregation of the Resurrection. It was Eugene's brother, the Reverend Dr. Louis Funcken, who noted that there were few Catholics in leadership roles, nor any in the vocation of the priesthood. In response, he founded and opened St. Jerome's College on January 1, 1865.[64]

Around the turn of the last century, the largest concentration of Lutherans in Canada could be found in the vicinity of Kitchener and Waterloo, so the Lutheran Church established a seminary in the area. The City of Waterloo offered the denomination a tract of land, and in 1911, the Evangelical Lutheran Seminary of Canada opened its doors. By 1925, its Faculty of Arts, under the name of Waterloo College, began offering honours degree programs in the arts. The seminary would later obtain a revised charter, changing the name of the institution to Waterloo Lutheran University. On November 1, 1973, the name was changed to Wilfrid Laurier University in honour of Canada's seventh prime minister.[65] Elisabeth O'Reilly, born in Canada to German immigrants and schooled in German during her primary years by the Quirings and then later by Mrs. Felton out of her home in Preston, received her Bachelor of German Language and Literature from Wilfrid Laurier University.

---

62 "About (Kitchener-Waterloo Collegiate & Vocational School)", accessed October 10, 2015, https://kci.wrdsb.ca/about/
63 "Kitchener Meets Its Waterloo", Macleans.ca, accessed May 18, 2015, https://www.macleans.ca/news/canada/kitchener-meets-its-waterloo/
64 "St. Jerome's History", accessed July 29, 2019, https://www.wcdsb.ca/about-us/st-jeromes-history/
65 "Wilfrid Laurier University - The Canadian Encyclopedia", accessed October 11, 2015, https://www.thecanadianencyclopedia.ca/en/article/wilfrid-laurier-university/

Conrad Grebel University College, chartered in 1961, was established by Mennonite community leaders, as more Mennonite young people began attending secular universities to receive training in specialities unavailable at traditional Mennonite colleges or bible schools. The College became an affiliate of the University of Waterloo, and the first classes were taught in 1963.[66]

Canada celebrated the centenary of Confederation in 1967. Communities throughout the country participated in arts, building, music, and other projects to mark the occasion. Centennial Stadium and Jack Couch Park on the Auditorium grounds were created as centennial projects. Furthermore, Owen Lackenbauer, one of the original Kitchener-Waterloo Oktoberfest organizers reports that,

> "as part of the 1967 Centennial celebrations, the Concordia Club had
> a small Oktoberfest, and we had a mandate with the Chamber of
> Commerce to develop a tourism event to attract visitors. When we saw
> what Oktoberfest looked like, we said [that] this is a great opportunity."[67]

The first official Kitchener-Waterloo Oktoberfest took place in 1969 and the tradition continues to this day.

The early 1970s saw numerous changes to the municipal landscape of Waterloo County. With the June 1972 first reading of Bill 167 "An Act to Establish the Regional Municipality of Waterloo," Waterloo County, itself first established in 1852, was coming to an end.[68] The bill was passed, and by November the new region's committee structure was in place.

All that remained were the final meetings of the eight municipalities that would pass out of existence on December 31, 1972. The oldest was Waterloo Township, which disappeared from the map entirely. New Hamburg, Elmira, and Ayr also ceased to exist as separate municipal entities, as did Bridgeport, Galt, Preston and Hespeler.[69] Hence, Waterloo County was effectively dissolved January 1, 1973, when the Region of Waterloo was formed.[70]

The recession of 1981-84 put tremendous pressure on the existing manufacturing sector, particularly those traditional, more labour-intensive industries like the tire industry, and those susceptible to international competition such as shirt manufacturing.[71] While the beginning of the 1980s saw a painful restructuring of the old, toward the end of the decade new opportunities for economic growth and prosperity presented themselves, in particular within a market sector developing an investment cachet, and quickly dubbed "high tech." New companies like Research in Motion, Descartes, Teledyne DALSA, and SAP (International) AG, became major

---

66 "History of Conrad Grebel | Conrad Grebel University College", accessed October 10, 2015, https://uwaterloo.ca/grebel/about-conrad-grebel/history-conrad-grebel

67 "Oktoberfest - Welcome", accessed October 18, 2015, https://www.oktoberfest.ca

68 Hayes, Waterloo County, 215.

69 Hayes, Waterloo County, 217. The city of Galt and the towns of Hespeler and Preston were amalgamated into the city of Cambridge.

70 Hayes, Waterloo County, 216.

71 English, Kitchener, 201.

economic drivers. Financial services companies such as Manulife Financial, Mutual Life (later acquired by Sun Life), and Waterloo Lutheran Life expanded their presence not only in Waterloo Region but throughout Canada. The universities and colleges also became significant employers. To great fanfare, Toyota announced in 1985 that it would begin building automobiles in Canada. The first Canadian-made vehicle, a Corolla sedan, rolled off the Cambridge plant assembly line in 1988.[72] Since then, two additional plants have been built, with a significant number of the employee pool drawn from the region.

Much of the recorded history of Waterloo County and Waterloo Region is centred on urban expansion, population growth, and economic opportunities in manufacturing. However, it is important to remember and acknowledge the importance of agriculture to the region. The opportunity to acquire farmland was one of the primary reasons for the first large group of German-speaking pioneers, the Pennsylvania Mennonites, settling in this area. The draw to acquire good farmland has never stopped among German-speaking immigrants.

Growing up in Bavaria, Christine Lindner's parents had a "kleine Landwirtschaft."[73] She worked on the family farm, milking cows and doing other chores. At nineteen, she married a farmer. She and her husband realized that there was an opportunity to buy a bigger farm in Canada rather than in Germany. In 1983, together with their two small children, Christine and her husband moved from Bavaria to a Wellington Region farm they had bought before even leaving Germany.

The end of the 1980s would see the fall of the Iron Curtain, the opening of the Berlin Wall, and the unification of a divided Germany. This all coincided, not surprisingly, with the smallest number of German immigrants arriving in Canada. For census year 1989/90, less than 1% of total immigrants listed Germany as their last country of residence before emigrating. This is a stark contrast to the 10.27% thirty years earlier.[74]

Wolfgang Wurzbacher is the only interviewee for this book who moved to Canada in the 1990s, though his arrival might be considered a homecoming; his parents originally immigrated to Canada in 1951, and he was born here. Following his parents' separation, his mother would eventually move herself and her son back to Germany and build a home for them in Baden-Württemberg. Almost all his schooling took place in Germany, in German-language public schools. Years later, on a trip to Canada to visit his father, Wolfgang met his future wife Almut, a young woman who had immigrated to Canada as a teenager with her farming family ten years earlier. To stay in touch, they became penpals. Their relationship deepened, and Wolfgang decided to move to Canada. In Wolfgang's own words, this was, in some

---

72 "History & Milestones - Toyota Motor Manufacturing Canada Inc.", accessed July 29, 2019, https://tmmc.ca/en/toyota-manufacturing-plants/

73 Translation: a small agricultural business.

74 "Table 13.2 Immigrants to Canada, by Country of Last Permanent Residence, 1959/1960 to 2009/2010", accessed November 18, 2015, https://www.statcan.gc.ca/pub/11-402-x/2011000/chap/imm/tbl/tbl02-eng.htm

ways, a return to the land of his birth, in other ways it was like he was entering the country for the first time.

The past twenty years have seen Kitchener, Waterloo, Cambridge, and the surrounding towns and hamlets deal with the familiar cycles of economic ebb and flow, political wrangling, questions around future immigration, innovation, industrialization, and investment. There is a communal desire to not only acknowledge but embrace the region's rich heritage and legacy of courage, hard work, perseverance, risk-taking, and creativity. As this brief historical overview has shown, the German-speaking immigrants to the Waterloo Region had a profound and significant impact locally, through which they also played a major role in the history of Ontario and Canada. The foundations are strong, and the Germans of Waterloo Region are likely to continue to be a relevant and vital piece of the Canadian mosaic.

Mennonites

Christine Kampen Robinson and Nikolai Penner

This chapter tells the stories of a group of German-speaking immigrants to Canada different than the rest of the book, namely the stories of people who are connected to the Mennonite faith. We start with their stories because Mennonites played an important role in the settlement and establishment of Waterloo Region, including creating Ebytown, which later became Kitchener-Waterloo. German-speaking Mennonites have a complicated migration history, and fall into a variety of diverse groups — Steiner estimates thirty-three different group affiliations in Ontario alone.[75] At a general level, these groups are characterized and categorized by a number of factors, including places of origin (e.g., Swiss Mennonites versus Dutch Mennonites), places along their migration path (e.g., Russian Mennonites and Prussian Mennonites), names of founders (e.g., David Martin Mennonites), and language (e.g., Low German-speaking Mennonites). The focus of this chapter will be on two groups primarily. The first group are Russian Mennonites who immigrated to Canada after World War II from Imperial Russia and the Soviet Union, from an area that today is in Ukraine. The second group are Low German-speaking Mennonites,[76] some also referred to as Old Colony Mennonites.[77] As a result, this chapter is not intended to be a comprehensive overview of Mennonite migration to Canada. Instead, we will introduce these two of the many sub-groups of German-speaking Mennonites and depict and compare the experiences of individuals within these two groups to tell their migration stories.

The Information Base for this Chapter

The stories presented in this chapter come from different sources than the stories found elsewhere in this book. We drew on information from our two dissertation projects, which include interviews with German-speaking Mennonite immigrants in Ontario, since the interviews of the Oral History Project only included one self-identified Mennonite interviewee: Victor Rausch.

---

75 Sam Steiner, In Search of Promised Lands: A Religious History of Mennonites in Ontario. (Harrisonburg and Waterloo: Herald Press, 2015).

76 Although both groups we refer to in this chapter lived in Russia at some point and used Low German, we use 'Low German-speaking Mennonites' to refer to one particular subgroup: Mennonites who migrated to Central and South America from Canada in the 1920s.

77 The Old Colony Mennonite Church is one of numerous subdivisions within the Mennonite faith characterized by a conservative theology in relation to salvation; members are recognizable in their dress, with women wearing a dark head covering and floral pattern dresses. The name "Old Colony" refers to the original migrants coming from the first settlement in Russia, the "old" colony. See Royden Loewen, Village among nations: "Canadian" Mennonites in a Transnational World, 1916-2006. (Toronto: University of Toronto Press, 2013).

The first of these projects was a dissertation by Nikolai Penner.[78] He looked at the languages spoken in south-western Ontario by Russian Mennonites who immigrated to Canada in the 1920s and after World War II. In 2007, Nikolai interviewed 24 Mennonites in Waterloo Region, all of whom were born in today's southern Ukraine between 1918 and 1938 and had immigrated to Canada between 1947 and 1967 from Germany directly or via South America. The interviews were conducted in High German,[79] and concentrated on various aspects of participants' life stories connected to language use, identity, and attitudes toward the languages they are using today.

Admittedly, Victor Rausch, the only self-identified Mennonite interviewee of the Oral History Project, was born and grew up in a smaller Mennonite settlement in a different part of Ukraine than the rest of the Mennonites interviewed by Nikolai. Nevertheless, the linguistic situation throughout Victor's life, his experiences with leaving the Soviet Union, fleeing to Germany, and then immigrating to Canada, as well as his use of both Plautdietsch (Low German language or dialect) and High German and his attitude towards the German culture in general resemble those of the other Russian Mennonite interviewees so much that we are not going to make a distinction, and will treat him as a part of the Russian Mennonite group.

The second set of stories was collected by Christine Kampen Robinson and formed the basis for her dissertation project, which examined the connection between language and identity within a group of Low German-speaking Mennonite women in Waterloo Region.[80] Christine took notes during and after their meetings, conducted individual interviews and group discussions, and recorded conversations. Of central importance to this dissertation project was eliciting narratives related to language and identity, rather than creating a complete picture of participants' migration experiences. Lastly, it is important to note that the participants in both dissertation projects participated with the understanding that their personal information would be kept anonymous. Therefore, the names in this chapter are pseudonyms, and some of the identifying details have been altered.

We will begin by sketching a brief history of migration of both Mennonite groups to the present day, paying particular attention to their arrival in Canada, and their use of Low and High German. Following this, we will introduce several individuals from both groups and use their own words to illustrate the ways in which language influenced not only their migration experiences, but also other experiences in their everyday lives.

Since both labels — Low German and High German — are used differently by different groups and differently yet again in Linguistics, we need to mention that we

---

78 Nikolai Penner, "The High German of Russian Mennonites in Ontario." (Unpublished Ph.D. diss., University of Waterloo, 2009).

79 High German is the label that Russian Mennonites use to refer to their variety of German. It bears a close relationship to dialects of southern Germany and to the written standard German.

80 Christine Kampen Robinson, "Contesting the centre: Low German-speaking Mennonite identity, language, and literacy constructions." (Unpublished Ph.D. diss., University of Waterloo, 2017).

are using both terms as members of these two Mennonite groups use them. Low German generally refers to the dialects spoken in northern Germany, whereas High German is a label for the dialects in the southern parts of Germany. We use Low German as the English translation of Plautdietsch — a Low German dialect or language — that is spoken by some Mennonite groups. We use High German as the Mennonites do: both for dialects that are based on regional dialects in the southern parts of the German lands, and for the literary language of the German Bible, in literature, and in education.

Mennonites: Their Origins and History

Mennonites originated as an Anabaptist religious group that traces its beginnings to Reformation-era Europe. Anabaptists differentiated themselves from the Roman Catholic Church through the belief that individuals could interpret the Bible for themselves, rather than relying on a church representative to interpret it for them. This belief was further supported by stressing adult, rather than infant, baptism, a commitment to non-violence, and a refusal to swear oaths. The Anabaptist movement began in Switzerland in the early 1500s, and due to continuous persecution from both governments and other Christian churches, the movement was driven underground. The persecution also forced the spread of followers across Europe when they tried to escape torture and death. After being driven underground in Switzerland, Anabaptists moved to southern Germany and Austria, eventually finding their way down the Rhine River to northern Germany and the Netherlands.

In the Netherlands, a former Catholic priest, Menno Simons — after whom the Mennonites are named — joined the movement in the 1530s. He became one of the most influential Anabaptist leaders.[81] Although the name was originally only used to refer to the Anabaptist groups settled in northern Europe, it was eventually applied to southern groups as well, the exception being two additional Anabaptist groups that still exist today, namely the Hutterites, named after Jakob Hutter, and the Amish, named after Jakob Amman.[82]

Due to extensive religious persecution, the different Anabaptist groups eventually all but left their countries of origin. The group known as Swiss Mennonites includes a wide range of religious affiliation and involvement. The most conservative of these represent the most visible population of Mennonites in the Waterloo Region due to their plain dress, and rejection of modern conveniences such as cars. These groups of Swiss Mennonites tend to be religiously conservative, and have kept their religious practices and way of life, having migrated to the United States at the turn of the 18th century, primarily to Pennsylvania, and eventually on to Ontario in the first half of

---

81 Cornelius J. Dyck, An Introduction to Mennonite History. (Scottdale: Herald Press, 1993), 102.
82 C. Henry Smith, Smith's Story of the Mennonites (5th ed.). (Newton: Faith and Life Press, 1981), 73.

the 19th century following the Revolutionary War.[83] Swiss Mennonites had a significant impact on the founding of Waterloo Region, including establishing the settlement of Kitchener-Waterloo, which they called Ebytown originally.

The group that settled in the Netherlands in the 16th century is sometimes referred to as the Dutch Mennonites. After leaving their homes in the Netherlands and northern Germany, they initially moved to Prussia, and remained there for a few centuries before migrating to southern Imperial Russia, where they settled in colonies and largely remained until World War II. Due to this aspect of their migration history, this group is more commonly referred to as Russian Mennonites, and we will also do so here. Unlike their Swiss brethren, Russian Mennonites did not begin migrating to North America until the late 19th century; they migrated in three separate waves — during the 1870s, the 1920s, and the 1950s. During the 1870s and 1920s migrations, the Swiss Mennonites already living in Ontario were instrumental in helping the Russian Mennonites make the transition to Canada, providing housing, food, and clothing for the immigrants when they arrived. However, very few Russian Mennonites from these waves settled in Waterloo Region, as most of them were headed towards western Canada.[84] The largest group of Russian Mennonites emigrating from Russia via Germany to Waterloo Region came during the 1950s.

A portion of the Russian Mennonite immigrants who arrived during the 1870s and 1920s settled in the prairie provinces of Manitoba and Saskatchewan, where they established farms and villages that very much resembled those in Russia. However, the most conservative of these immigrants moved on to Paraguay and Mexico after provincial legislation resulted in changes to the Mennonite private school system.[85] Prior to this legislation, private schools operated without significant government oversight allowing Mennonites to use High German as the language of instruction. The new legislation gave the government more authority over what was being taught in schools, and specifically the language in which that material was being taught. As a result, some settlers felt that their freedom of language and religion was being encroached upon, and thus emigrated to Mexico and Paraguay in search of that freedom.

The willingness of the Mennonites to uproot their entire lives to maintain instruction in German, the language deeply connected to their religion, is linked to one of the tenets of Mennonite self-understanding, namely the desire to remain separate from the 'world'. Along with plain dress and a rejection of various worldly luxuries, choice of language has historically been an effective way in which Mennonites establish and maintain their separateness from the dominant 'world', whether in Europe, Asia, North or South America. This is especially true for more

83 Paul H. Burkholder and John M. Bender, "Ontario (Canada)." Global Anabaptist Mennonite Encyclopaedia Online. 1990, accessed August 15, 2015, https://gameo.org/index.php?title=Ontario_(Canada)&oldid=114359
84 Burkholder and Bender, "Ontario (Canada)."
85 Cornelius Krahn and H. Leonard Sawatzky, "Old Colony Mennonites." Global Anabaptist Mennonite Encyclopaedia Online. 1990, accessed February 16, 2016. https://gameo.org/index.php?title=Old_Colony_Mennonites&oldid=113570

conservative Mennonite groups, such as the Old Colony Mennonite Church, one of the primary church affiliations of Mennonites in Mexico. Old Colony Mennonites established settlements primarily in Mexico and Paraguay, but as more conservative leaders perceived those colonies becoming too worldly, additional colonies were established in Bolivia, Belize, and Argentina.

Generally, and even within Canada, there is a wide range of interpretations as to the centrality of dress code, gender roles, amount of interaction with non-Mennonites, and church practices to religious life. In Paraguay, for example, the dominant group are not members of the Old Colony Church, but rather more progressive Mennonites who have much more in common with progressive Canadian Mennonites in terms of their religious faith and overall lifestyle. In Mexico, where these more progressive Mennonites can also be found, on the other hand, just as in the initial settlements on the Canadian prairies, immigrants connected to the Old Colony Church organized their lives as they had in Russia and Prussia: in villages with a central main street, houses on either side, with a meeting house and a school, in a close-knit community overseen by the church authorities, including a bishop and a committee of Älteste (elders). As theologian David Schroeder writes, Old Colony theology is a community-based one of Christian formation, while the Russian Mennonite theology is more individual and centred on grace, the love and mercy given to humans by God.[86]

For much of their history, Mennonites were a primarily agrarian people. While Canada provided a climate that was familiar to them after their lives in Russia, for many, life in the arid deserts of Paraguay and Mexico did not allow them to farmstead successfully. As a result, during the 1950s, Mennonites began returning to Canada from Paraguay and Mexico, but rather than returning to Manitoba or Saskatchewan, many chose south-western Ontario. The majority settled in the Niagara Region, and Aylmer area, but a portion of this group also settled in Waterloo Region.[87]

Moving to Canada

The Old Colony theology continues to permeate the lives of Low German-speaking Mennonites who have settled in Canada since the 1950s. Since then and continuing today, the question of where to settle has not been an easy one for many, as they continue the rhythm of the seasonal worker even when they work a different job. Neta, one of the women who will be introduced later, talked about the complication of travelling back and forth between Mexico and Canada, and the associations people had with the journey:

> "I think for some people when you lived in Mexico, you didn't —
> you never really got to go anywhere. It was work, work, work, but
> when you drove to Canada then you could go to a place like drive

---

86 David Schroeder, "Evangelicals Denigrate Conservatives", Preservings 15 (1999): 47-48.
87 Burkholder and Bender, "Ontario (Canada)."

through the US and that was exciting until you got to Canada and
had to work, ha ha ha."

Today, for Mennonites returning from Mexico to Canada, the community ties
either disintegrate completely or must be renegotiated, because in Canada families
sometimes live in very isolated contexts — either on their own farms or in towns and
villages with non-Mennonite Canadian neighbours, as opposed to the villages and
colonies they are used to in Mexico. This isolation from church and community
results in an orientation towards Canada, which creates a tension between the fear of
sin and the promise of freedom. But as Steiner writes:

> "Those leaving for Canada had no religious support from the
> communities they left, since the leadership in Mexico saw the negative
> impact of those who left on the community that remained. Some of
> those who left were already on the margins of the communities because
> of their desire to access greater technology, a different religious
> experience, or simply greater economic opportunity in Canada."[88]

Language and Mennonite Identity

As previously mentioned, the name Mennonite was originally a religious term that is
used to refer both to the religious faith, as well as the European ethnic background
and culture described in the previous sections. As such, it has become an ethno-
religious term, and this is one of the reasons why it is so difficult to come up with a
comprehensive definition or description of what Mennonite means. As Loewen
outlines, Mennonite constructions of identity always revolve around faith *and*
ethnicity, even when one or the other is being rejected as the basis for the identity
construction.[89] We have used Mennonite to refer to the ethno-religious category but
also use it to define the group along linguistic and cultural lines. Language,
specifically the German language, and how different groups orient towards it have
significantly shaped the experiences of those groups, whether they assimilated to
Canadian culture, as most of the Russian Mennonites did, or whether they remained
more staunchly separate from Canadian culture, as those closely connected to the Old
Colony Church have done. However, all these groups have approached the issue of
assimilation from different angles in relation to the significance of the German
language to their religious identity. This can be seen in the ways in which groups
adapted their language use in official institutions, such as their churches. For pre-
World War II Mennonite immigrants, the shift to English was an intentional move to
demonstrate their allegiance to Canada.[90] Overall, as Henry Paetkau describes,
Russian Mennonite immigrants to Canada have had an "outward" focus in terms of

---

88 Sam Steiner, In Search of Promised Lands: A religious history of Mennonites in Ontario
   (Harrisonburg and Waterloo: Herald Press, 2015), 488.
89 Royden Loewen, "The poetics of peoplehood: Mennonite ethnicity and Mennonite faith in
   Canada." In Christianity and Ethnicity in Canada, edited by Paul Bramadat and David
   Seljak, (Oxford: Oxford University Press, 2008), 330-364.
90 Steiner, In Search of Promised Lands, 355.

self-concept, which "transcended language, culture, class or clan."[91] While most Russian Mennonite groups integrated into the dominant Canadian culture, taking over the English language as their own, Low German-speaking Mennonites from Mexico continue to use Low German in Canada today. However, the lamentations of the earlier generations about the younger generation giving up their language (and by extension their identity) echo through both groups.

Both Russian Mennonites and Low German-speaking Mennonites use High German in a different way than the Swiss Mennonites do. When Swiss Mennonites arrived in North America they spoke and wrote different High German dialects. In Pennsylvania, the differences between their dialects were levelled and a new High German dialect, Pennsylvania Dutch, emerged. The Russian and Low German-speaking Mennonites, on the other hand, speak Plautdietsch (Low German)[92] as their community language, while maintaining the importance of High German as the language of school, literature, and most importantly, church.[93]

Despite living for over a century in southern Ukraine, which was then part of Imperial Russia, many Mennonites never learned to speak Russian, because they lived in isolated villages, where it was not necessary for them to interact with non-German speakers. In 1936, when German-language Mennonite schools were forced to close under Soviet purview, and the language of instruction became Russian, community members learned Russian to different extents.[94] Once they came to Canada, migrants were confronted with and had to learn English. Low German-speaking Mennonites in Mexico had a very similar experience to the Mennonites in Russia. In both places, life was organized into villages and colonies that were for the most part self-sufficient, and the everyday language of the community was and still is Low German. However, whereas Russian Mennonites hold non-religious High German literature and culture in high regard, these do not play a significant, active role in the lives of Low German-speaking Mennonites, due to the more conservative nature of the Old Colony Church. While the official language of instruction in Low German-speaking Mennonite parochial schools remains High German, and their books are written in High German (printed in Fraktur, an old German typeface), most community members cannot communicate orally in High German.[95]

---

91 Henry Paetkau, "Separation or Integration? The Russian Mennonite Immigrant Community in Ontario, 1924-1945." (Unpublished Ph.D. diss., University of Western Ontario, 1986), 380.

92 Mennonite migrants carried Low German, Flemish, and Frisian dialects to Prussia, where these mixed with local Low German varieties. Over time, dialect levelling occurred, and Plautdietsch was formed and became their identity marker.

93 Jakob Warkentin Goerzen, "Low German in Canada: A Study of Plautdietsch." (Unpublished PhD diss., University of Toronto, 1952), 22.

94 Wolfgang Wilfried Moelleken, "The Development of the Linguistic Repertoire of the Mennonites from Russia", In Diachronic Studies on the Languages of the Anabaptists, edited by Kate Burridge and Werner Enninger, (Bochum: Universitätsverlag Dr. N. Brockmeyer, 1992), 64-93.

95 Kelly Lynn Hedges, "'Plautdietsch' and 'Huuchdietsch' in Chihuahua: Language literacy and identity among the Old Colony Mennonites in Northern Mexico." (Unpublished Ph.D. diss., Yale University, 1996).

In Mexico, exposure to Spanish is limited, as the exposure to Russian was limited in Russia, due to the inward focus and insular nature of the community. Nevertheless, precisely because of the isolation of their communities, it is typical for many Mennonites to try to find a common relative or at least acquaintance when they get to know another Mennonite, by asking questions about each other's immediate and extended families, such as what their last names are, which village in the Old Country they were from, who they were married to, or who their teacher or church minister was in a specific year. Very often, they can go two, three, or four generations back to find that connection, but most likely, a connection of some sort will soon be established, even if it is too distant to be even considered plausible by non-Mennonites. This is known as the Mennonite Game; most Mennonites and their descendants not only find great pleasure in playing it, but have also mastered it to perfection, and know the genealogy of their families by heart.

Russian Mennonite immigrants from 1945 onward, almost all of whom were well into their seventies and eighties at the time of the interviews, do not look any different from most other people of European descent their age in Canada. They drive ordinary cars, wear contemporary clothing, shop at malls, go to movies, parties, concerts, and church events. What unites them is their Mennonite faith, their love for Borschtsch, Pirogen, and Zwieback,[96] and a wealth of life experiences with unbelievable stories of childhood in 'the old land', their flight to and then from Germany, and finally their migration to Canada. Life stories of Russian Mennonites are full of both happy memories and tragic stories from the past. The stories of picking cherries, apricots, and watermelons in their gardens, swimming in the Dnjepr or Molotschna rivers with other children, or pleasant memories of coming and settling in Canada after the war are intertwined with the horror stories of relatives being taken away at night by the KGB, surviving the famine of 1933, going through the pain and suffering of the war, avoiding being deported back to the Soviet Union soon thereafter. These and many other memories were quite painful for most interviewees to talk about. In fact, it was not uncommon for both men and women to burst into tears when talking about their lives, and some have refused to be interviewed altogether for the same reason. However, these experiences, both good and bad, are common to most if not all first-generation Russian Mennonites living in Canada today. Although the life story of every single member of this group is unique, the life paths of these Russian Mennonites nevertheless show several similarities, which we will try to illustrate here by telling the story of one person.

From Russia to Canada: Gerhard's Story

The slim, smiling old man with lively grey eyes who is sitting across the dinner table, and looking at the audio recording device between us is Gerhard Enns, born at the end of the 1920s in a Mennonite village in the steppes of southern Ukraine. As a child, he spoke Low German with his family, friends, and other villagers, and picked

---

96 Translation: borscht (Ukrainian beet soup), pierogi (filled dumplings), zwieback (a form of rusk).

up some High German before he started attending the village school. Taught entirely in High German by a teacher from a neighbouring Lutheran village, the school was forced to switch to Russian as the only language of instruction after Gerhard completed the third grade. During the war, he was drafted into the German army, taken captive by the Allies, and spent several years in Austria. In a refugee camp, he met several Canadians working there, and was greatly impressed by them: "That's where I developed deep respect for Canadian people. And that's holding up until today. If there are good people, then it's Canadians. It's Canadians." In 1948, he was able to immigrate to Canada thanks to the Mennonite farmers who offered him a job for a year:

> "I had a grandmother, two uncles and a few cousins in Canada. But
> they were poor as church mice. I could come because a Mennonite
> farmer in Manitoba signed a paper that he would give me work for a
> dollar a day. They were the Mennonites who came here in 1874.
> That's how I came to Canada."

The linguistic situation in Manitoba among the first-wave Mennonite immigrants, where Gerhard found himself at the end of the 1940s, was very similar to the one he knew as a child in his Mennonite village in southern Ukraine: Low German was the only community and family language, whereas High German was reserved for writing and for religious and official functions within the community. Although Mennonite children in Manitoba were exposed to the English language in schools, its use was largely restricted to communicating with non-Mennonites.

Gerhard stayed in Manitoba on the farm for several years, until his brother emigrated from Germany and came to Kitchener, where Gerhard joined him in 1952. Knowing no English, finding a job in Kitchener-Waterloo turned out to be challenging partially because of their German background:

> "We didn't know any English, went to a factory and he [the owner]
> said: 'We don't hire Nazis!' And he himself was German! So, we
> went to a Jewish lumber dealer, and he said: 'Sure, we'll take you
> guys!' So, that was our first job here. There were so many furniture
> factories here in Kitchener-Waterloo, and that's where they dried
> lumber. We worked there."

Despite having the entire interview conducted in very good High German, Gerhard claimed to have only spoken Low German with his wife, relatives, and friends before they had children. Major changes came when the children were born. Like most Russian Mennonites in Canada, both Gerhard and his wife viewed High German as a more useful language compared to Low German and switched entirely to High German when raising their children. At the same time, High German remained the only language of the church Gerhard and his family attended in Kitchener-Waterloo. For the most part of the 1950s, High German was the only language used during the church services, Sunday schools, and summer camps, although the pressure grew to introduce more English. This pressure came primarily from the Mennonite immigrants of the previous migration wave, whose children were born in Canada and were already more proficient in English than in High German. This resulted in a few heated debates, and it was a significant source of conflict in the church community, as Gerhard describes:

> "There were all kinds of quarrels about this and I have fought really
> hard to keep German because of our mother, my wife's mother who
> could speak English, but it always remained a foreign language for
> her: 'It doesn't touch my heart', she said."

Gerhard further remembers:

> "Even our children, her grandchildren, were for the German
> language when filling out the ballot in the church: Do you prefer
> English? Do you prefer German? So, our children chose German.
> 'Only because of you, Oma!' they said. Oh yeah, there were sparks
> flying back then."

Interestingly, once the children went to school, and Gerhard and his wife's parents passed away, their opinion about the German language in church changed drastically:

> "Only when the kids grew up a bit and went to school, then we
> started to support English in the church too. One can't hold on to
> what's gone. Our generation will die next, the new ones are coming,
> and you have to use their language. English is their home language
> now, so that's what you have to use."

Like most other Russian Mennonites, both Gerhard and his wife have completely switched to English today, when communicating with their children and grandchildren. They occasionally use High German when talking or corresponding with their relatives in Germany and Russia. Nevertheless, they feel very close to Low German and consider it 'their language', when they say:

> "We only speak Low German with my wife and friends, even today,
> and we think it's the best language in the world, and if you know the
> language, you can say so many things which can't be translated at all."

Stories like the ones Gerhard is telling have come up time and again in our interviews with Russian Mennonites. Circumstances, names, and emphases vary slightly, of course. Yet, the members of this group share a lot of experiences, their faith, and their outlook on life.

From Mexico to Canada: Justina, Neta, Greta, and Patty

The experience of our other group, Low German-speaking Mennonites, closely mirrors that of Gerhard's generation in terms of language and the pressures that parents feel to keep their children connected to the language of their family and their heritage. As has already been mentioned, we call this group Low German-speaking Mennonites because this allows for the inclusion of people who are no longer an official part of the Old Colony Church. Attitudes about migration, and especially about language, are complicated and varied, and as such, both unite and divide community members.

Neta and Justina, who are both members of the Old Colony Church, have family in both Mexico and Canada who speak little to no English. They both feel a strong sense of obligation to raise their children to be able to communicate in Low German. Neta is a round-faced woman with blue eyes and a contagious belly laugh. She has six children, aged three to twelve, and came to Canada as a fourteen-year-old. Justina is a tall woman with eyes that betray a wicked sense of humour. She has four children, aged new-born to nine, and she came to Manitoba as a fourteen-year-old with her father, a bishop, and her six sisters. Both women identify Low German as the language they are most comfortable speaking. Both married within the Old Colony community, and neither have spent a lot of time in Mexico since immigrating to Canada, although they both talk about continuing to feel a connection to Mexico and wanting to go back to visit family. The theme of family connection, and the link that language provides for them is prevalent in the stories these women are telling. For example, when Justina is asked why she wants her children to speak Low German[97] at home, she says:

> "Because their grandparents speak German and they wanted to talk
> to the kids, and nowhere else would the kids learn Low German
> except at home from the mother and father. If they were allowed
> English all the time, they wouldn't know Low German and then the
> grandparents could never speak to their grandchildren."

Both Neta and Justina talk about how difficult they found it to raise their children to be fluent in Low German. Neta especially comments on how there are times when her kids have questions, and if she speaks German, they don't understand.

As a result of her children's disconnectedness from Low German, Neta has lobbied for her church to change the Sunday School curriculum to be taught in English, rather than in High German, so that the children would be more connected to the Bible stories, and as a result, more connected to the church and their faith. This effort was not easy for her, and she was met with opposition from the leadership, although many parents, and especially the children, were very much in favour of the change. Like Gerhard's realization, for Neta it is more important that the children stay connected and are a part of the church than that the language is maintained. She has English Bible storybooks at home that her children read, and she says: "Now I have [a Bible] that [has] from one side Low German and one side English that I can understand more than before."

The relationship to language is complicated, however, and the positive association and sense of obligation to pass Low German on to their children is not one shared by all people in this community. Patty and Greta are two women who

---

97 In her interviews, Justina also refers to Low German as German; she uses both interchangeably.

have both left the Old Colony Church. They wear pants and earrings, cut and dye their hair; and although both attend church, one attends a Lutheran and the other a Pentecostal church. Patty immigrated to Canada with her family when she was only seven, is one of nine children, and says she only uses Low German to "have fun with [her] sister," or to make jokes, and that she does not "even speak it that well." As a result, she has intentionally not taught her children Low German, and holds a very different attitude from the one held by Neta and Justina, when she says:

> "In my opinion, why live in a country like Canada where the first language is English? Why would you teach them a different language, right? If you're gonna live here the first thing you should know is English because everything has to do with the English, right? Like, they go to school — kids go to school knowing only German, and then so they're set back just as far as those who come from Mexico — don't know the language, don't know anything about the culture or anything so they're set back by having to first of all learn the language and then catch up with the rest of the kids, right? Like, to me it just makes sense that you would teach them English first, like the German will come naturally even if they don't speak it, they can understand it, right? Like, if you still speak it at home as a family."

Greta, on the other hand, although she is no longer part of the Old Colony Church, actively teaches her daughter and son Low German, for precisely the same reasons that Neta and Justina do. Greta came to Canada when she was a teenager, but she did not come with her family. She came against her family's wishes, following a husband, who subsequently left her. When she first came to Canada, she says, she thought she could "put [her] Low German away,...put it on the back burner," box up that part of herself to live only in English. But her plan did not work, and she realized when her son was born that he simply would not learn Low German by osmosis and decided that a passive proficiency in Low German (only being able to understand it), would disconnect him from his history and his family. As a result, she compels her children to use Low German regularly so that they can communicate with their grandparents and cousins. Because of Greta's financial situation, her family is also able to return to Mexico at least every two years, which helps the children to feel connected to their family there and to form bonds with the country of their parents' birth in a way that Neta and Justina's children are unable to do.

What Do Two Different Mennonite Groups Have in Common?

A commonality in the information gleaned from the two projects is the overwhelming tendency for participants to use the terms Mennonite and German (either the High German version "Deutsch" or the Low German version "Dietsch") in reference to themselves.[98] This may at least in part be connected to the fact that in both cases the

---

98 Penner, The High German, 184.

group constituted a minority of German (dialect) speakers in a dominant population of speakers of other languages, whether that was Russian, Spanish, or English. In any case, it is significant that this category of Germanness seems to be one that transcends any specific migration history of Mennonites, which is notably different for the two groups, and connects them inextricably to the centrality of language in terms of self-identification.

In addition to language being a significant unifying factor in their identity construction, their stories of migration and displacement serve a similar function. Epp writes that

> "Ethnoreligious groups such as the Mennonites…maintain significant collective myths — patterns of thinking and telling their story — that are shaped by both cultural tradition and religious belief. With respect to their many global migrations, the story has been one of adventurous and visionary leaders, all male, guiding a particular group forward historically to a new land where the integrity of religious belief and cultural custom could be preserved."[99]

Both groups were unable to mirror in Canada the lives they left behind in Russia and Mexico. Due in large part to space limitations, neither group was able to establish colonies and self-sufficient villages, enclaves where everyone knew each other, ate the same food, and spoke the same language. The groups' responses to this challenge were vastly different, however. For the Low German-speaking Mennonites from Mexico, Canada was simultaneously a promised land and a danger, and part of the tension they experience in establishing themselves here is that their very existence in Canada is fraught with the deep-seated belief that their connection to the world draws them away from their faith. While many maintain traditions and connection to the Old Colony Church, many others do not, as with the four women whose voices were presented here. At the same time, the Low German language remains an important connector, allowing identities and ways of being Dietsch to be reshaped beyond church affiliation.

Russian Mennonites, on the other hand, tend to frame an arrival in Canada very much along the lines of an arrival in a promised land, a final settling down after generations of migration across continents. They do not experience the same tension, in part because of the parallels they draw between themselves and the Israelites finally arriving in Israel. But while the Jews viewed Israel as a promised land, in the Russian Mennonite narrative, Canada becomes the country that was shaped into the Promised Land, in part because of their hard work and initiative. Re-establishing village life seems to have been less important to Russian Mennonites and does not remain the near constant struggle it appears to be for the Low German-speaking Mennonite community.

---

99 Marlene Epp, "Pioneers, refugees, exiles, and transnationals: Gendering diaspora in an ethnoreligious context", Journal of the Canadian Historical Association 12 (2001): 137-153.

In conclusion we can say that the members of the two Mennonite groups with whom we spoke talked about migration experiences, struggles and successes, and attitudes towards and beliefs about language, which are quite different from those shared by the other German-speaking immigrants whose voices can be heard in this book. What the Mennonites have in common with the other groups, however, is not only the German language but also the experience of having grown up in a different part of the world, and of now making Canada and specifically Waterloo Region their home.

They Came from South-eastern Europe
Lori Straus and Emma Betz

In English, there is a saying: "Home is where the heart is." This suggests that there can only be one home; to have two would split the heart. Germans of Yugoslavia, Hungary, and Romania ponder this, especially when deciding where Heimat is. Whether meant figuratively or literally, the German concept of Heimat does not translate easily into English. Yes, we try, for example, with home or homeland, but neither captures the spirit or soul of a people. Home and Heimat for a bilingual German can be two different locations. For the participants in the Oral History Project who grew up in Hungary, former Yugoslavia, and Romania, Heimat is usually where the heart was born. It may beat and thrive in Canada, but it was born in the Gottschee, the Banat, the Batschka, Siebenbürgen, and other regions in those three countries.

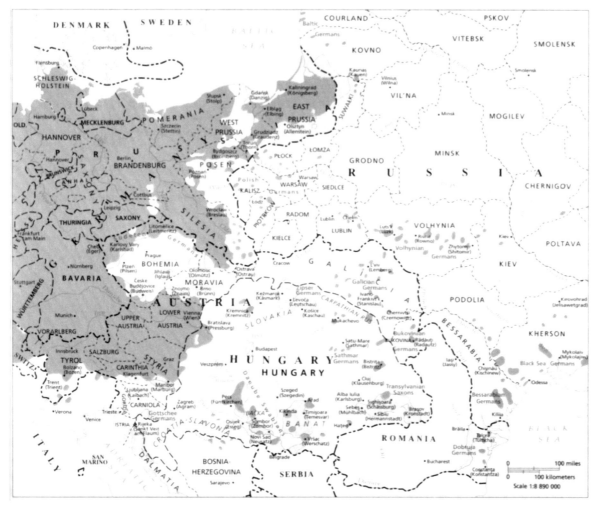

Germans in east-central Europe, ca. 1900. Reproduced with permission from Paul Robert Magocsi, Historical Atlas of Central Europe, 3rd revised and expanded edition. (Toronto: University of Toronto Press, 2018), p. 104.

What was this Heimat like? What did it feel like to live there? And if these people truly felt at home, perhaps even felt like their spirit was created there, why did they leave? The German populations in what are today Hungary, Romania, Croatia, Serbia, Slovenia, and Bosnia came from many different places in west-central Europe and soon became known by names that do not actually indicate where they originated from. For example, the Transylvanian Saxons did not come from Saxony, nor did most of the Danube Swabians come from Swabia.

The earliest wave of German immigration to these eastern regions was most likely in the 12th century to Siebenbürgen, an area in the Carpathian Mountains often referred to as Transylvania. They remained in this area for about 800 years, continuing their culture and language as a minority in their country (first Hungary, then Romania). This group became known as the Siebenbürger or Transylvanian Saxons. The earliest mention of the name Saxon appears in 1206 in a Hungarian royal document. It referred to the German settlers who lived around the episcopal residence of Weißenburg in Siebenbürgen.[100] According to a book published in 1795, the Saxons originated from Flanders and the south of Germany and arrived between 1143 and 1161.[101] A later observation noted that these people were occasionally called Flandrenses in the 12th century. This supports the possibility that they may have come from Flanders and surrounding regions, or that they originated specifically in Brabant, also a part of Flanders.[102]

Siebenbürgen comprises nine regions: Hunyad, Weißenburg, Klausenburg, Bistritz-Nassod, Hargitta, Kovasna, Kronstadt, Hermannstadt, and Mieresch.[103] It was unique among the German settlements in south-eastern Europe because, for a time, it had its own government and political boundaries, and because the dominant religion eventually became Lutheranism. Most of the later German settlements would remain Roman Catholic.

The likely next oldest settlement is the Gottschee, an area in what is now the south-central part of Slovenia.[104] The inhabitants of this area and their descendants are called Gottscheer. Starting in 1320, the Counts of Ortenburg, a noble family from Upper Bavaria, began to settle this area by transferring farmers from Kärnten and East Tyrol. Later, they brought in settlers from Franconia, Thuringia, and Swabia. The earliest piece of evidence of this community is the appointment of a priest in 1336.[105]

---

100 Holm Sundhaussen, Deutsche Geschichte im Osten Europas, edited by Gunter Schold, (Berlin: Wolf Jobst Siedler Verlag GmbH, 1995), 31.

101 August Ludwig von Schlözer, Kritische Sammlungen zur Geschichte der Deutschen in Siebenbürgen. Unveränderter Nachdruck der Ausgabe Göttingen 1795 – 1797, (Böhlau Verlag: Cologne, 1979), 4.

102 Sundhaussen, Deutsche Geschichte, 31.

103 Günther Meizer, "Siebenbürgen." accessed August 11, 2015, https://www.siebenbuerger.de/portal/land-und-leute/siebenbuergen/wo.php

104 Gottscheer Heritage and Genealogy Association, "Brief History of Gottschee," accessed July 30, 2019, https://gottschee.org/history/

105 Harald Zimmermann, Die Deutsche Südostsiedlung im Mittelalter (Berlin: Wolf Jobst Siedler Verlag GmbH, 1995), 74.

In the 16th century, the Ottoman Empire had conquered much of the then Hungarian territories. In Siebenbürgen, national and religious liberties and traditions were allowed to flourish, and these rights were later physically defended against the Habsburg monarchy.[106] Two hundred years later, when the Habsburgs conquered territory that had been left bare and devastated after 150 years of wars with the Ottoman Empire, they sought a specific group of people to re-settle and redevelop it, so they appealed to Catholic Germans to immigrate. The new settlers would increase the presence of the German language and the Catholic religion in these areas, but they would also serve as a buffer against further invasions.[107]

The Germans immigrating via the Austrian Empire in the 18th century came in three main waves, often referred to as The Great Swabian Migration or The Great Swabian Trek:

- The Caroline Colonization between 1718 and 1737 under Charles VI. Most of these immigrants settled in Swabian Turkey (west of the Batschka) and the Banat and a few in Sathmar and Ofner Bergland.[108]
- The Maria Theresian Colonization between 1744 and 1772 under Maria Theresia. They settled predominantly in the Batschka.[109]
- The Josephine Colonization between 1782 and 1787 under Joseph II. They settled mainly around the Banat.[110]

New settlers were sought to work the land; because of the wars with the Ottoman Empire, many inhabitants had fled. For example, the area of Baranya, which lies in southern Hungary and borders on Croatia, had 922 towns and 27 cities with 15,018 taxpayers. By 1696, just four years before the Peace of Karlowitz when most of Hungary had been returned from the Turks, only 2,554 taxpayers remained inhabiting 110 towns or cities.[111] The monarchy needed farmers, preferably German and Catholic, so they looked to the Holy Roman Empire for new people. The settlers of the first two Swabian migrations were Catholic, whereas Joseph II allowed both Catholics and Lutherans to settle in the Banat.[112] Although there were many German settlements in the area of Yugoslavia, Romania, and Hungary over the centuries, the participants in the Oral History Project spoke mostly of five regions: the Gottschee, Siebenbürgen (Transylvania), the Banat, the Batschka, and Baranya.

The Banat is a region that belonged to Hungary and was annexed to Romania after the Treaty of Trianon in 1920 (see below for more details). Its borders are made up of the Marosch River in the north, the Carpathian Mountains in the east, the rivers Donau (Duna, Dunav, Danube) in the south and Theiß (Tisa, Tisza) in the west.

---

106 Katherine Stenger Frey, The Danube Swabians: A People with Portable Roots (Belleville: Mika Publishing Company, 1982), 13. Sundhaussen, Deutsche Geschichte, 205.
107 Susan Clarkson, "History of German Settlements in Southern Hungary," accessed August 11, 2015, www.banaters.com/banat/clarkson.asp?category=history
108 Stenger Frey, The Danube Swabians, 19.
109 Sundhaussen, Deutsche Geschichte, 153.
110 Stenger Frey, The Danube Swabians, 19.
111 Sundhaussen, Deutsche Geschichte, 95.
112 Stenger Frey, The Danube Swabians 24.

The Batschka was originally in Hungary and Yugoslavia but is located mostly in Serbia today (with a small part still in Hungary). The Danube forms the borders in the west and south, and the Theiß in the east. Although there is no natural boundary in the north, the frontier lies between the cities Baja and Szeged.[113]

Baranya is another area in pre-Trianon Hungary that had a sizeable German population. It is located between the Danube and Drau rivers. A small piece of it currently lies in Croatia, with the rest remaining in Hungary.[114]

The Germans who settled in these three areas are often called Danube Swabians. This term refers to all Germans who arrived during the three colonisations and settled not only in these three regions but also in Swabian Turkey and the Hungarian Highlands in Hungary, Syrmia and Slavonia in what would become Yugoslavia, and Sathmar in Romania.[115] The majority of the Danube Swabians did not, however, originate from Swabia. Although many began their journey down the Danube in Ulm, which lies in Swabia, many of these families originated from diverse areas of Germany, such as Württemberg, Baden, Alsace, Lorraine, Rhineland, Westphalia, Bavaria, and Swabia.[116]

Whether in Siebenbürgen, the Gottschee, or any of the Danube Swabian areas, all these groups came to view these places as their Heimat. Even the drastic political upheavals of the 20th century could not change that. South-eastern Europe, like most of Europe frequently struggled with cultural and national identities, different forms of government, invading forces, and social strife. We will start with the conclusion of World War I. In south-eastern Europe, the fighting did not end on November 11, 1918. During the first few years after World War I, invasions in and around eastern Europe continued. For example, Yugoslavia and Italy invaded Albania on December 25, 1918. On April 10, 1919, Romanian troops attacked Hungary and occupied Budapest by August 1. Greece invaded Anatolia on May 15, 1919, with Allied help, as part of the continuing Greek-Turkish dispute.

In addition, 1918 saw the first of several major changes to the political map in Europe. On October 17, 1918, the Hungarian parliament declared independence from Austria.[117] On October 19, 1918, the national council at Zagreb announced the Yugoslav union. On December 1, the formal declaration of the Kingdom of Serbs, Croats, and Slovenes was declared, with Prince Alexander of Serbia as the leader. On

---

113 Stiftung Donauschwäbisches Zentralmuseum, "Travel, Encounter and Experience: German Heritage alongside the Danube," accessed August 11, 2015, www.danube-places.eu/ index.php?option=com_content&view=article&id=260&lang=en&Itemid=252

114 Johann Krumpholz, Judy Ott, and Thomas Willand, "Siedlungsgebiete." Kolut in der Batschka, accessed August 14, 2015, https://kolut.wordpress.com/siedlungsgebiete/

115 Nick Tullius, "A Short History of the Danube Swabians." Donauschwaben Villages Helping Hands. accessed August 11, 2015, https://www.dvhh.org/heritage/society/nationality~Tullius.htm

116 Anneli Ute Gabanyi, "Geschichte der Deutschen in Rumänien," siebenbuerger.de portal, accessed August 11, 2015, https://www.siebenbuerger.de/portal/land-und-leute/siebenbuerger-sachsen/

117 Joseph Held, The Columbia History of Eastern Europe in the Twentieth Century, (New York: Oxford: Columbia University Press, 1992), xi.

November 16, 1918, a Hungarian republic was proclaimed in Budapest, after a revolution that had started 16 days prior.[118]

The following year, on June 13, 1919, the Entente Powers of World War I divided up the Banat region, including its German and Hungarian populations, between Romania and Yugoslavia.[119] The Treaty of Trianon, a peace treaty signed between Hungary and the Entente victors on June 4, 1920, officially dismantled historic Hungary. Romania, Czechoslovakia, and Yugoslavia each received territories from Hungary, thus considerably reducing pre-World War I Hungary.[120] This would pave the way for many more years of struggle before World War II broke out in 1939.

After the Austro-Hungarian Empire had been dismantled, the efficient, fluid trade systems that existed among its many parts had also been disrupted. However, instead of re-establishing the old system, isolationism became the trend, wherein each country assigned high tariffs to imports and tried to produce everything it needed to survive and flourish. This new isolationism had serious effects: new tariffs introduced everywhere in the former Austro-Hungarian empire increased import prices by an average of 30% (three times more than under the former monarchy). As a result, for example, Austria and Czechoslovakia imported their grain from America rather than elsewhere within the former Austro-Hungarian Empire.[121]

Communism was gaining ground in Romania, Hungary, and Yugoslavia, and World War II helped solidify that political change. As the Red Army moved through eastern Europe from 1944, forcing the German Wehrmacht to retreat, they remained in the countries they occupied. The presence of the Soviet Red Army also had a strong effect on local politics. For instance, Romania fought on Nazi Germany's side during most of the war, but once the Soviet army arrived, King Michael of Romania turned against Germany.[122]

One event that is perhaps less well known than the others was that Yugoslavia also fought a civil war between 1941 and 1945 "that caused suffering greatly in excess of that in World War I."[123] After Nazi Germany occupied Belgrade on April 11, 1941, two antifascist resistance movements formed in Yugoslavia: the anti-communist Četniks (also referred to as The Yugoslav Army in the Fatherland), led by Draža Mihailović, and the pro-communist National Liberation Army, also known as the Partisans, led by Josip Broz Tito.[124]

The end of World War II on May 8, 1945, did not end the persecution of people. While many of Hitler's concentration camps were being liberated, many ethnic Germans in Soviet-occupied zones were being deported to Soviet labour camps or

---

118 Held, The Columbia History. xi-xii.
119 Held, The Columbia History. xii.
120 Sten Berglund and Frank H. Aarebot, The Political History of Eastern Europe in the 20th Century: The Struggle Between Democracy and Dictatorship, (Lyme: Edward Elgar Publishing Inc., 1997), 20.
121 Held, The Columbia History, 175-176.
122 Berglund and Aarebot, The Political History, 57-62.
123 Held, The Columbia History, 324.
124 Held, The Columbia History, xxiv, 325.

into Tito's prison camps in Yugoslavia. Some of the participants in the project experienced extreme poverty; others witnessed the atrocities of guerrilla war. However, despite all the political uprisings, the shifting of borders, and the continual conflicts, the ethnic Germans in these countries managed to adjust to their circumstances. The following sections will outline various aspects of daily life for Germans living in Yugoslavia, Hungary, and Romania. We will look at schooling, religion, language, interaction with other cultures, every-day economy, and finally, their expulsion from their Heimat.

Daily Life

The constant changes in the political structure of the 20th century affected educational structures. The participants in the Oral History Project who were born in and spent at least some of their childhood growing up in Hungary, Romania, or Yugoslavia had vastly different experiences in school. For some, the language of instruction only switched between the majority language and German. In John Heffner Sr.'s hometown of Gara, Hungary, for example, the language of instruction switched between German and Hungarian five times between 1902 and 1941.[125]

However, for towns like Schöndorf, located about 540 km northwest of Bucharest in the Banat, border changes affected the language of instruction even more drastically. Schöndorf, which first belonged to Hungary, was then annexed to Romania after the Treaty of Trianon. At the turn of the last century, two hours a week were devoted to German; the remaining hours of instruction were in Hungarian. In 1907, only schools connected to a church could teach German.[126] As World War I neared its end, both Serbia and Romania were hoping to keep the Banat in its entirety. They therefore promised that instruction could once again continue in German for all schools. The Treaty of Trianon, though, assigned this part of the Banat to Romania, removing it from Hungary. Within four years, instruction in the minorities' mother tongues was increasingly repressed. However, religious schools retained some freedom, so the teachers in Schöndorf continued teaching in German for a time.[127]

After World War II, various statutes once again changed the language of instruction in Romania. On February 6, 1945, a statute that seemed to guarantee equality for minorities excluded Romania's ethnic German population. The Catholic Church in Schöndorf, however, attempted to continue teaching in German by classifying it as a charitable cause, since churches were allowed to continue charitable work. Then again in 1946, another statute guaranteed instruction in German, if the school was denazified.[128]

---

125 Stefan Keiner, Gara: Beiträge zur Geschichte einer überwiegend deutschen Grenzgemeinde in der Nordbatschka/Ungarn (Langenau: Honold GmbH, 1991), 200.
126 Nikolaus Engelmann, Heimatbuch der deutschen Gemeinde Schöndorf (Vocklabruck: Kroiss & Bichler GmbH, 1989), 100.
127 Engelmann, Heimatbuch, 101.
128 Engelmann, Heimatbuch, 101.

So even within one country, Romania, language education varied throughout the years and across the different regions of the country. Even though the school in Schöndorf found ways to keep teaching in the German language, schools that were not attached to a church did not have that consistency. Steve Schatz, born in Transylvania in 1934, recalls receiving instruction from Grades one to four in German. From Grade five on, the language of instruction was Hungarian or Romanian. "It depends on who we belonged to at the time," he says. John Penteker, born only six years later, completed Grades one and two in Romanian. "And for Grade three and four, we got German teachers, so it switched to German."

One female interviewee, born in 1944 in Romania, stayed in her home country after the war, and both her children were born there. By the time her children started school, they could choose Romanian, Russian, French, or English as subjects. She had her children learn French and English, but not Romanian or Russian. German does not appear to have been available.

Not only did the wars and their aftermath affect these participants' schooling, living in rural communities also resulted in inconsistent education. Mathias Wolf, who was born in 1933 in Romania, only completed three years of schooling in his home country. Furthermore, there were too few kids to start a new grade each year, so new students were only taken in every two years in his school. This meant that some children automatically started school a year later than others.

Regina Karschti, born in 1934 in Transylvania, was held back two years. Her birthday fell just inside of the school year, and the teacher gave her mother the option: have Regina attend, even though she was younger than her peers, or have her stay home. Her mother decided to hold Regina back so she could accompany her mother and the new baby to the fields. While the baby slept, she could help with the hoeing. Mathias Wolf's hometown offered schooling up to Grade eight. On the other hand, John Heffner Sr. had only five years of elementary education in his hometown Gara, Hungary, before he had to travel by train to the neighbouring city for further education.

The German communities in these areas were mainly Roman Catholic or Lutheran. Celebrating the birth of Jesus was one of their most important holidays. The extensive gift-giving tradition that often comes to mind nowadays was not central to celebrating Christmas in the ethnic German communities. Steve Schatz said that gifts were often just a few apples and nuts, and maybe some hand-made mittens. Children might also get a pencil and a small pad of paper. "But we waited months for Christmas to come," he says. According to both Steve Schatz and Mathias Wolf, the wooden rod was also a possibility for children who had not behaved well during the year. For one of the female interviewees, Christmas was both a happy and a sad event. People would go door-to-door to collect flour, sugar, or whatever someone could give. The women would then bake cookies at the church, which was located on a hill, and the children would learn songs and poems. The Christmas tree at church would be decorated with paper stars, candles, apples, and pinecones. "There weren't any round ornaments," she says, referring to the glass and plastic balls used as ornaments today. The sadness came when the bells rang. Everyone who had a loved one in the cemetery and could afford candles had a little Christmas tree or made a flower arrangement and lit the candles. "And it was so nice, how you went up the hill and then thought about those who'd passed away."

Many of the participants grew up in rural villages, where farming was the main occupation. In fact, Yugoslavia was still a predominantly agrarian country in 1941, and peasants made up 75% of its population.[129] In 1930s Hungary, farmers owing service made up 19.2% of the population, and subsistence peasants 16.3%. Farming was the main way of life for many of the older participants in this project. For example, Steve Schatz describes his family as "average farmers." Anna Kreischer's family lived in a farming community, where her parents owned a farm and horses. "There was nothing else to do, anyway," she says. "Everyone had to work very hard."

One word unique to the German language of the Batschka and Banat regions is Sallasch: farmland with an additional dwelling, located outside of a town's borders. This is not the typical Canadian-style farmhouse; it functioned like a long house as it could accommodate several families, usually the farmhands' families. This helped spare time and effort, since the owner and farmhands might need to travel up to five kilometres to reach the family's farm. Each farmhand (called a Sallaschmann) had a kitchen, large pantry, and a room for his family within the larger building, which also housed the animals' stalls. Members of the owner's family could also live in the same house, especially if the family had enough children to manage the farm without external help. If farmhands did live there, the owner often still had an apartment he would use during the week. He lived at home on Sundays and throughout most of the winter unless work needed to be done.[130]

Although farming was the most common occupation, there were, of course, other jobs. Joe Piller, for example, comes from a long line of blacksmiths. Helen Neumayer's husband was also a blacksmith, but he had first tried his hand at something else. Helen Neumayer explained that her father-in-law wanted his son to study veterinary medicine. However, once he had completed his schooling and returned to their town in Hungary, he could not make a living because there were no animals that needed his care. He therefore trained with his father to become a blacksmith and eventually took over the family business.

Other participants' families owned dry goods stores, built wagons and wagon wheels, operated vineyards, or worked for the government. However, farming was the main source of income for most of the ethnic Germans in Romania, Yugoslavia, and Hungary. Children worked too, whenever they could. In their youth, Joe Piller and his sister helped their family keep bees.

---

129 Held, The Columbia History, 323.
130 Keiner, Gara: Beiträge zur Geschichte, 85.

"And if we caught a swarm of bees, then we got a little money for
that. And with that money, I bought a bicycle in the end, and I got
around all over the place."

Steve Schatz had to start working at home at around age six or seven. "Our
parents said, 'As soon as you're able to hold a rake or a shovel, you can work'," he
recalls. However, after the war, things changed. Communism, deportations to Soviet
labour camps, and the aftermath of war all contributed to increased poverty. One of
the female interviewees describes how Romanian laws and policies permanently
changed her family's situation. She says her parents were farmers for a short time, but
they had to stop farming in 1945 because they lost their land. "We were dispossessed
of everything," she says, and then emphasizes, "of everything we had." She describes
further:

"It happened like when you sweep a house. Our farm and house,
everything. Everything was swept out. We stood there. My parents
told us that we all cried. Back then it was very hard."

The immediate poverty inflicted on her family meant that they sometimes had
little to eat. Her father had gone away to war and when he returned, there were no
jobs for farmers. He found a job as a roofer in the city, which was 80 km away. He
only returned home once every month or two and brought along a little sugar or oil.
She also told this story:

"and my parents told me that he came home one Christmas with
money. They were going to buy a pig,…we of course had nothing at
home to raise a pig with. We had no feed and no money to buy [it]
with. Then he came with the money. It was the annual market at our
village, and overnight, the money changed. So, we no longer had any
money. We no longer had a pig for Christmas."

The same thing happened to others in her village. For some, she says, it was even
worse, especially for older people who could not work any longer. Eventually, she
says, the Romanians, who now owned the land, hired the Siebenbürger Saxons to
work it, but for half the wage. It was sufficient to start to earn some money again, but
in her memory, it was a bittersweet improvement: "Then you went and worked your
own fields. But you were no longer the owner." The work, though, allowed them to
afford a few chickens, and they could raise a pig again. Her parents bought a goat so
that the children had milk. They were also able to bake bread, which had two
purposes: for nourishment, and as a coffee substitute. She recounted:

"I can still remember how we baked bread. You baked 10 or 12
breads. Then you left a few with black crusts and you first ate the
other ones. After two weeks,…you only had the bread left in the root
cellar. It had mold. You scratched away the mold and ate the bread.
You soaked the black crust and boiled it. …You then poured the
black water into the milk. That made the goat's milk dark. And that
was our coffee."

She also recalled that she had only one dress to wear. She would wash it on Saturdays, and then wear it again all week. She also had the same pair of shoes for four years. When she grew and the shoes became too small, her father cut open the heel of the shoe. When she grew some more, he cut open the toe.

The post-war downturn in the economy pushed many Germans to leave Hungary, Romania, and Yugoslavia. Many others were expelled from their homes, with no financial compensation. The political and economic developments over the years had seriously affected their Heimat.

Languages

The initial German immigrants into Romania, Hungary, and Yugoslavia were predominantly farmers, and they therefore settled in rural communities. Their descendants stayed in these communities for several centuries and maintained the German language. Steve Schatz explains that, in his experience, no one ever left the village unless they were in the military or when work was occasionally sought out of town. "If you were born there, you died there," he says.

Ethnic Germans in eastern Europe had developed social patterns regarding which language to speak and when. For example, they might have used German at church and with the family, and the majority language (Hungarian, Romanian, or Serbian) at school. These areas of life, such as religion, family, employment, and education, are called domains.[131] In the case of societies and communities where two or more languages are used, one language will usually dominate in each domain.

What did this look like in everyday life? John Penteker, born in Transylvania in 1941, remembers speaking Saxon German at home, standard German at school, and Romanian on the streets and sometimes at school. Joe Piller, born in 1929 in Yugoslavia, spoke German at home and Croatian on the street. One of the female interviewees, a Siebenbürger Saxon born in 1944, spoke their dialect at home and with other Siebenbürger Saxon families but used Romanian in school and on the streets.

When a language community has established domains of use for at least two different languages or dialects, this is referred to as stable diglossia.[132] Stable diglossia is important, because it provides the basis for maintaining a language. It ensured that people continued to speak German in countries where German was not the official language, several centuries after their ancestors had left Germany.

But how does diglossia accomplish this? Why is it so important to have contexts and situations in which one language is systematically and predominantly used? The answer is simple — efficiency. If all speakers used both languages in all

---

131 Joshua Fishman, Language Loyalty in the United States: The Maintenance and Perpetuation of Non-English Mother Tongues by American Ethnic and Religious Groups (The Hague: Mouton & Co., 1966), 428.
132 Joshua Ferguson, "Diglossia," Word (1959), 325.

situations, one language would eventually become superfluous, and the community would no longer use it.[133]

Living apart from mainstream German culture for so many centuries also meant that the German spoken in Yugoslavia, Hungary, and Romania differed in many respects from German spoken in Germany, Switzerland, and Austria. Descendants of the immigrants who arrived via the Great Swabian Migrations generally refer to their dialect as Danube Swabian, in German Donauschwäbisch, in their dialect Donauschwowisch or just Schwowisch. Those whose ancestors had arrived in Siebenbürgen in the 13th century refer to their dialect as Saxon, Siebenbürger Saxon, or Siebenbürgisch in German. For the purposes of simplicity, and to distinguish their dialect from the Saxon spoken in Germany, we will refer to it as Siebenbürger Saxon.

How different were these dialects? Although he was not born in Europe, Willy Heffner grew up speaking Danube Swabian with his parents and grandparents. He explains: "I remember sometimes when I spoke with somebody who was real German, some of the words, they'd looked at me. 'What are you talking about?'"

Some of the differences lie in pronunciation, others in vocabulary. Here are some examples of common words used in Danube Swabian, Siebenbürger Saxon, and Gottscheerisch and then compared to standard German, as shown in the following table.

Danube Swabian	Sieb. Saxon[134]	Gottscheerisch[135]	Std. German	English
Grumbiere	Krumpirn	Erdepfel	Kartoffel	Potato
Kukurutz	Kukuruz	Tirkisch-boitse	Mais	Corn
Ziweva	Zibebe		Rosine	Raisin
Paradeis	Paradeis	Paradeis	Tomate	Tomato
Hingel	Hin or He[136]	Zibe	Henne	Chicken

The prevalence of these dialects in their respective areas has changed. Alex Müntz, born in the 1980s in Romania, says that very few there still speak Siebenbürgen Saxon. His parents, though of German heritage, spoke Romanian at home but sent him to a German school where instruction was in German, and where he could finish his Abitur.[137] The German he learned, though, was different from what is spoken in Germany now. As a result, when he went to Germany for university, he was also in for a bit of a shock: "I talked like, oh, I don't know, like they did 200 years ago," he recalls of his experience.

---

133 Joshua Fishman, The Sociology of Language (Rowley: Newbury House, 1972), 96.
134 "Wörterbuch siebenbürgisch-deutsch", Kirchberg in Siebenbürgen, accessed July 30, 2019, https://kirchberg-siebenbuergen.de.tl/W.oe.rterbuch-siebenbuergisch-_-deutsch.htm
135 Walter Tschinkel, Wörterbuch der Gottscheer Mundart. Mit Illustr. v. Anni Tschinkel. (Vienna: Verlag der Österreichischen Akademie des Wissens, 1973).
136 Adolf Schullerus et al., Siebenbürgisch-sächsisches Wörterbuch: mit Benützung der Sammlungen Johann Wolffs (Berlin: W. de Gruyter, 1971), 141.
137 Translation: high school diploma in the German school system.

Interaction with Other Cultures

Let us now look at how Germans interacted with other cultures to see the beginnings of this change.

> "Russians, Bulgarians, Saxons, Serbians, Jews, gypsies, Schokatzs, Bonyvatzs, and other known and unknown races and tribes, each with distinctly different dress, languages, and customs practically unchanged by transplantation into Hungarian soil, so bewitched us with the charms of constant variety and novelty that our trip was one round of exhilarating and delightful impressions."[138]

Such was the observation of writer F.D. Millet, who reported on a canoe trip down the Danube River from December 1891 to May 1892. Millet subsequently describes a visit to the Hungarian (later Yugoslavian, then Serbian) town of Apatin:

> "Almost the first person we saw was a little old German woman spinning flax on a tiny wheel, looking exactly as if she had been transported bodily from the Black Forest."[139]

As his party continued along the street, they "met unmistakable Germans" and heard them speaking German.

> "At the nearest corner was a brewery, with tables under the trees, and guzzling sluggards devouring strong sausage and stronger cheese. Everything was of the most commonplace German order, from the architecture of the houses to the beer mugs."[140]

It is remarkable that already more than 120 years ago, this author noted how each culture retained its uniqueness as it lived and thrived among other diverse cultures, and that he so readily recognized representations of German culture.

Tony Fieder's hometown of Ridjica in Serbia is an example of a small town with a sizeable German population. By 1820, Ridjica had 2,000 Germans in addition to other nationalities. In 1931, the town had 2,359 Germans, 1,369 Slavs, 467 Hungarians, and 37 other minorities, totalling 4,232 inhabitants.[141] Joe Piller lived in a town called New Slankamen, also in Serbia. It had a population of about 5,000 when he was young. From his recollection, the population was made up of roughly 50% Croats, 25% Germans, and 25% Serbs, with a few Slovaks, who worked in the vineyards.

---

138 F.D. Millet, "From the Black Forest to the Black Sea", Harper's New Monthly Magazine, December 1891, 918.
139 Millet, "From the Black Forest", 923.
140 Millet, "From the Black Forest", 923.
141 Michael Hutfluss, Familienbuch Ridjica: Batschka 1804-1943, B 475:5. Schriftenreihe zur donau-schwäbischen Herkunftsforschung 155 (Plaidt: Cardamina Verlag Susanne Breuel, 2010).

The linguistic makeup of all of Yugoslavia on March 31, 1931, was as follows[142]:

Language	Population	Percentage
Serbo-Croatian	10,730,829	77%
Slovenian	1,135,410	8%
Albanian	505,259	4%
German	499,969	4%
Hungarian	468,185	3%
Romanian	137,879	1%
Turkish	132,924	1%
Other	3,323,589	2%
Total	13,934,038	100%

Germans, at first glance, made up only about 4% of the population. However, some areas had higher concentrations of Germans: 22% of the population in the Batschka was German, compared to 20.6% in the Banat, and 29.8% in Baranya.[143]

Although Germans made up a sizeable proportion of the population in these parts, several other ethnicities lived there, too. The general feeling among the participants was that relations between the various ethnicities were good until World War II. Joe Piller mentioned: "It was a very peaceful village that I could remember. That was before the Second World War, right before the Germans entered Yugoslavia."

Helen Neumayer was born in 1919 in what she called Croatia, which by then had become part of the new country of Yugoslavia. She said there were many Serbs in her hometown: "We got along well." However, during the Second World War, Tito's Partisans attacked, tortured, and killed many people. Helen Neumayer witnessed atrocities she would prefer to forget. For example, she and her brother-in-law set out one night to see what was going on and stumbled upon a fresh mass grave:

> "And then I saw…this much of a foot. A man fell on his back like
> this. I saw the feet. And I of course saw the forehead. And I saw the
> cane and the hand that held the cane. And then I saw that his lunch
> bag had a piece of bread in it. He believes he's going to work. Had a
> piece of bread in there and a piece of salami. And it was a salami
> sandwich in there. And the man was lying there. And half the shoe. I
> still [see] half the shoe."

Although Helen Neumayer grew up getting along well with Serbians, her opinion about them changed after she witnessed the atrocities committed by the Partisans.

---

142 Bundesministerium für Vertriebene, Flüchtlinge und Kriegsgeschädigte, Das Schicksal der Deutschen in Jugoslawien, vol. 5, Dokumentation der Vertreibung der Deutschen aus Ost-Mitteleuropa (Düsseldorf: Oskar Leiner-Druck K.G., 1961), 11E.
143 Held, The Columbia History, 329.

Over 60 years later, her traumatic personal experiences still coloured her view of Serbians as a people. Helen enjoyed sitting at the nearby mall and meeting different people. She told a story about the time when a man from Serbia sat down next to her:

> "A man comes and sits down next to me. 'Can I sit here?' 'Yeah.'
> Then he talked and talked and suddenly he said to me, 'I bet you
> come from Yugoslavia.' I say, 'You mean former Yugoslavia,' I said
> to him right away. 'Yes, Yugoslavia.' 'It was such a good country
> before and now it's completely ruined. But,' I say, 'You ruined it.' I
> said, 'You Serbs ruined it'."

As World War II progressed and ended, the status of the German language within the towns seemed to have changed. Gisela Steckel, for example, was born in Serbia, in a village close to the borders of both Hungary and Romania, in 1957. She grew up speaking Hungarian first, and then learned Serbian at school. She only learned a little German from her mother:

> "German was, like, one of the things my mom used to speak, but not
> really. It wasn't really welcome in that area. So, we, or my
> grandparents, tried not to speak it and just tried to speak Hungarian,
> or only [speak German] inside of the house. So, I did not speak very
> well German at all."

She would learn German later once they moved to Germany.

Expulsion

Many of the Germans in Hungary, Romania, and Yugoslavia were forced to leave or flee for different reasons, including the incoming front, deportation to Soviet labour camps, poor economy, ethnic tensions, and state sanctioned expulsion.

Anne Kroisenbrunner was born in Yugoslavia in 1939. In 1941, Yugoslavia capitulated to Hitler. He divided up the country such that Baranya and the Batschka were returned to Hungary, the Germans in the Banat had an independent Volksgruppenorganisation (association of the ethnic group) under Sepp Jankos, and the Gottschee became part of Italy. Shortly thereafter, the Kroisenbrunners were relocated to Lower Styria in Austria. Anne said that her family received a few horses and a small farm. "I have good memories of the horses," she says. "But I also experienced horrible things."

Steve Schatz's family had two weeks to pack any important belongings before leaving. Anna Kreischer's family seems to have had the shortest notification — 30 minutes. Because cars were rare in these towns, those who fled during or shortly after the war hitched up their horses and packed their wagons. Steve Schatz explained that on the day of his village's departure, September 12, 1944, people in the village opened all the stalls and chased all the animals onto the streets. They then hooked up their wagons to horses. The Schatz family wagon was third from the front in the "train" of evacuees. He continues:

"And there the bells, the bells started to ring. And outside of the
community, the entire group stopped, and the bells kept ringing.
Then each person turned around one more time and each person
cried. But back then, I could not understand that. I was, of course,
only ten years old."

Steve Schatz said his family and friends travelled a felt 1,000 km from their
home in Weilau (now Uila), Romania, to Lower Austria. The refugees lived off the
kindness of strangers who would cook basic soups for them when they could. If the
group got to spend a night in a barn, sleeping on some hay, it was a wonderful night,
Steve Schatz says, because normally they slept outside under their wagons.
Sometimes, they had to travel at night. The entire journey took six weeks, but those
six weeks were filled with bombings and the fear of running into soldiers.

Travelling by wagon had its own difficulties: roads were not always paved, and
the journey included mountainous passages for which the wagons were not well
equipped. As John Heffner Sr. remembers, refugees from Gara, Hungary, had to have
someone run next to the wagons with a stick. Because Gara was on flatland, the
wagons did not need brakes. The sticks were inserted through the wagon wheels to
stop the wagon when necessary.[144]

Not all Germans were convinced that they needed to leave. The older generation,
according to Joe Piller, assumed things would be the same after the war as during,
namely, that they would move out of the area until the front had passed and then
return. So many chose to stay. "And that was the worst thing they could have done,"
he says. Others, like Helen Neumayer, were on the fence. In 1944, she tried to flee.
She had her children packed up in a wagon and was ready to leave, when her sister
convinced her to stay. "That was the biggest mistake I had ever made in my life," she
says. Because Helen Neumayer stayed behind, she was later deported to a Soviet
labour camp in the Ukraine and became separated from her children and husband for
five years. Tony Fieder was interned, along with his family, in the Gakovo and
Kruševlje camps at age two for about one year. Although he does not remember
anything from the camps, he said his parents never spoke about that time. He
concluded from this that "the experiences that they underwent must have been
horrific." Elizabeth Schultheiss was one of only eight or ten women in her town in
Baranya to be deported. She spent over two years in Soviet coal mines.

Residents of Yugoslavia had a particularly difficult experience. Not only were
they on the front between the Red Army and the Germans, but they also lived
through a civil war in their own country from 1941 to 1945.[145] Helen Neumayer, who
was in her twenties during this time, recounts one particularly gruesome scene she
witnessed: two doors down from her family home was a large house, owned by a rich
farmer. The farmer's wife fled with the son, but the husband stayed home. "Then

---

144 Keiner, Beiträge zur Geschichte, 32.
145 Held, The Columbia History, 324.

they got him. He screamed so horribly, the man." Helen Neumayer then explains how she crept into the neighbouring house and secretly watched the farmer's demise.

> "It's gruesome. There were so many Partisans there in the farm. Very
> big house. And then they threw the man down and four or five stood
> on his feet, and one at his head, and one at his body. And he screamed.
> They took a piece of wood. Then they hit him on the head with the
> wood. And the other came with an axe and chopped off his head."

Some managed to stay and survive the aftermath of World War II. Life for them, however, was not easy. In Romania, where communism had taken hold, one of the female interviewees eventually found a job working in a grocery store many years after the war. She said she was instructed to keep much of the stock in the backroom for consumption by members of the party. Although there was not enough to satisfy the local demand, she was not allowed to sell any of the additional stock:

> "I can remember this picture as long as I live. A mother came. She
> had four children. 'Give me a little piece of bread.' I said no. But in
> the back, the bread was hidden for the communists who were with
> the government. And there I said, 'I can't do this anymore. I can't
> watch this anymore.' That pushed me to leave for Canada."

Germans who left much later, including Alex Müntz (only 28 at the time of his interview), sought new opportunities. Another interviewee left Siebenbürgen in 1957, twelve years after World War II, to join her parents in Austria. John Heffner Sr. had always dreamed of opening his own mechanic shop. He and his mother avoided deportation in the 1940s, but after the failed Hungarian Revolution in 1956, he decided it was indeed time to go. He left for Canada with his wife, his mother, his in-laws, and his four-year-old son.

> "Then in '57 in January, I see everything's turning back to
> communism again, and I fear that I will never have my own shop.
> So I said to my family, let us pack and we go."

Heimat

Although their ancestors left west-central Europe up to 800 years ago, the ethnic Germans of Yugoslavia, Hungary, and Romania had created tight-knit German communities that became their Heimat. They maintained their culture, their families, and their friendships throughout many hardships. They may feel that their home is here in Canada, but their Heimat is back in the countries of former Yugoslavia, Hungary, and Romania. One interviewee, who fled Romania when he was twenty years old, said: "Wenn ich auch träume in der Nacht, wird immer von zu Hause, vor allem von der Kindheit geträumt. Die Heimat vergisst man nie."[146]

---

146 Translation: When I dream at night, I always dream of home. I especially dream of my childhood. You never forget your Heimat (homeland).

They Came from East-central Europe

Stephanie Cooper and Sebastian Siebel-Achenbach

Amongst the German-speaking population living in the Waterloo Region, there are many who were born in areas outside of Germany and Austria. During the Third Reich, these Germans were often referred to as Volksdeutsche (ethnic Germans) because they lived in areas outside of the Reich (Imperial Germany). This chapter will focus on these German immigrants to Canada who came from what were then Czechoslovakia and Poland, and including Germans from the Baltic states.

German-speaking groups have a long history of living in east-central Europe. German settlers arrived in the areas of Czechoslovakia, Poland, and the Baltic states as early as the 12th and 13th centuries, as part of the Ostsiedlung, the settling of German groups east of the borders of the Holy Roman Empire in the Middle Ages.

German minorities in Eastern Europe (Deutsche Siedlungsgebiete in Osteuropa), 1925. Bibliographisches Institut AG Leipzig. Spiridon Ion Cepleanu / Historischer Schul-Atlas, Velhagen & Klasing publ., Bielefeld and Leipzig 1897. https://commons.wikimedia.org/wiki/File:Deutsche_Siedlungsgebiete_in_Osteuropa_1925.jpg

In the first half of the 20th century, there were still many communities that had held onto their German culture and were predominantly German speaking. With the rise of the Nazi Party in Germany and the horrors of World War II, these groups in east-central Europe were no longer accepted within the wider majority communities. They fled from their homes, were evacuated, or deported. They were often blamed for what happened in Germany and across Europe under the Nazi regime. Owing to this, their evacuation experiences were largely unpleasant, as they experienced harsh conditions and were often separated from loved ones along the way. They started looking elsewhere for new opportunities, causing many of them to leave Europe, which is what brought a significant number to Canada. Relatives, who were already in Canada and were prepared to sponsor family members, made this an appealing option for many who had limited opportunities and no home left in Europe.

The personal stories shared by our interviewees reflect the history of German-speaking settlement groups before, during, and after World War II. Because of the time period covered, many interviewees were very young during these years, and their earliest recollections pertain to the 1930s and 1940s, or they are memories their parents shared with them. These memories often revolve around the difficulties and struggles they encountered when leaving their homes. Stories relating to different stages and aspects of their lives after their exodus will be covered in the later chapters of this book.

This chapter has two main sections, the first pertaining to the Germans in what became Czechoslovakia, and the second pertaining to those from Poland and the Baltic states. Each section will begin with an overview of the history of significant German-speaking settlements of the area, explaining briefly how and why certain areas came to be settled by German speakers. The second part of each section will focus on the personal stories that people have shared regarding their experiences living in these areas of east-central Europe. Topics such as interaction with other cultural and ethnic groups, language, religion, and economy will be discussed. Also included in this part of the chapter will be experiences of population transfer, flight, and expulsion — all of which affected their settlements in the years surrounding World War II.

Germans in Czechoslovakia

Prior to World War II, Czechoslovakia had a population of approximately 3.15 million Germans living in what has been referred to as the Sudetenland since 1918. The contiguous region derived its name from the Sudeten mountains which form the northern border of Bohemia, Moravia, and Czech Silesia. Following World War I, these regions along with their largely German-speaking populations were incorporated into the newly formed Czechoslovakia.

The history of the ethnic Germans living in this area can be traced back to the 12th century, when the medieval ruling family of Bohemia, the Přemyslids, encouraged settlement of their lands by peoples of the Holy Roman Empire.[147] These settlements allowed for the incorporation of new agricultural lands and the creation of new towns which were governed by German law. The expertise of the settlers also allowed for new mines to be created and become economically beneficial. In 1526, the Bohemian crown descended to the Habsburgs, and remained a part of the Austro-Hungarian Empire until the end of World War I.[148] During this time, the German-speaking population of Bohemia was considered a very modern and wealthy group within the empire. German was considered a language of culture, and members of the German-speaking population held significant positions of privilege and leadership in the Empire.[149]

Due to economic and cultural changes in the 19th century, tension escalated between the German and Czech populations. As more Czechs moved into areas predominated by Germans, they felt pressure to assimilate to the majority's German culture. In turn, when the Czechoslovak Republic was formed after World War I, it was the German population who felt pressure to assimilate.[150] They went from being part of the dominant culture of the Habsburg Empire to living in a country where they were now a cultural minority. The opportunities that the German-speaking population once had to maintain their German language and culture started to diminish, as Czech became the official language. Germans found that their minority German-language schools and cultural associations were not receiving the same official support they once had.[151] Land redistribution programs left wealthy Germans feeling their land was given unfairly to Czechs, and Germans also complained that Czechs were getting preferential treatment for state jobs and contracts.

The fate of the Sudeten Germans changed greatly again with the rise of Hitler and the Nazi Party in Germany, most notably with the Munich Agreement that provided the cession to Germany of the Sudeten German territory. The remaining Czech area was annexed to the Third Reich in 1939, becoming the Protectorates of Bohemia and Moravia; Slovakia became a nominally independent but compliant state of the Reich. During the war, Bohemia and Moravia remained under German control. As the war evolved, these Protectorates became relatively safe zones attracting refugees.[152]

Johann Leinweber grew up in the Sudetenland. When asked about his language use, specifically whether he knew how to speak Czech, he answers that he did not, because, when he was growing up during the war, they spoke German. However, his grandparents and parents, who would have been living in the Sudetenland when it became part of Czechoslovakia, could speak fluent Czech. This reflects the situation

---

147 Ulrich Merten, Forgotten Voices: The Expulsion of the Germans from Eastern Europe after World War II (New Brunswick: Transaction Publishers, 2012), 95.
148 Merten, Forgotten Voices, 95-96.
149 Arnold Suppan, "'Germans' in the Habsburg Empire: Language, Imperial Ideology, National Identity, and Assimilation", in The Germans and the East, edited by Charles W. Ingrao and Franz A.J. Szabo (West Lafayette: Purdue University Press, 2008), 149, 175.
150 Merten, Forgotten Voices, 97-98.
151 Antony Alcock, A History of the Protection of Regional Cultural Minorities in Europe: From the Edict of Nantes to the Present Day (London: Macmillan Press, 2000), 72.
152 Merten, Forgotten Voices, 100-102.

of the ethnic German population in Czechoslovakia before World War II, when they were a minority culture, and what changes took place when the Sudetenland was transferred to Germany. For most people, who only lived in Czechoslovakia for a short period of time when they were very young, their language use would have likely been similar to what Bill Kunsch describes as speaking a regional dialect of German at home and learning "Hochdeutsch" (literary or standard German) in school. In contrast, for the older generations, who spent longer periods living and working in these German-speaking communities, it may have been essential for business reasons to also speak the Czech or Slovak languages.

Nearing the end of World War II, the fate of the ethnic Germans living in Czechoslovakia became increasingly evident, as the local population often blamed ethnic Germans living outside of Germany for the actions of the Nazi regime. Johann Leinweber describes an interaction between the different cultural groups during the end of the war, where the lives of the men of his family were being threatened by some young Czech men with guns. A local Czech professor came in to intervene, stating that these Germans had done nothing wrong and should not be killed. Luckily for Johann's family, the Czech professor was able to convince the young Czech men to spare the lives of the men. However, stories like this demonstrate the type of tension that occurred. Although Germans were productive members of society, there was the pressure of war, nationalism, and hatred towards the Nazi regime that fuelled tensions.

Although there was great suffering during the final years of World War II, with many people being ripped from their homes and killed, Germans in Czechoslovakia suffered much after Nazi Germany's defeat at the end of the war. The expulsion of the German minority from the Sudetenland involved executions, stripping them of all their property and possessions, and shipping them off on trains and on foot to the west and north. People like Dagmar Schilha, born in Trautenau (today Trutnov, Czechia), experienced hardship when they were forced to leave their homes in 1945. She describes that she, along with her mother and siblings, had to walk on foot for a whole day with more and more people joining them along the way, and then they were put onto freight trains. They were able to make their way to Dresden, where Dagmar's aunt took them in and helped them out.

Johann Leinweber, who was from Stašov, also recalls the difficulties of leaving home, and how his family was separated. With his father being a casualty of the war and his mother unable to take care of him, Johann left their home with his grandparents; they were squashed into a train car for three days as it made its way into occupied Germany. Johann describes the relief they experienced when they opened the train cars after three days; there was water nearby and they were finally able to wash themselves. The approximately 3.15 million Germans who lived in Czechoslovakia before the war years were reduced to approximately 200,000 by 1948.[153]

---

153 Alcock, A History, 92.

In today's Slovakia, another significant, although much smaller, German-speaking community existed. Historically a part of the Kingdom of Hungary, these German-speaking settlers were first invited to settle in the Carpathian Mountains in the 12th century, hence they are commonly referred to as Carpathian Germans. They were valued because of their trades or skills and because they helped smaller communities to grow and establish themselves.[154] The community settled mainly in three different areas: in Bratislava, and in the Hauerland and Spiš (Zips) regions.

When Czechoslovakia was formed after World War I, the Carpathian Germans also found themselves to be a minority group in their new country. However, unlike the Sudetenland Germans, the Carpathian Germans were well integrated, and did not initially experience the same struggles over language and culture that the Sudeten Germans did.[155] In an anecdote told by Bill Kunsch, born in a village called Eisdorf in the Carpathians, he comments that his mother and aunt knew how to speak Slovak because they had to live with a Slovak family for a year in their youth as "exchange students." He explains that although he did not speak any Slovak, it was common for youth in his village to participate in an exchange with Slovak families, and for Slovak youth to spend a year living with German-speaking families in their village. However, near the end of World War II, life was made difficult for the Carpathian Germans. In 1944, the German Wehrmacht resettled the German-speaking populations of the Carpathian Mountains to Germany and Austria as the Red Army advanced.[156] The expulsion of Germans continued after World War II, although there were significantly fewer than were expelled from the Sudetenland. Bill Kunsch recalls his experiences as a child during the final years of the war. He remembers Czech partisans coming through his village, and the death and destruction that accompanied them. Bill also recalls being sent to the Sudetenland on a train with his mother and siblings, without any of their possessions, leaving their home behind, and being separated from his father.

After World War II, Slovakia again became part of the re-established Czechoslovakia, losing part of its eastern territory to the USSR. In the post-war years, remaining ethnic German population numbers continued to decline, and those who remained in the Carpathian Mountains were forced to assimilate and suffered great discrimination.[157] For Bill's family, who were still in the Sudetenland after the war, they were again forced to leave, this time by the Soviet Red Army, who drove them into occupied Germany. Hilde Kreitzer, born in Honneshau, another village in the Carpathian German area, also recalls being forced from her home after the war. She remembers having to leave in 1945, going first to Vienna and then to the Soviet occupation zone, where they had family. From there, they waited to hear news of her father, who eventually came out of Soviet imprisonment in 1949.

---

154 Lucy P. Marcus, "The Carpathian Germans", in German Minorities in Europe: Ethnic Identity and Cultural Belonging, edited by Stefan Wolff (New York: Berghahn Books, 2000), 98.
155 Marcus, "The Carpathian Germans", 101.
156 Marcus, "The Carpathian Germans", 106.
157 Marcus, "The Carpathian Germans", 108.

As the personal accounts of Bill Kunsch and Hilde Kreitzer from the Carpathians, as well as of Dagmar Schilha and Johann Leinweber from the Sudetenland, demonstrate, many of these families had to leave without fathers, husbands, sons, and brothers during the evacuations in Czechoslovakia, as they had been conscripted in the German Wehrmacht. Many families were torn apart. Often, German speakers were no longer welcome in their communities. They were forced westward and northward, often struggling to start their new lives in occupied Germany, where there was very limited food and resources, and many people struggled to put a roof over their heads.

These difficulties are also reflected in other individual stories. Ingrid Hann, for example, was born in Stuttgart to German parents who had been forced from their homes during World War II. Ingrid's mother was born in Bratislava, and her father came from Romania. Ingrid describes the family's difficulties finding a place to stay as refugees, where they would also accommodate her as a child. She ended up having to stay with friends, separate from her parents, due to these difficulties.

Other individuals, such as Bill Kunsch, comment on the extreme conditions that they had to endure in the years after World War II. He recalls the horrible winters in the eastern occupied zone of Germany. Bill remembered that it was so cold they would steal coal from the railway tracks to heat the stove at home. In 1947, when there was not enough coal to heat the school buildings, the children had to be sent home with their assignments.

Due to the mass flight and expulsion across Europe during the war and post-war years, many other German-speaking people from different areas of Europe passed through Czechoslovakia, and particularly the Sudetenland, which was an area that attracted many refugees during the war because it was relatively safe. Waldemar Scholtes' family story is an example of this, as they ended up in Reichenberg (Liberec) in the Sudetenland after they were evacuated from their home in Transylvania in 1944. Waldemar's mother, who was pregnant with him at the time, and his father were separated during this evacuation, but were later able to find each other, and ended up moving to Austria at the end of the war. Bill Kunsch also recalls the flight and evacuation of people, as he remembers seeing German-speaking people heading west with their wagons and horses near the end of the war, either evacuated or fleeing. Although Bill was too young to realize, his parents knew that this would be their fate as well, which turned out to be true, as they soon evacuated to the Sudetenland, and then into occupied Germany at the end of the war. These stories demonstrate the uncertainty that many people experienced during the war, as they were forced to leave their homes without indication of where and when they would be able to rebuild their lives.

Germans in Poland

During the medieval period, the area of land that became Poland was also heavily influenced by German-speaking settlements. In the 13th century, Polish Duke Conrad of Mazovia invited the Knights of the Teutonic Order to settle along the north-eastern border, to help protect against the pagan Prussians.[158] This lay order was a powerful force against the pagans, but this also proved detrimental for Poland because the Knights were an expansive military force. After bringing the first German settlers to Prussia in 1230, they began to rapidly conquer territory in what is now northern Poland.[159] They played a significant role in developing cities, having founded Thorn (Toruń), Kulm (Chełmno), Elbing (Elbląg), and Königsberg (Kaliningrad). The Knights of the Teutonic Order fought against the Prussians to expand their land and to convert them to Christianity. Later they targeted the Lithuanians with the same intention.[160]

In the 13th century, dukes from Pomerania and Silesia also invited German migrants to settle their land. The eastern German settlements allowed for new towns and villages to be created, and because of the large German population, these areas were greatly influenced by German language and culture. By 1772, these territories along with East and West Prussia became a part of the Hohenzollern dynasty of Brandenburg-Prussia, a progenitor German state. German language and culture predominated. After the formation of the German Empire in 1871, there was increased German nationalism and with Otto von Bismarck's attack on the Catholic Church, there was heightened tension between the German and Polish peoples.[161] During this time there was pressure to assimilate to German culture. This drastically changed in Posen (Poznań) and West Prussia after World War I, as these areas became part of reconstituted Poland, and Germans were pressured to assimilate to Polish culture. Posen and West Prussia also experienced a land reform shortly after World War I which favoured the Polish inhabitants. Due to the assimilation pressures and the changes they were experiencing as Germans, many of them decided to leave Poland and go to Germany.[162]

For decades or centuries, many German families had been living in Poland, and they had strong ties to the communities they lived in. Many had successful businesses or farms that they ran. Our interviewees spoke about their time living in Poland, and the success of their parents' farms or businesses. Nelly Kilianski, for example, was born into a German family that had been living in Poland for over 300 years. In her interview, she talks about the success of her parents' butcher shop, which they opened after they married. She spoke proudly about how her parents' shop was the first in their city to have an electric refrigerator, and how, during World War II, Nelly's mother ran the shop, until it was no longer safe to do so. Her mother eventually had to leave so she could safely make it out of the country with her children. In her interview, Nelly reflects on how Poland was their Heimatland (home country); they did not feel like foreigners there and, until the war came, they had lived comfortable lives in Poland.

---

158 Jean W. Sedlar, East Central Europe in the Middle Ages, 1000-1500 (Seattle: University of Washington Press, 1994), 20.
159 Sedlar, East Central Europe, 21.
160 Merten, Forgotten Voices, 88.
161 Merten, Forgotten Voices, 87.
162 Merten, Forgotten Voices, 90.

Alice Bromberg also talks about her family's history in Poland, stating that her forefathers originally came to Poland in the 1700s. Alice recalls that her parents, whom she describes as "Polish by birth but German by nationality," owned a successful farming business in Karlshof (Biały Dwór). They ran a farm and had hired Polish help for operating a threshing machine. Her parents had also hired a Polish girl to look after Alice, which led to Alice learning Polish as her first language, the only language she could speak when the family fled to Germany. Heiderose Brandt-Butscher and Bernd Brandt, siblings who were born in Thorn (Toruń), also talk about their lives and their parents' business in their interviews. Heiderose describes that her parents owned a mill, and it was the business connections that her father had made that led to them having a place to stay as refugees in the west. These stories demonstrate the lives that these families had built for themselves in Poland. They were productive members of society who were forced to leave everything behind when they had to go west.

The languages people used also provide insight into the kinds of contact Germans had with other cultural or linguistic groups in their communities. Bernd Brandt recalls that his father knew Russian from learning it in school. For him, Polish was the language used outside the home, and German was spoken at home. Except for Germans who were resettled in Poland, it would have been quite normal for our interviewees to be exposed to both the Polish and German languages. Most of them recall that their parents spoke Polish because that was the language that was spoken in the community and for business purposes. German or sometimes Plattdeutsch, a Low German dialect, would have been spoken at home and in church. Although Germans would typically live in communities with other Germans, there would have been pressure throughout history to assimilate to the Polish culture, and to learn and use Polish. Kaethie Pfeifle, who was born south-east of Thorn (Toruń), remembers going to a Polish school in fourth grade, where they had to speak primarily Polish but also had German classes. Kaethie comments on their daily language use, recalling that church as well as interactions with friends and neighbours was in German, and that Plattdeutsch was spoken at home. Kaethie's parents, who worked as farmers, spoke Polish, but Kathie's exposure to Polish was limited to the classes and interactions she had in her Polish school.

The Baltic States

The Baltic states were also conquered by the Knights of the Teutonic Order in the medieval period, which contributed to the German expansion into the south and east shores of the Baltic Sea.[163] At the beginning of the 13th century, Albert of Buxhoeveden, who held the title of the third Bishop of Livonia, became the first to

---

163 Raisa Mazeika, "An Amicable Enmity: Some Peculiarities in Teutonic-Balt Relations in the Chronicles of the Baltic Crusades", in The Germans and the East, edited by Charles W. Ingrao and Franz A.J. Szabo (West Lafayette: Purdue University Press, 2008), 49.

successfully conquer Livonia (present day Latvia and Estonia).[164] Under his rule, the city of Riga was built, and the military contingent of the Order of the Knights of Christ (also known as the Sword Brothers) was formed. Their ability to convert Livonian chieftains to Christianity aided them in their goal of expansion.[165] Not long after the Knights of the Teutonic Order were invited by Polish Duke Conrad of Mazovia, they absorbed the Order of the Knights of Christ, thereby not only having the goal of extending their control over Prussia, but now also protecting Livonia against the pagan Lithuanians.[166]

Prior to the 19th century, the Baltic Germans (Baltendeutsche) represented less than 10% of the population of the Baltic states, and yet they were the dominant force in the economic, political, and social spheres.[167] Although the Baltic states came under Russian rule in the 18th century, the German speakers living there were able to keep their culture and their land-owning status up until the 1880s, when "Russification" policies were enacted.[168] With these campaigns, the Baltic Germans were stripped of some of their authority, and there was an attempt to minimize the influence of German culture by changing the language of instruction in schools from German and Latin to Russian and by making Russian the official language of government.[169] After World War I, Lithuania, Latvia, and Estonia became independent countries, and assured the German-speaking minority that they would be allowed to keep their culture and language. They allowed them to set up schools in which German was the main language of instruction.[170] However, the Baltic Germans were no longer able to enjoy the position of power they once had, as their land was taken from them and given to the people who made up the majority group.[171] This change in fortune for the German-speaking minority caused some to leave their homes and move to Germany. However, after the Hitler-Stalin Pact of 1939, which awarded control of the Baltic states to the USSR, many Germans still living there were relocated by the Nazi government as part of the campaign called Heim-ins-Reich.[172] When the German population of the prior Baltic states were directed to "return home," most of them complied, and exited the country in the later months of 1939 and in the first half of 1940. Approximately 53,000 Baltic Germans from

164 Andrejs Plakans, A Concise History of the Baltic States (New York: Cambridge University Press, 2011), 36.
165 Plakans, A Concise History, 37.
166 Paul W. Knoll, "The Most Unique Crusader State: The Teutonic Order in the Development of the Political Culture of NorthEastern Europe during the Middle Ages", in The Germans and the East, edited by Charles W. Ingrao and Franz A.J. Szabo (West Lafayette: Purdue University Press, 2008), 38.
167 Knoll, "The Most Unique", 53.
168 Plakans, A Concise History, 51, 68.
169 Plakans, A Concise History, 68-69.
170 Kevin C. O'Connor, The History of the Baltic States. 2nd Ed. (Santa Barbara: ABC-CLIO, 2015), 130.
171 O'Connor, The History of the Baltic States, 130.
172 Plakans, A Concise History, 338-339. Translation: returning home into the empire/Reich.

Latvia, 14,000 from Estonia, and 52,000 from Lithuania left their homes and were resettled in the western areas of Poland that had been annexed by the Third Reich.[173]

Andrea von Weyhe's parents are one example of Baltic Germans who were forced to leave Latvia. This happened before they knew each other. Her mother had to flee from Latvia to Germany, where she was able to find work as a kindergarten teacher. Her father, also from Latvia, returned from imprisonment in 1954 where he had apprenticed as a gardener. Andrea's mother and father came to Canada independently from each other, but both being from Latvia, they met at a Baltic German function in Canada.

Willi Ristau was born in Latvia to German parents. In 1939, the whole family was moved to Warthegau (a much-enlarged Posen-Poznania). When the Baltic Germans were resettled in Poland, they were given homes and land that the German government had taken from Polish inhabitants.[174] When Willi's family came to Poland, they were given two farms, one of which had previously been owned by another German farmer. Willi remembers that German farmers would have clay tile roofs, and Polish farmers would have straw roofs. He also recalls that his father was drafted into the war in 1944 and ended up being a prisoner of war for two years in the Soviet Union. The circumstances of war for the Baltic Germans were like those of other German minorities, as they were recognized as ethnic Germans by the Nazi regime. The men were required to fight in the war, many of them imprisoned, others never able to return to their families. Near the end of World War II, many Baltic Germans fled Poland, trying to escape the threat of the approaching Soviet Army, and trying to make it to West Germany.

Having to Leave Home

In 1944 and 1945, the ethnic German population of the territories in the east started to evacuate as the threat of the Soviet Red Army came closer. They would either go on foot or by train. For a short period of time, it was also possible to take a ship from Danzig (Gdańsk) to the west, either to Germany or to Denmark. For some time, it was forbidden by Nazi order to "escape" west. By the time communities were granted permission, it was simply too late, either because the Red Army was too close, transportation was not available, or harsh winter conditions would not allow for it.[175] For those who were not able to escape in time, many were imprisoned or killed, and others were deported to the USSR.

Willi Ristau remembers leaving with his mother and eight siblings in January of 1945, loading some of their possessions onto two wagons, and leaving the rest behind. He describes that his father had been drafted in 1944 and held as a prisoner in the USSR; his mother had to take care of a small farm and eight children before Willi's father was released in 1947. Willi also recalls that they "survived on potatoes

173 Plakans, A Concise History, 339-340.
174 Plakans, A Concise History, 338-339.
175 Merten, Forgotten Voices, 44-50.

and bread," commenting: "a lot of people did a lot worse than what we did." Alice Bromberg also comments on the conditions at the end of the war, recalling that when they got word that the Red Army was approaching, they were forced to leave immediately. Alice told us that they travelled by train at times, but due to the extensive bombing of train cars and of the tracks, most of the time they had no choice but to walk, with no shelter and with nothing to eat.

After the war, many people who had fled or been evacuated wished to return to their homes in Poland, and although they were forbidden by the Polish government to do so, many managed to make it back to their homes.[176] Upon returning, these former residents were not welcome, as they were often blamed for the war crimes committed under the Nazi regime. Returning residents, as well as those who had remained there after the war's end, found their property confiscated, many were tried for treason, some were sent to camps.[177] The fate for many able-bodied people was to be put to work in Soviet or Polish labour camps, where the conditions were so severe that many people died. Those who were deemed unable to work in the camps and those who became sick in the camps were deported.[178] When the labour camps ended in 1949, the people imprisoned were returned to occupied Germany.[179]

Kaethie Pfeifle talks about being taken to a camp in Siberia. When they were trying to flee, it was already too late, and she was captured by the Red Army. Kaethie recalls that it took them four weeks to trek to Siberia. After falling ill shortly after her arrival there, Kaethie was put on a sick list and was released of her duties earlier than many others. She was, remarkably, able to find her father upon her release, and together they were able to safely make it to the western part of Germany. Many men who had fought in the German Wehrmacht were also taken prisoner in the Siberian camps. They had to find their families in Germany once the war was over. Willi Ristau's and Alice Bromberg's fathers, for example, had to find their families, with hopes that they had survived and made it out of Poland during the war.

Because many of our interviewees had to leave their home countries behind when they were very young, their childhood memories revolve around the extreme difficulties of war, and the horrible losses they, along with their families, suffered because of the war. Our interviewees recount their lives to varying degrees, some willing to share more of the horrible conditions than others. However, many of them share the difficulties of leaving their homes, starting new lives, and losing family and friends. People were forced to move, in some cases more than once, along different paths and by different means of transport: on foot and with hand cart, by train, and by boat. Some interviewees also spoke about their hired Polish help leaving with them during their flight from Poland. Regardless of the path, their journeys were long, and they had to risk their lives as there was still a war going on. Families were separated because the men were required to fight in the war. This meant that many women

---

176 Merten, Forgotten Voices, 57.
177 Merten, Forgotten Voices, 64-69.
178 Merten, Forgotten Voices, 75.
179 Merten, Forgotten Voices, 62.

were forced to flee their homes with their children, not knowing where or how they would ever be able to see their husbands or other male family members again. Many of these men would have perished in the war, others would have been taken prisoner, and some were to survive and reunite with their families in Germany after the war.

The stories the interviewees share give us a glimpse into what life was like for Germans living outside of Germany's borders during the war and in post-war times. The interviewees who came from Czechoslovakia, Poland, and the Baltic states had lived in German communities. The majority spoke a regional dialect of German at home, and for those who were able to go to school, it seems that many went to German school. However, it also appears that these German families were well integrated into their communities. The interviewees often recall that their parents were able to speak the language of the majority culture, and multiple people recall stories of their families' interactions with people from other linguistic and cultural backgrounds.

The focus of the individuals' memories and stories shared from their time spent in Czechoslovakia, Poland, and the Baltic states are, of course, centred on their flight or expulsion from their homes, simply due to the age of many of the people who were interviewed. And because their only memories of their homes may be limited to horrible memories, some people's accounts of their time in Czechoslovakia, Poland, and the Baltic states are very restrained. What this chapter discussed happened at the beginning of the lives of interviewees from these areas; it does not represent the entirety of their lives, as they all eventually made their way to Waterloo Region. In other words, this chapter depicts a consequential but relatively short period of their lives; the following chapters will detail the time afterwards: their arrival and life in Canada.

They Came from Germany and Austria

Stefanie Templin and Sebastian Siebel-Achenbach

For quite a few of the refugees described in the previous chapters, the way to Canada led through Germany. This chapter, however, gives voice to the immigrants to Canada who were born within the area of Germany and Austria.

Between 1947 and 1955, when most German-speaking immigrants came to North America, the only method of transportation was by boat; immigration via an airport was done only later.[180] The vast majority of our interviewees went through Bremerhaven (Bremen's port). From 1946 to 1967, nearly 300,000 people, most of

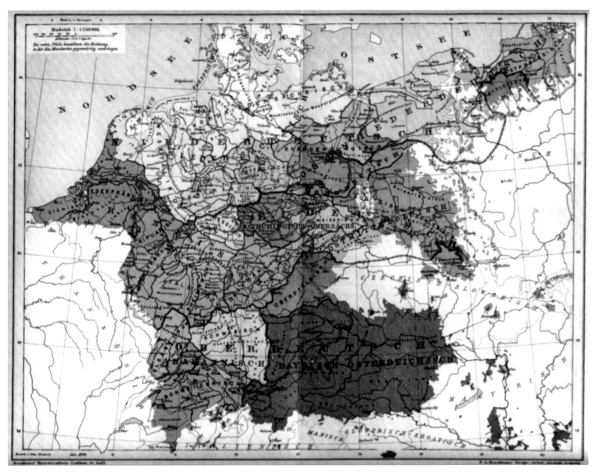

Map of the German Dialects. Brockhaus (German encyclopedia), Leipzig 1908. Karte der deutschen Mundarten. Brockhaus' Konversations-Lexikon, 14. Auflage, 4. Band. https://commons.wikimedia.org/ wiki/ File:Karte_der_deutschen_Mundarten_(Brockhaus).jpg

whom were displaced persons or refugees, emigrated from Germany to Canada.[181] It is important to keep in mind that this was only one of many changes in location; in a considerable number of cases, people had already been on the move for quite some time and spent months, if not years, in different cities, camps, or countries.[182]

Whatever the decade, many Germans, as well as Austrians, state that the main reason they left was that they saw no future for themselves and their families, where they were. By the end of World War II, entire towns and many businesses had been destroyed; people had lost everything or had no means to take care of their houses, gardens, or land. Jobs and accommodation were scarce, and evacuation, flight, and imprisonment had family members scattered all over Europe. With Germany divided into two states by 1949, a whole new set of problems arose. While the Cold War posed a constant threat on both sides and drove parts of the population to move out of the country, many people in the German Democratic Republic were especially dissatisfied with their government. Only the German unification in 1990 finally allowed many of them to pursue, among other things, their dreams of travelling and seeing the world. Before and after this date, though, professional and personal barriers, desires, and opportunities motivated individuals to leave for Canada. This chapter depicts the historical circumstances, living conditions, and journey of those immigrants to Canada who had lived in Germany or Austria.

Before and During World War II

Few of our interviewees can still recall life under the Nazi regime during World War II and later the separation into two German states. A female interviewee who requested to be anonymous was born before Hitler became chancellor of Germany in January 1933. Being an only child, she naturally found the Girl Scouts atmosphere and steady company offered by the Bund Deutscher Mädel[183] rather appealing. She received an extraordinary education: instead of twelve, she only had to go to school for ten years, as she was sent to a special facility for students whose intellect was above average. After graduating from high school, she became an apprentice at a bookshop specialized in theatrical works and underwent training at the Reichsschule des Deutschen Buchhandels.[184]

What is rather unknown to many people today is that, before having any chance of getting a job, young women in Nazi Germany had to complete a mandatory year of national service. They had to sign up for either farm labour or housework. Often, they were assigned to a household with a mother with three or more children, who had requested that help. One of the interviewees, who had worked such a housework job,

---

180 Dirk Hoerder, Geschichte der deutschen Migration vom Mittelalter bis heute (München: C.H. Beck oHG, 2010), 101-105.

181 Ronald Schmalz, "Former Enemies Come to Canada: Ottawa and the Post-War German Immigration Boom, 1951-57." (Unpublished PhD diss., University of Ottawa, 2000), 20.

182 Hoerder, Geschichte der deutschen Migration, 11.

183 Translation: League of German Girls.

184 Translation: Academy of Book Trade of the German Reich.

felt like she was a house slave, having to do the cleaning, vacuuming, washing, and whatever other chores the older woman did not want to perform herself.

For most interviewees, childhood experiences in Germany and Austria left strong memories. Manfred Richter grew up just outside of Dresden before, during, and after the war. He spent his first six years in an apartment in the city's historic centre, facing a plaza where, in the early thirties, demonstrations took place. One of Manfred's earliest memories is watching through a window how the tram had to stop for yet another demonstration — probably a dispute between people associated with the Social Democratic Party on one side and the National Socialist German Workers' Party (Nazi Party) on the other. His mother quickly pulled him away. At the time, merely months before Hitler took over the government, these events were often accompanied by violent outbreaks and gunfire. Remarkably, Manfred said that, despite the trouble that comes with war and although he had to interrupt his schooling several times and saw the destruction of Dresden firsthand, he had a generally happy childhood. One night when he was sick in bed, he decided to ignore the air raid sirens announcing an attack and watched through his window how the city lit up with fire and explosions. For the subsequent two attacks, he joined his mother and siblings in the nearby bunker.

Tony Bergmeier remembers that the constant hunger and search for food did not prevent him from being content. Rather, he found the anti-aircraft batteries behind his family's house highly interesting and exciting. As a young boy, Tony did not have any sense of the danger and the threat surrounding him every day. For him and his friends, shards of exploded bombs that had set neighbours' houses on fire became collector's items like they were postage stamps.

According to Siegfried Schranz, who was six years old when the war finally ended, his childhood in Bavaria during the war was not unpleasant. The German troops would sometimes play music when marching in the streets, there were airplanes to watch in the sky from inside the house, and once, one of those planes even crashed — an exciting event for the young boy. Siegfried thought at the time that "war was…normal." Similarly, post-war children did not pay attention to the debris framing their path to school because they had never known anything different.

Astrid Braun even goes so far as calling herself "spoiled" because she grew up in Berlin, with maids in a gated property. This protected environment was largely due to her aunt's wealth; Astrid Braun's own parents had left Poland with her before she entered elementary school in the hope that they could escape the war. With her father being sick most of the time and her mother working full-time, the rest of the family took care of her and made sure she had everything she needed, including food and education.

Others were less fortunate: Kinderlandverschickung[185] was a common practice. Children living in especially endangered areas such as larger cities were taken from

---

185 Translation: sending children from war-ridden cities to less dangerous places, e.g., rural areas.

their parents and sent to camps or host families in the countryside.[186] This happened, for example, to Martin Giebel's mother, who was born in Dortmund in 1929. Her home was bombed out three times during the war, and her parents stayed in emergency housing until 1973. In the case of Minnie and Kurt Boese, who grew up in Bremen, the separation from parents and home lasted between six and eight months. They were still able to attend school in rural Saxony, where they lived with host families until the war was over. Their teacher had been evacuated with them. At the age of seven, Rita Schirm, also from Bremen, spent a year evacuated in Saxony with "foster parents," as she calls them.

Growing Up in Post-war Germany and Austria

Another group of our interviewees grew up after the war. Recollections of the immediate post-war period vary, with some remembering little, while others recall collecting and swapping bomb shards for fun, constantly moving and relocating from one part of the country to another, or spending months in camps. It was not unusual for some, even if they had the chance to continue their education, to work hard alongside their mothers to get food for the family. Fathers and brothers who had been drafted often spent years as prisoners-of-war before being released back home. Very often, their families did not even know if they were still alive until they returned.

Many others interviewed for this book had to take breaks from their education or stopped going to school altogether. Astrid Braun was an excellent student to the point of being able to skip grades. However, she was set back by almost a whole year when her mother fled the Soviet occupation zone with her, and subsequently spent six months in a refugee camp before leaving for Canada in 1949. Hans Peter Kahlen had to leave school after Grade eight to learn carpentry and join the family business. A couple of years later, he went to evening school to get his Fachabitur.[187] According to Christa Streicher, girls had a harder time pursuing further education because boys' careers were deemed more important or promising at the time.

Considering the trauma this generation experienced, it was quite surprising that many interviewees said that they had a normal, protected, and happy childhood. They were affected by bombing raids, evacuations, times of hunger, and destroyed urban centres; a significant number of German emigrants witnessed the devastating results of warfare with their own eyes. After the war, faced with forced relocations and the knowledge that Germany had lost the war, other horrors were just about to begin. For those who had already suffered, it intensified: "My people had gone from bad to worse," Helga Sarkar says about the situation in Saxony after the Soviet military government took over. Kids saw dead soldiers piled upon dead soldiers, fathers had lost limbs, and mothers and daughters were raped. There were people who sought refuge in death, some because of the horrors, others for fear of having to live through

---

186 "Kinderlandverschickung", Wikipedia, accessed May 16, 2019, https://de.wikipedia.org/wiki/Kinderlandverschickung
187 Translation: vocational high school diploma.

such things themselves. According to an article in the German magazine *Spiegel*, at least 100,000 people killed themselves in the immediate after-war period. They feared the revenge the Red Army would take after the German military had brutally slaughtered their way through eastern Europe. They were desperate in the face of the German Reich's downfall or unable to deal with the trauma of their rape.[188]

Helga Sarkar was barely two years old when her mother decided that she would rather die than suffer the same fate as so many other women. To kill herself and her baby, she turned on the oven gas. Before that she had written a letter to her husband, who fought in the German army, asking him to follow her example "so that we will at least be reunited in that way," explains Helga. The infant's life was spared because the smell of gas alarmed the neighbours; her mother, though, was already dead. This event took place two days after the official announcement of Hitler's suicide when the Red Army was already in control of Berlin. The young mother had been terrified of what might happen to her and her family if Soviet soldiers found them; after all, they did have the reputation of raping women of all ages and abducting them to do restitution work back in the Soviet Union. These recollections are a recurring motif in the stories of people who fled from what had been eastern German territories. In large part, this negative assessment seems to be due to evacuations forced by the occupying military and, later, the post-war allied government.

After her mother's suicide, the rest of Helga Sarkar's childhood was defined by moving around from parents to different grandparents every few years. Her father remarried very soon, and she remembers being raised by her stepmother and her father. When she was six years old, her paternal grandparents took her in because her father and his new wife, expecting another child, had decided to illegally cross the border to West Germany. For her, this was a rather lucky turn of events since her grandparents treated her much better and more lovingly. After two years, however, her father wanted her to join his family in the West, and the rough treatment began anew. She was almost ten years old when her stepmother's parents took pity on her and took her in. Meanwhile, she had found out by accident that the woman she used to call "Mutti" was not her real mom. When finally, she decided to ask her parents for clarification, they casually mentioned that "yeah, it's true. Your mother died and this is your Mutti now." Now she was again supposed to refer to people she was unrelated to as family members; she did not have a room of her own, but at least she was taken better care of. In the summer of 1956, when Helga was turning into a teenager and they no longer knew how to deal with her, she was sent to her other grandparents again for a few months before returning to West Germany. So apart from the struggle against hunger and having a father with deep psychological wounds from both the war itself and its accompanying effects, Helga was subjected to a tremendous amount of emotional trauma.

---

188 Norbert F. Plötzl and Klaus Wiegrefe, "Die Heimkehr des Krieges", Der Spiegel, no.5 (2005): 50-61, accessed October 12, 2015, https://www.spiegel.de/spiegel/print/d-39178608.html

Hans Peter Kahlen remembers "sehr böse Erlebnisse in Aachen"[189] where he grew up. Since his family was living so close to the Dutch and Belgian borders, the family was one of the first to witness the occupation of their city. They tried to stay for as long as possible, hiding in a basement alongside several soldiers, many of whom were dead or fatally injured, for two months. After that, they were taken to the mountains in central Germany on a military truck.

Horst Wiesner remembers some terrible scenes in his youth, too. When his father, who had not yet recovered from the wounds he received in the war, tried to leave his home in Breslau with his son and get the rest of the family later, he found that he was not the only one with this plan. Breslau's main train station, as well as the trains, was overflowing with people trying to escape, mothers begging strangers on the moving carriages to take their babies to save them. It took Horst and his father several days of waiting and another two attempts before they were able to leave and get a few things to their grandparents. The second part of the undertaking, namely getting his mother and infant brother out of Breslau (today's Wrocław) to his grandparents' farm failed because the city was already encircled and under siege. The thirteen-year-old and his father took a wagon and horses and hid in the mountains around Waldenburg in Silesia.

Growing up in post-war Germany and Austria was anything but easy for many people. Things had to be rebuilt; people needed a new perspective, and a better outlook on the future than they had before 1945. With both the emotional and physical injuries our interviewees and their relatives had experienced, this was hard to achieve in a country suffering from war debt, destruction, and people trying to find places to live. The next part focuses on the specifics of this last aspect: the flight of interviewees from other places in Europe to Germany and Austria before their eventual migration to Canada.

On the Run from the Red Army and the Soviet Occupation Zone

Although people from all over Germany were subjected to relocations, it was especially women in eastern Germany who felt the need to escape the invading military for reasons mentioned above. John Schultheiss recalls his mother Elisabeth telling him that the Red Army took women from the eastern German villages rather than men, and that his mother lost many friends due to shootings, landmines, and sickness, among other things. One of the women we interviewed received a message from her husband, who had been a prisoner-of-war with the Americans and later the British, in which he asked her to join him in West Germany. Meanwhile, the Red Army had reached her hometown. "Und vor den Russen musste man flüchten als junges Mädchen,"[190] if you did not want to be raped, she told us. This made her decide to flee across the "Grüne Grenze."[191] Her grandmother bribed a trucker with

---

189 Translation: very bad experiences in Aachen.
190 Translation: And as a young woman, you had to flee the Russians.
191 Translation: unfenced sections of the demarcation line between Western occupying forces and the Red Army territories.

cigarettes to take her close to the border, where she then found an English driver willing to give her a ride. He did not smuggle her over to the West, though, as he was afraid the Soviet authorities would imprison him or worse. She still had a bottle of vodka with which she tried to convince a Soviet officer to let her pass. Not wanting to have the procedure watched by the British military on the other side, the officer sent her into the forest with a soldier instead. Once they reached a safe spot, however, the soldier demanded something other than a bottle of alcohol, which she refused. After she wandered around blindly for a while, she ran into another group of soldiers wearing an unfamiliar uniform — she panicked for a moment because she had nothing to trade for favours anymore, but the two men addressed her in English. She had made it to the British zone.

Elizabeth Schilling's family had similar experiences when they fled the Soviet occupation zone. After being moved from a small village in Hungary to a camp in Pirna, Saxony, they were placed in the apartment of an elderly lady. Elizabeth's older brother worked for a farmer there, who was kind enough to sometimes give him a few extra potatoes, vegetables, or other food so that they would not suffer too much from the constant hunger and malnutrition. A few months later, her brother went across the border into West Germany illegally, got work, and sent back some money so that the rest of the family could follow.

Elizabeth remembers the story of their journey into West Germany in detail. Having arrived in a village close to the border, they were given orders to go down a street and wait until a certain woman on the opposite side stepped into a house. Only then they were to enter a barn two houses further down and wait until nightfall when someone would accompany them to the border. At four in the morning, they followed a man on a narrow and very steep path. It was raining hard that night, and they had to give up their raincoats so they would not alarm the sentinel with any rustling sound. Finally, they arrived at a friendly farmer's house on the other side. Even after that, the family still experienced several hardships like moving forward with no identification or other documents, waiting on a train station for days until Elizabeth Schilling's sister sent them money to buy tickets so all could reunite, and find work and a place to stay.

Loss of Property, Political Dissatisfaction, and Professional Barriers

For many, the way to Canada led through Germany or Austria, especially for people who had lived in the part of the Third Reich east of current German borders. Nearly everyone interviewed from these areas experienced the loss of their property due to expropriation, bombings, or expulsion. People in the western parts were sometimes able to return to their homes after the evacuation if their houses were still standing. Dorothea Snell's family had to leave behind their farm when evacuating from a village near Tilsit, East Prussia, in January 1945. Once her father returned from captivity in the Soviet Union, he began work as a fisherman in Bremerhaven. He enjoyed his new trade and the feeling of freedom that being on a ship conveyed, but a lung disease ended this occupation. He became a typewriter salesman, cruising the villages on a bicycle. Since this was not an ideal situation, the family's goal was to immigrate to North America, be it Canada or the United States. At the age of eighteen Dorothea moved to Canada, where she first finished her last year of high school and later her post-secondary education at the University of Toronto. Dorothea had her parents follow later. They were able to purchase a farm and manage it successfully for 35 years.

Similarly, Christa Streicher's father lost his business due to a bomb raid during World War II, and they moved in with her grandmother in Essen, West Germany. Although she really wanted to, Christa could not do her Abitur[192] and go to university, since the family did not have the financial means. They also considered the education of their four sons to be more important than that of their daughter. When her parents denied her the means to pursue her dream, namely, to become a teacher, she was so devastated that she decided to "rebel" against her family in every way possible.

Economic shortages were more or less the norm everywhere after World War II, but people in the Soviet occupation zone of Germany, the later German Democratic Republic (GDR), felt political pressure as well. Many interviewees from the GDR felt uncomfortable living under an imposed authority whose ideology they disagreed with. The absence of fundamental freedoms was most acutely felt. Mathias Schulze speaks of a "geografische Enge"[193] in the GDR due to travel restrictions and, of course, the Wall, which had been erected in August 1961, and was to remain a physical impasse until November 1989. This is especially hard for a teenager who wanted to see what the rest of the world looked like. It is no wonder then that Mathias remembers the possibility of travel as one of the most persistent demands voiced in the demonstrations of 1989, in many of which he participated as a student. He also remembers the positive feeling that accompanied these demonstrations, which was the belief that things could be changed. Mathias had faith that with enough support from the population, policies could be influenced, most importantly, in a peaceful manner. Shortly before the Wall fell, he did consider crossing the border to Austria while he was on vacation in Hungary. What kept him from doing that was the fear of never seeing his parents again and never being able to return.

As was the case with Mathias Schulze, even those who were born in the GDR, and did not know any other system, were sometimes extremely dissatisfied with certain policies. In 1989, Ronny Horvath and his family fled to Munich because the sixteen-year-old wanted to learn the same trade as his father — plumbing — to take over his business one day. The GDR government, however, denied him the apprenticeship to avoid the creation of self-perpetuating dynasties. By illegally leaving the country, his father lost the company, but Ronny was amazed at the new freedom of choice and speech. Confronted by similar restrictions, Helga Sarkar always believed that she would never have the chance to a higher education in the GDR because none of her family were members of the communist party.

---

192 Translation: high school diploma.
193 Translation: geographical constriction.

Additionally, her father had fled to West Germany, so her marks could never be high enough to make up for that perceived treachery.

Political and social dissatisfaction can be a decisive factor in life decisions anywhere, including in the West. As Ursel Wandschneider reports, it was not always easy to succeed or rise to a higher position if you did not agree with the desired political standards. Ursel was raised in North Rhine-Westphalia and started a promising career in engineering. But she also reported how later, in a second career in teaching, she experienced rejection because she was not measured by her performance but her disinterest in supporting political matters. In her account, she lacked the appropriate connections, and did not always toe the party line, which led to disagreements with her superiors. Ursel did not want to be part of a system where connections were worth more than hard work, so she decided to emigrate to Canada.

For Ronny Horvath, things also did not turn out quite as he expected after his move from the GDR to West Germany. While he did get his apprenticeship as a plumber, he went back to business school a few years later and, afterwards, founded his own restaurant. The venture was so successful that he expanded, even though there was a recession looming. Then, Ronny had problems with his main creditor. No longer able to sustain the restaurants, he was forced to close the entire business and returned to his job as a plumber. In 2004, the company he worked for let him go. It was next to impossible for him to find employment anywhere in Germany, so when he found an advertisement in a newspaper that offered a job in Canada, he took the chance.

Language and Cultural Experience before Emigration

Quite a few German and Austrian emigrants already knew another language, had lived abroad, or were otherwise involved with different cultures, languages, and dialects before they arrived in Canada. Obviously, children whose parents came from another eastern-European country like Poland, Hungary, or Romania, for example, grew up hearing those languages. The latter experience was especially common among people who lived in areas which were repeatedly transformed politically. This was the case with Kathie Pfeifle, who was born in a village south-east of Thorn (today's Toruń), which changed political jurisdiction a few times. Though the members of her family were all born in the same area, her parents were born in Imperial Russia, she herself was born in Poland, and her sister in a territory annexed to Germany during the war. Kathie learned Polish during the first few years of her life, when she went to a Polish school; at home, however, the family spoke "Plattdeutsch" (Low German). Her father had learned Russian when the region was under Russian sovereignty, and both her parents were fluent in Polish. The whole village spoke and identified as German since they were on the border with West Prussia, and in church one spoke German. Even when the area belonged to Poland, children had German as a subject in school.

While later generations of immigrants or those who came from West Germany were mostly taught (British) English as a second language, and thus had at least a basic means of communication, many interviewees did not speak English before coming to Canada. Former prisoners-of-war sometimes picked up a few words of English during their time in captivity with the British, Canadian, or American army. In other cases, people were able to take advantage of their language skills, to make their time in labour or prisoner-of-war camps more bearable. In the case of Pauline Schmidt, it even helped her father save himself and his family. Her father had left home as soon as he knew that he would be drafted again; having served in the Serbian army during World War I. Once he heard about the terrible situation in Yugoslavia, where he thought his wife and daughters still resided, he tried to go back to sell the house before the communist Partisans would expropriate him. When he reached the border, he was discovered and detained. From then on, he moved from one camp to another until he found his wife with Pauline and her baby sister. With some diligence, risk-taking, and luck, he was able to use his Serbian on one of the soldiers guarding the camp to help his family and a few others escape.

Helga Sarkar's experiences also included a language connection. She grew up in Zschopau in the German Democratic Republic and was taught Russian from Grade five. She was enthusiastic about trying out what she had learned in real life by talking to Russian soldiers on the street. Like the stories people tell about the American military handing out chocolate, fruits, and other kinds of food to children, the Soviet soldiers in East Germany liked giving children candy and practised Russian with them. This in turn motivated Helga to get better and learn even more Russian.

In her desire to find her own way, Christa Streicher left Germany and her family once she finished her apprenticeship. She spent a year in France as an au-pair before she worked at a hospital in England to practise the language. After that, a friend from school who had already immigrated to America helped her find work overseas, where Christa married and had her first child. As her husband was a translator and interpreter with NATO, they often moved, later returning to Germany. When he grew tired of his job, the family visited two of Christa's brothers, who were living in Canada then, and they decided to stay here.

Initially, Ronny Horvath had a hard time learning English. After his family's arrival in Munich, he repeated Grade nine to make sure he would get good marks when graduating. The only problem was that, whereas his classmates had received English lessons for five years, he had to start from scratch. It was not that he was bad at learning new languages; merely that he was behind his peers. In Saxony, he had been taught Russian in school, which he spoke well enough. With his father being Hungarian, Ronny knew three languages before facing the task of catching up on five years of English instruction within two years.

Siegfried Schranz always had a very good relationship with the American soldiers who came to his school and gave the children food. They were also the reason he no longer drinks Coca-Cola; he had too much of it as a young boy when they kept serving him the drink. What really piqued his interest in North America, though, were Karl May's novels, especially the ones about Winnetou.

While most of our interviewees came to Canada fifty to sixty years ago, there is still a substantial number of people who immigrated much later, and whose decision was not at all affected by war or political or economic circumstances. One of these later immigrants, Alex Müntz, born in Siebenbürgen, Romania, grew up bilingually: at home, he spoke Romanian with his parents even though his father is of German descent, whereas in school, nearly all subjects were taught in German as he was living in a German-speaking community. Public German schools in Romania, however, struggled to exist. In Alex's experience, many people left for Canada and the United States during the sixties; with the fall of the Soviet Union in the 1990s and the possibility of travelling worldwide, there was another wave of emigrants. It was the German influence, though, that eventually led him overseas as well. From 2005 to 2011, he studied optometry in Jena, Germany. This choice was obvious to him since he wanted to leave the place where he had spent his entire life and wanted to experience something new. Furthermore, he already knew the language. His sister, four years younger than he, was studying in Germany, too. During his master's studies, he went to an international conference in Florida, along with a few faculty members. His supervisor and a colleague at the time decided that it would be a good idea for Alex to write his thesis in Canada, which he did. In the summer of 2010, he participated in a project in Canada, and, a year later, he and his best friend and fellow student returned to do their doctorates.

Annika Nicholson came to Canada in a similar manner. When she started attending university in Germany in 1999, students in her program of Tourism Management were encouraged to travel. Annika did her first internship in England and found living in another country fascinating. She went on to study in Spain, did another internship in Mexico, and wrote her thesis in Switzerland in cooperation with a Swiss firm. It was this business which offered her a job with a partner company in Vancouver, after she had spent half a year working on a farm in Iceland.

Conclusion

There always have been a multitude of reasons why German-speaking immigrants decided to come to Canada. This chapter has sketched the lives they had in Germany and Austria, the conditions that were prevailing at the time of their departure, their fears and deprivation, as well as their wishes and desires. A large group of immigrants came after World War II, when many people were displaced, and dissatisfied with, or even scared of their home environment. It is not surprising that they started looking for new opportunities elsewhere. Even then, however, people did not only seek security and stability. Some longed to be reunited with their family; others chose to start over far away by themselves. While a considerable number of our interviewees had previous experience with foreign cultures and languages, just as many seem to have ended up in Canada almost by accident and with no English-language experience beforehand.

Illustrations

Birthplace of Dorothea Baltruweit (Snell): a farm in East Prussia, in 1936. © Dorothea Rosemarie.

Paternal great-grandparents in Dittersbach, formerly Sudetenland, now Stašov, Czechia, in 1929.
© Johann Leinweber.

Home of paternal grandparents in Dittersbach, formerly Sudetenland, now Stašov, Czechia, in 1936.
© Johann Leinweber.

Steve Schatz's
family as refugees in
Austria, 1944.
© Steven Schatz.

Refugees from
Romania.
ca. 1950.
© Steven Schatz.

Grandmother, parents, aunts, uncles, cousins, siblings; Elizabeth Reuss is the baby in her mother's arms, next to her father (on right). ca. 1948. © Elizabeth Reuss.

Danube Swabian wedding in the Batschka, Hungary in 1950: John Heffner Sr. and Mary Zimmermann, who later immigrated to Canada together. © John and Willy Heffner.

Astrid Braun in braids.
ca. 1942
© Astrid Braun.

Bernd Brandt in grade 1 in Hoffenheim, in 1949. © Bernd Brandt.

Dagmar Schilha on her own bike, which her stepfather made out of three old bicycles in 1952.
© Dagmar Schilha.

Dagmar Schilha in her first dirndl (traditional
dress), in 1955. © Dagmar Schilha.

Bernd Brandt on the right with his "Zuckertüte,"
a bag full of candy as a gift for the start of school.
Grade 1, 1949. © Bernd Brandt.

Elizabeth in a traditional
costume. 1940s.
© Elizabeth Schilling.

Rosina Mühlberghuber's father
holding his first grandson (second
grandchild), Rosina's child. 1960s.
© Rosina Mühlberghuber.

Many Germans in Eastern European countries were dispossessed either during the war or later. Here, Elizabeth Schilling's aunt and uncle stand on the right, with the Czech family who became the new owners of their home. Post-WWII. © Elizabeth Schilling.

Danube Swabian basket weaving continued in Pinsdorf, Austria after the family fled from the Banat, Romania, during World War II, ca. 1960. © Gerda Wolf.

Outside the barracks at the work camp in Passau. 130 people at a time slept in one of these former army barracks. 1940s-1950s. © Elizabeth Schilling.

Weilau wheat harvest, in the 1980s. © Steven Schatz.

1000-year parade in Großenhain, Germany. Guenter Lotzmann is the first on the right. 1954.
© Guenter Lotzmann.

A travelling Carnival group, Germany, 1958/59. © Dagmar Schilha.

Rosina on the boat from Germany to Canada, coming alone. Landed in Montréal, June 22, 1960. © Rosina Mühlberghuber.

First car, at 21 years. 1958. © John Naas.

The MS Transatlantic. 1950s. © John Naas.

Schwaben Club musicians, with John Heffner Jr. the accordion player at the right;
Mr. Quiring, far right. Late 1960s. © John and Willy Heffner.

Transylvanian Hofbräu Band in Kitchener, Canada, in 1967/68. © Steven Schatz.

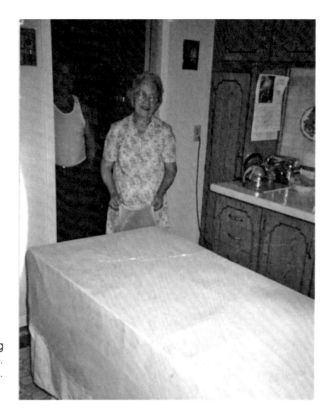

A dough tablecloth; Mother making
her favourite strudel. ca. 1965.
© Elizabeth Reuss.

Elizabeth Reuss and a Catholic priest, instructors at the German Congregation (St. Mary's, Kitchener) for
First Communion. ca. 1965. © Elizabeth Reuss.

A (Canadian!) fun afternoon at Laurel Creek
Conservation Area in Waterloo. Dorothea is
with her two children, Elinor and Robert, in 1980.
© Dorothea Rosemarie.

Start-up of "Finest Sausage & Meat". Guenter Lotzmann on the left, with partner Martin Gedja. ca. 1975.
© Guenter Lotzmann.

Hilda and Paul in traditional
Transylvanian Saxon costumes
(sächsische Tracht) at the
Trachtenball, Transylvania Club,
Kitchener, in 1987.
© Paul Konnerth..

Montréal Men's
Wear Show,
"Cool Wool"
exhibit in 1987.
© Ingo Schoppel.

Germans of Waterloo Region

The Berlin Wall on November 12, 1989, three days after it opened. © Paul Schulze.

An East Berliner driving to West Berlin, November 12, 1989. © Paul Schulze.

90

Christine Lindner receiving her Canadian citizenship in 1996. © Christine Lindner.

Tony Bergmeier with Mayor Carl Zehr at the Kitchener Christkindl Market, in 2000.
©Tony Bergmeier.

Dagmar Schilha next to polka musician and Grammy winner Walter Ostanek. She is holding her grandson. 2003. © Dagmar Schilha.

Arrival in Canada

Judith Linneweber and Harald Bauder

"Canada is often described, with good reasons, as a country of immigrants."[194] When immigrants arrive in their new country, they confront many challenges but also have a range of positive and often surprising experiences. This chapter captures the arrival period of the interviewed immigrants: their reasons for choosing Canada, their expectations, their journey, first impressions, and feelings about their new home country. It describes the initial settlement period and problems they had to face during their reception in a new society. How did they prepare for their immigration, and who came with them? Did they feel welcome? Were there any people they already knew, or did they have another previous connection to Canada? Furthermore, this chapter provides additional details about when German speakers initially arrived in Canada and where they resided.

Reasons to Immigrate and Expectations

Scholars of migration often separate push factors that cause people to leave their countries of origin from pull factors that attract the migrants to a particular country in which they settle. Many important push factors were covered in previous chapters, which dealt with the experience of war, expulsion, and the flight of people who saw no future in Germany or Austria for themselves and their children. These immigrants arrived in Canada during the late 1940s to the 1970s to build a better life. In this chapter, we also focus on the reasons why migrants from Germany chose Canada in the late 1970s up to the 2000s. Their reasons are more cheerful than those of earlier cohorts, even compelling a laugh at their experiences when they reflected on them in the interviews. Nevertheless, there is no simple explanation why all these migrants chose Canada. Rather, the reasons why people decided to immigrate to Canada are diverse and changed over the decades. In fact, when the interviews were analysed, the push and pull factors were not always easy to separate.

Some immigrants came with the expectation to eventually return to Germany. In 1956, Tony Bergmeier and his wife went on a honeymoon; they planned to stay just one year, but then never returned to Germany. According to Tony Bergmeier, this honeymoon simply lasted a lifetime: "Wir sind eigentlich gar nicht ausgewandert in dem Sinne, wir sind noch immer auf Hochzeitsreise."[195] Franz-Josef Burgund came with his wife in 1958 and told a similar story — they are also having a lifelong honeymoon. These two couples "accidently" ended up immigrating to Canada. Almut

---

194 Myer Siemsiatycki, "Continuity and change in Canadian immigration policy", in Immigrant Experiences in North America. Understanding Settlement and Integration, edited by Harald Bauder and John Shields (Toronto: Canadian Scholars' Press Inc, 2015), 93.

195 Translation: Actually, in a sense, we never emigrated; we have continued on a honeymoon trip.

Wurzbacher presents another unusual reason to immigrate: her family decided to move to Canada in 1981 because the family's farm in Germany had to be relinquished due to the construction of a highway. For Hans Peter Kahlen, the migration meant the fulfilment of his childhood dreams; he had always wanted to emigrate either to Canada or Australia. However, he lived in Germany until he was forty-seven years old. Then finally in 1980, he convinced his wife to visit Canada for the first time. His wife, Christiane, described his actions as very sneaky, "dann hat er sehr raffiniert immer Zeitungsausschnitte ausgeschnitten und mir so wortlos neben den Frühstücksteller gelegt, über Kanada und so."[196] In 1984, and after several visits to Canada, the couple finally decided to stay permanently.

A more conventional reason for choosing to immigrate was receiving a job offer in Canada, which came about in different ways and for various reasons for different people. Some of the interview participants were looking for a job offer in Canada, while for others it was just coincidence that their job led them here. One of the people who coincidently was "stranded" in Canada is Michael Drescher. He started university in Germany and decided that he would like to expand his horizons by going abroad. He spent a few years in the Netherlands, went to France, and then to South Africa. He never had intended to go to North America; his image of North America was focused on the United States and shaped by his political opposition to the fact that the USA was deploying nuclear warheads. During this period, Michael went to demonstrations, and boycotted McDonald's in opposition to US policies. During the interview he admitted that "everything [he] associated with North America was these pop cultural identities." He did not differentiate between the United States and Canada. Later, he worked as a visiting scholar in the field of environmental studies, and in this context met a professor from Canada at a symposium who offered him a job. It turned out that previous migration experiences — leaving his parent's place to study, living abroad — helped him to integrate into Canadian society, and made it easier for him to stay here.

Martin Giebel also came to Canada without any intention to stay. He completed his university studies in Germany and thereafter became a priest. However, he was never satisfied with the German tax system, especially the church tax. In his job as a priest, Martin was often responsible for hosting visitors from the United States. These contacts made him curious of how churches function outside of Germany. On these grounds he became interested in working in a different context and luckily, through a friend, learned that he could apply for a pastorate abroad. In 1979, Martin came to Canada on a six-year contract with the full intention of returning to Germany — but then stayed.

Manfred Strauss is another pastor who left Germany. He briefly explained that there are two kinds of duties for a pastor: first, the work in his home country and in the community, and second, the mission abroad. Manfred had the impression that his calling was to do missionary work. Hence, he signed up to work in Papua New

---

196 Translation: Then, cleverly, he put newspaper clippings about Canada silently next to my breakfast plate.

Guinea; however, for medical reasons he was not permitted to go there. Then the opportunity arose to go to Canada; a community in Alberta was searching for a pastor. He came to Canada in 1976, worked in Alberta for five years, and then in Kitchener until he retired in 2011.

Like Martin Giebel, the parents of Paul Schulze came to Canada with the expectation of returning to Germany after a few years; they saw the opportunity to make some money abroad, go back, and create their own business. Werner Bromberg had a similar idea. He wanted to complete his skilled-trade schooling in Germany and needed money to pay for it. Consequently, he came to Canada to earn money, but then never returned to Germany.

Mathias Schulze came to Canada in 2001 to improve his working conditions. He was unhappy with the organisational restructuring at the university in England where he worked as an assistant professor. Therefore, Mathias searched for a job which better matched his skills and interests and found it in his job at the University of Waterloo. Another interview participant who received a job offer in Canada is Ronny Horvath. He came in 2005 after closing his restaurant in Germany because of a poor economy. Since he was unsuccessful in finding a new job in Germany, he applied for a job as a technician in Canada that he saw in an advertisement. He immediately received a phone call from Canada inviting him for a job interview. Ronny never expected this response. Since he was unemployed, his friends in Germany paid for his flight. The interview was successful, and his future employer handled all the paperwork for his immigration to Canada.

Reinhold Schuster also received a rather unexpected job offer. In 1957, he had emigrated with his family to the United States. He completed his studies there, and taught architecture while finishing his doctorate. Reinhold remembered a gifted student who must have been twenty years older than he was. Several years later this very student walked into Reinhold's office and told him that he came to hire Reinhold. It turned out that in the meantime, this gifted student had become the inaugural director of the School of Architecture at the University of Waterloo. He praised the way Reinhold taught his classes and offered him a professorship at his new school. At that time, Waterloo sounded to Reinhold like "south of Alaska" — somewhere in Canada. However, this was a welcome offer since the Dean of the Faculty of Engineering at his university had started to restrict the study of architecture, and Reinhold might have needed to find a job elsewhere in any case.

Other immigrants to Canada were driven by strong feelings. Manfred Richter came to Canada because his fiancée was Canadian. Ekkehard Burow and the parents of Monika Hoedl, for example, were among the immigrants who had an urge for adventure and wanderlust. Irmgard Burow also left her home country for love. After her loved one made her a marriage proposal, she followed him to Canada in 1965. Her future husband, Ekkehard Burow, had different motives for leaving Germany. On the one hand, he was bored in Germany and driven by wanderlust, longing for a time like when he worked in Switzerland for several years. On the other hand, he had lost his mother during his early childhood and when his father remarried, he felt out of place within the family. He felt there was nothing left to keep him in Germany, which is why he emigrated immediately when he saw an ad for a job in Canada. The father of John Schultheiss also broke up with his family in Germany and set off to Canada. Similarly, Christa Streicher wanted to get away from her German family, because they did not want her to study to become a teacher. When her husband quit his job in Germany, they decided to join Christa's brothers who were already in Canada.

Other interviewees came to Canada to reunite with their families. So did Helene Schramek's mother, who was born to German parents in Yugoslavia. When Helene's mother was seventeen years old, she was taken to a labour camp in the Soviet Union for almost two-and-a-half years. After her release, she searched for her family members, which was complicated by the rudimentary communication channels at that time. She finally managed to find family members in Vienna and discovered that she had relatives who had moved to Canada. These relatives sponsored them, and the family was reunited in Kitchener.

Finally, there are also those who had lived in Canada but had to return to Germany, and they kept wishing to return to Canada one day. Ingrid Hann originally came to Canada one year after her parents had arrived in the country. She had remained in Germany with friends until her parents were settled, and then they called for her. She made the journey via ship with her aunt and uncle. The family returned to Germany after seven years in Canada, but Ingrid never forgot her childhood in Canada and, as an adult, she returned, which is described in the next section. Hugo Schwengers came to Canada for an adventure the first time, and the second time returned to build a life in Canada.

These various reasons for coming to Canada illustrate that the immigrants confronted different circumstances and had different expectations. Some came for a job, to earn money, and to build a career in Canada; others came to reunite with their families or followed the person they love. The stories of these immigrants also show that the reasons for leaving Germany and for choosing to come to Canada are often intertwined, and not always easily separated into push and pull factors.

Preparation and Journey

Many people we interviewed who immigrated to Canada after World War II had family members or acquaintances somewhere in Canada. Hence, they followed an established path of what historians and sociologists call chain migration. Their contact persons in Canada sometimes even had the opportunity to sponsor and support our interviewees when entering the country. These lucky ones include Astrid Braun, Alice Bromberg, Gerald Drews, Tony Fieder, Evelyn Guderian, John Heffner, Bill Kunsch, and Joe Piller. The contact persons often prepared a location for their immigrant to stay, and some were able to line up a job in advance.

The immigration visa was an important factor in the preparation for the journey to Canada. However, most immigrants spoke only very briefly about this process in the interviews. For Ingrid Hann, however, this application was a major step in her life, as she wanted to immigrate without her parents at the age of seventeen. After growing up in Canada until she was twelve years old, she decided to return and make Canada her home. As a seventeen-year-old, she went to the Canadian Consulate in Stuttgart and said "I'm emigrating to Canada. What do I have to do?" At the consulate she was informed that she could not leave the country without her parents due to her age; this only would have been possible if she had found a sponsor in Canada. Thus, she was back on the consulate's doorsteps at the age of 18, handed in her paperwork, bought a flight ticket, and emigrated in 1969. Her decision to leave adversely affected her relationship with her parents. She recalls her father's last words at the airport: "but don't come to me for money." By that time, she had saved a thousand Deutschmark, and thought she was rich.

The interviewees prepared in various ways for their departure. The family of Harry Drung emigrated in 1950. Harry was a nine-month-old baby at that time. When his parents learned that there was no universal health coverage in Canada, they decided to have the baby born in Germany, and leave when the child was old enough to travel. Other people prepared by having conversations with their families discussing the topic of emigration. Mathias Schulze and Hans Peter Kahlen convinced their wives to go with them. Martin Giebel also had many talks with his family. His father encouraged him to go to Canada by admitting that he himself would have left the country, but having lost a leg during the war, he was unable to leave. Martin's siblings, in contrast, were surprised, and regretted Martin's decision. However, his nieces and nephews thought it would be "cool" to have an uncle in Canada.

Compared to earlier immigrants, many who emigrated in the 1980s, 1990s or 2000s had the chance to explore Canada before deciding to immigrate. For example, Christiane and Hans Peter Kahlen or Michael Eckardt vacationed several times in Canada before they made the final decision to stay. Many of these immigrants could engage in a "step-by-step" immigration, as Michael Drescher and Martin Giebel called it. In other words, they had the chance to travel within and outside of Germany, work somewhere in Europe, move back and forth, and test themselves before taking the step of emigration. Michael admitted that it would have been very likely that he would have returned to Germany if he had gone directly to Canada without all the little steps in between.

The immigrants who came immediately after World War II often said that they came with nothing; they had no belongings left in the Old Country. Either their property had been destroyed during the war, or they had to flee and leave their homes behind. In 1951, the Canadian government implemented the Assisted Loan Scheme, covering the transportation fees for European immigrants.[197] Finally, the Immigration Act was passed in 1952, offering the chance to recruit Europeans "who had skills urgently needed in Canada but who could not pay the full costs of transportation to

---

197 Canadian Council for Refugees, Brief history of Canada's responses to refugees, accessed August 20, 2019, https://ccrweb.ca/sites/ccrweb.ca/files/static-files/canadarefugeeshistory.htm

this country."[198] Other immigrants sold their business or belongings in their home country, and used the money for a new lease on life in Canada. This is what the parents of Dieter Conrad did. Their eldest son had already immigrated to Canada, and they also came for a year initially, to see what it was like. As they decided to emigrate as well, they had no one to take over their business since Dieter had learned a different profession and had moved to another town in Germany. Therefore, his parents sold it. Ernst Friedel sold his motorbike and used the money to buy tickets for the ship voyage. People who emigrated in later decades like Martin Giebel said that they had steamer trunks for their belongings and had to warehouse their furniture in Germany. Martin Giebel remembers his last hours before his departure from Germany quite vividly. All the preparations for the journey were completed, the house was empty, and he went into the garden, sat down on a wall, and started crying, because he realized that this was the beginning of a journey into the unknown.

Regarding transportation, there was only one affordable way to come to Canada in the 1940s up to the early 1960s — by ship. Many German immigrants sailed with the 'Beaverbrae'. It was a big ship that immigrants also remembered because of its size. The most common experience many interviewees had during their journey was being seasick. Only very few immigrants had fond memories of the time on the ship. One of them is Manfred Richter who remembers the moment when the ship reached the Saint Lawrence River, and he first smelled the Canadian conifer forest. Monika Hoedl arrived in the 1960s, at the age of eight on a luxury liner, the 'Arkadia', from Greece. For her, the journey on the ship was a pleasure; she remembered the fabulous meals and the kindergarten on board.

Some people had trouble on their journey. When Danuta Grigaitis arrived with her brother and a cousin at the harbour in Bremerhaven in 1949, they realized that their transport was for men only. Danuta Grigaitis, 18 at the time, was left behind, and could only follow on a freighter via Italy eight days later. Irmgard Burow forgot her last visa stamp from the consulate in Cologne. Unfortunately, her English was insufficient to be able to persuade the officers that this stamp was not needed. Luckily, she was allowed to enter Canada, but she was obliged to leave the country within one year and get that missing stamp. Most immigrants who came by ship entered the country through Québec City or Montréal, sometimes Halifax, and then took a train to their destination which, in the case of our interviewees, often was Kitchener. Immigrants who arrived in the late 1960s or thereafter, usually arrived by plane at the Toronto airport. Ingrid Hann, Gerhard Griebenow, and Almut Wurzbacher were among those immigrants. Their journey had become faster, more convenient, and in most cases less strenuous than that of earlier cohorts.

---

198 Valerie Knowles, Strangers at our gates: Canadian immigration and immigration policy. (Toronto: Dundurn, 2007), 170.

First Impressions

Many interviewees left their home country with mixed feelings: there was an adventure waiting, they were excited, but at the same time many felt a loss of family and friends they left behind. Some people had concrete expectations of their life in Canada, and some came with curiosity and "naiver Offenheit,"[199] as Mathias Schulze called it. The parents of Tony Fieder escaped from an internment camp in Yugoslavia to Austria. They did not want to live anywhere in Europe and were looking forward to building their new home in Canada. Before arriving, Bernd Brandt associated Canada with the Wild West. He fancied big trucks, and thought he was in heaven when he arrived in Toronto and saw all the beautiful cars lined up. Astrid Braun also thought she had "died and gone to heaven" when she first saw the beauty of Leamington at the north shore of Lake Erie. Hugo Schwengers arrived in Toronto on a Sunday in 1952, when nearly all the stores and restaurants were closed. Even the curtains of the Eaton department store were closed, and he thought: "my gosh where did I end up here." Kurt and Minnie Boese arrived in Québec City in the same year and travelled by train to Toronto and then to Clifford, Ontario. Kurt describes Clifford as at the end of the world. It was a small village with less than 500 inhabitants, the people had no curtains, no carpets, and no toilets; they had to use outhouses. He did not want to acknowledge these circumstances to his family in Germany. Tony Bergmeier arrived in 1956 in Québec City, made the same journey, and experienced Canada as very different from Germany and also from today.

Being homesick is a common experience when newcomers adapt to a new environment, and it was also an issue for many immigrants who were interviewed. Homesickness, especially at the beginning, was an issue for Ernst Friedel, who had never been so far away from home. The situation improved for him when he met his wife Ruth. Connected with the feeling of being homesick is the feeling of being alone and having left one's friends. Ronny Horvath described himself as "a lone wolf" when he first arrived when nobody called to do something together, like playing volleyball. Mathias Wolf, and many others, also mentioned missing friends and family. Apart from missing family and friends, Michael Drescher reported that, when he came to nearby Guelph, he missed that people were not connected to their land through centuries of history, which he had experienced, for example, in an old city in the Netherlands where he once lived. He found it fascinating how this history manifested itself in a collective mental state of mind among people in Europe, and he missed finding this sense of attachment among Canadians.

In contrast, others did not experience homesickness. Tony Bergmeier, who came in 1956, reported that he adapted very quickly. Bill Kunsch also says that he felt like he fitted in right from the beginning when he arrived in 1948. Elizabeth Schultheiss immediately liked living in Canada in 1954. Jörg Stieber, who arrived 1983, also

---

199 Translation: naïve openness.

found it relatively easy to adjust to Canada, since he already spoke English and did not experience a language barrier.

Some people were disappointed because their expectations of Canada did not match the reality they encountered. Before coming to Canada, Dieter Conrad was promised that he could have a job as a bassoonist in Kitchener. However, he quickly learned that the symphony in Kitchener practised only once a week, and only paid ten dollars per week. Thus, Dieter had to search for an additional job to make a living and started repairing instruments. He was very unhappy with his situation. He knew that he could return to Germany within the next four months and resume his former position. He really wanted to take that chance, but his wife, who had felt uncomfortable during the journey on the boat, gave birth. The child had poliomyelitis, which required a ten-year rehabilitation program. Therefore, Dieter and his wife agreed to return to Germany at a later point in time, but they never did.

In more positive terms, most interviewees were fascinated by the landscape, the vastness of Canada, and the friendliness of Canadians. The distances were not interpreted negatively but associated with liberty. For Martin Giebel, the vastness of the country meant he could afford to buy a cottage, which would never have been possible in Germany. Ernst Friedel and Tony Bergmeier also associated Canada with liberty. For Ernst, this liberty meant that he was away from home, and was now able to do whatever he wanted. Tony encountered less bureaucracy in Canada. Many interviewees perceived Canadians as very supportive and welcoming. According to Jörg Stieber, German immigrants were not used to this supportive and welcoming attitude. He was used to foreigners in Germany being treated with suspicion and disregard. In Canada, he felt welcome, and no one criticized him for the English-language mistakes he made.

The interviewees reported many small details in their everyday lives which made their acculturation in Canada easier. One of the female interviewees remembers people patiently helping her to find the right products while she was grocery-shopping in case she did not understand the English product descriptions. Whenever Brigitte Bergmeier walked in the rain, cars would stop, and people would offer her a ride. Hans Peter Kahlen was impressed by the Canadian openness, and Bernd Brandt, as well as Ruth and Ernst Friedel, admired the Canadian sense of trust. Ernst recalled that many homeowners would not lock the front door in the 1950s. Many Canadians left money in a milk chute next to the side door, which only the milkman would take. For Ernst, it was unfathomable that people did not think about the possibility that anyone could steal the money.

The interviewees had experiences that many immigrants around the world share, especially when unquestioned habits and assumptions of a society cannot be relied upon in the same way in their new environment. Many talked about how they learned to interpret the mannerisms that identify some people as fellow immigrants and others as non-immigrants. Monika Hoedl, for example, explained how she could tell from the outside of a house whether Europeans or Canadian-born people lived there: Europeans had net curtains on their windows and Canadians regular drapes. It turns out that the interviewees had diverse opinions on how large the differences between Canadian and German cultures really were. Some of the interviewees said that there were no big differences, as Michael Eckardt put it. Martin Giebel supported this statement by saying that he could not understand how people would experience a culture shock in Canada. Not until he had lived several years in Canada, did he discover differences. For example, he described his relationship to Canadian friends and to German friends. According to him, Canadians have a different concept of friendship as they keep their distance and family is more important to them. For him, this is why friendship with Canadians always felt superficial and distant. With his German friends he can talk about profound matters, including the relationship to the friends themselves, which is something he would not do with his Canadian friends. Jörg Stieber talks about a related experience and compares the German directness with the Canadian tendency of beating around the bush. Almut Wurzbacher made similar remarks and said she never felt accepted. The relationship to Canadians still concerns her. At school, she said, Canadians welcomed her warmly, but that was it. They turned their backs on her when they were among themselves. Playing in a sports team, everything was alright on the surface, but Almut missed close friendships with Canadians. She also noted the small things that changed in her everyday life: she ate different food, the doors had knobs and not handles, the landscape was different, the language, the cars, the houses, and so on. Despite the impression that everything was different, Almut Wurzbacher said she did not experience culture shock. In fact, she preferred the Canadian school system, which offered fulltime school with music programs and sports at school.

Immigrants are not only confronting different habits and cultural norms, but also new institutional and administrative practices. Tony and Brigitte Bergmeier, for example, recalled how surprisingly easy it was to receive a building permit, a hunting license, or a driver's license. Brigitte Bergmeier went to the building inspector in Bridgeport, a part of Kitchener, and told him that her husband wanted to build a garage. The inspector asked her what kind of garage he wanted to build. When he learned that Brigitte knew nothing about the details, he decided that it would be a wooden garage of specific dimensions and gave her the license. Getting a hunting license was even less complicated. Tony Bergmeier walked into a cigar store, ordered a hunting license, paid for and received the license, and left the store. Being used to German bureaucracy, he could not believe that he was not required to undergo a lengthy training program. Similarly, to receive their driver's license, they went to the owner of a gas station who tested them. They were told to drive around the block, and then received their license for ten dollars.

Conversely, many interviewees found it astonishing that they had to show their ID cards when ordering beer, which in Germany they were never asked to do. One interviewee jokingly suggested that accompanied by your parents, in Germany, you could drink beer at the age of five. Ursel Wandschneider expressed a similar sentiment as she described the Canadian attitude towards alcohol as puritan. She recalled that restaurants that served wine closed their curtains. For her this was strange. Dieter Conrad once sat in front of his house enjoying his beer at the end of the day, when his brother came over and told him that drinking in public was illegal. For Dieter, who wanted to return to Germany, this was another reason to do so. Martin Giebel celebrated New Year's Eve with a traditional Feuerzangenbowle, a mulled wine with a rum-soaked sugarloaf lit above it, and showed his Canadian friends how to prepare it. Afterwards, his friends complained about the amount of alcohol in it. Canadians do not party as exuberantly as Germans, according to Martin: "Canadians always stay well-mannered."

A few interviewees also commented on ideological differences. Christa Streicher mentioned the lack of ecological awareness among Canadians. According to her, Germany was far more progressive than Canada in this regard in the 1980s. She speaks of waste separation and energy conservation in Germany, which was not a discussion topic in Canada until decades later. Her children, on the other hand, were more concerned about not getting Nutella, an Italian chocolate spread that is now widely available in Canada as well; but they enjoyed the snow which they had not seen in Germany for a few years. Christa's four-year-old daughter would not come in from outside play at lunch time for fear that someone would steal her snow.

Living Among Canadians

When they first arrived in Canada, many immigrants were welcomed by acquaintances, landlords, or employers. When one of the female interviewees immigrated in the 1980s, she lived with her almost grown-up children at her uncle's house. Although she felt lucky to be in Canada, she was unhappy with living at her relatives' place and with doing things as they wanted them done. Soon she told her children that they needed their own space. She and her children worked very hard to earn money. She herself had up to three jobs at a time: she worked at a factory at night, slept a few hours, and then worked in the kitchen of a local German club during the day. Her daughter had several jobs — working in a hospital, and as a waitress in a German club. Their efforts were rewarded after a year when the family moved into their own house. Many other interviewees were eager and worked hard to rent their own flat or even buy a house within the first years of settling in Canada. Isa Schade landed in Canada in 1953 with her husband and her first son. They had a penpal in Canada who organized a room for them. The landlord, however, had already rented the apartment to young men from Yugoslavia and the Czech Republic. The Schade family therefore had to share the living room and slept on a sofa bed. Their living situation did not please Isa. They were fortunate when their Canadian neighbour offered them the living room for rent. Martin Giebel described the initial settlement period generally as a slow process of "being home in Canada" and "becoming a stranger in Germany." The usual work the immigrants could do after their arrival in Canada was working at a farm or in construction. Those who immigrated in the 1950s had to work on a farm, or at a public institution, since those were the requirements, as Harry Drung explained. In the 1950s, job hunting brought disappointments for many, but language issues were just a minor problem. Often, they had to learn that their apprenticeship was not accepted by Canadian employers. Franz-Josef Burgund, who was a plumber, had to repeat his apprenticeship certification exam. And even by the 1970s the situation had not improved a lot. Martin Giebel's wife worked as a physiotherapist before she came to Canada. At first it took a long time to get her degree recognized, and finally she was informed that she had to do a Canadian bachelor's degree to be able to do the same work in Canada.

Prejudice is something many immigrants experience, not only in Canada. In fact, the textbooks are full of stories of waves of immigrants to North America being ridiculed, discriminated against, and excluded from full social participation.[200] Compared to some immigrant groups, such as the Chinese in the early 20th century, German immigrants faced much lower barriers to social acceptance.[201] Nevertheless, many of the interviewees remembered experiencing prejudice. For instance, there were challenges for immigrant children in school. They were often humiliated due to insufficient English-language skills. Many children were also separated from other children of their age group and had to start a Grade or two lower, since they were not able to speak English proficiently enough. Evelyn Guderian describes this experience as "demoralizing." In 1950, Alice Bromberg was embarrassed to go to school: she had to attend a class for mentally-challenged students. The situation improved for her when she was allowed to return to her regular class in Grade two.

At times children were ridiculed not because of their lacking skills, but simply because of who they were. Alice recalled, "it was mainly at school, you know, you're nothing but a DP [displaced person]." Immigrants who entered the country in the late 1940s and early 1950s especially faced anti-German sentiments and struggled with insults. As many others, Alice experienced this. One day, a boy in school blamed her for his father's disability after World War II: "Your dad put my dad in a wheelchair." In contrast, Bernd Brandt reported that he had mostly good experiences at school. He had just one teacher who was bigoted. In Grade seven, the teacher gave the students an example of the worst kind of human being: it was a cross between a German and a Japanese. After that class, fellow students apologized to Bernd for their teacher's ignorance, which showed Bernd that they were aware of the effect that those words could have had on him.

Other children were mocked at school because of the "German things" they had. Monika Hoedl remembered that kids made fun of her German rye bread, and Theresia Burgund told us that her sons got laughed at when they appeared with their new Lederhosen[202] at school. As a supply teacher, Theresia Burgund had children running after her yelling "Hitler Hitler Hitler." Sometimes, people blamed her for actions that she personally had nothing to do with. A neighbour, for instance, blamed her when it became known that thalidomide, sold by the West German drug company Chemie Grünenheim under the brand name Contergan in the 1950s and 60s, had

---

200 Harald Bauder and John Shields (eds.) Immigrant Experiences; Knowles, Strangers at Our Gates (Toronto: Canadian Scholars' Press Inc, 2015); Jonathan Wagner, A History of Migration from Germany to Canada 1850-1939. (Vancouver: UBC Press, 2006).
201 Kay J. Anderson, Vancouver's Chinatown: Racial Discourse in Canada. 1875-1980. (Montréal and Kingston: McGill-Queen's Press, 1991).
202 Lederhosen are traditional leather shorts common in Bavaria. The word lederhosen has since been included in English dictionaries.

negative effects on pregnant women. Tony Fieder was called a "dirty German" in elementary school — luckily just once. Gerda Wolf entered Canada in 1953 as an eight-month-old baby. When she grew older and started to speak, her parents were afraid that their German heritage could affect her negatively; she was not allowed to speak German outside the house. Her mother would always give her instructions not to talk German with her in public, she herself would answer only with gestures, because she was worried that people would recognise her German accent. Ernst Friedel, who spoke of his experiences a decade or so later, said in his interview that he always perceived Canadians as friendly and open-minded. However, he had the feeling that they did not immediately trust him due to his German background; he always had to prove himself. He sensed that what he perceived as repeated anti-German propaganda led to a general suspicion towards Germans. Nevertheless, he found that this suspicion quickly disappeared once he made personal contacts with people.

Living Among Germans

Waterloo Region is known for its large population with origins in German-language regions of Europe. Monika Hoedl recalls that the man at the immigration office in Germany sent her family to Waterloo Region, because he knew that many German speakers lived there. The German-speaking population was the main reason why the parents of Paul Stagl decided to come here in 1949. The parents of Alice Bromberg chose the cities of Kitchener-Waterloo for the same reason. Once they arrived, German immigrants often benefitted from the presence of a German-speaking community. Especially in an era preceding today's multiculturalism policy, and considering residual prejudice after two world wars, the German community could provide emotional comfort and tangible benefits to new arrivals. Gisela Steckel embraced the German community in the region, it made her feel at home, and she felt accepted. Martin Giebel, who first lived in Toronto with his wife, recalled that life became easier for his wife when they moved to Waterloo Region due to its presence of German culture and language. The German language is an issue many interviewees mentioned because most of them did not learn English before they came to Canada, and therefore had language problems. To mitigate these difficulties, one interviewee worked at a German club where she did not have language barriers. The same held true for Ronny Horvath whose employer was also of German background. Tony Bergmeier recalled the German clubs to be supportive environments, where he could meet people who had similar experiences to his own. Many interviewees mentioned how they felt strong bonds of solidarity in these environments. Christine Burow recalled that for her parents the German-speaking community played a big part in their acculturation. When Christiane and Hans Kahlen arrived in Waterloo Region, they did not know that they were in a German area. When reading the phone book, they laughed at all the Meiers, Schmidts, and other German names they found in there. It made them feel at home, and they enjoyed the Germanness in the twin city Kitchener-Waterloo. They made German friends in the area, but they did not explicitly search for these contacts.

Ingrid Hann found it challenging to find a job in Toronto. In Germany, she had worked for three years as a short-hand typist, but the English language, keyboard, and shorthand requirements meant she was not successful in qualifying for suitable employment. Because she did not have a Canadian high school education, she was not accepted to a community college. It was recommended that she attend a private business school, which happened to be in Kitchener. There she mastered her secretarial profession and graduated with honours one year later.

When Michael Drescher left Germany, he made it a point of not teaming up with other Germans. He wanted to integrate and leave his German background behind, though his Canadian wife kept telling him how German he still was. Whenever he got in touch with German clubs, Michael, who had emigrated from Hannover in Germany, often felt that they emphasized aspects of German culture that he did not feel connected with, thus he had very little contact with these German clubs. Unlike other interviewees, Michael says that he did not benefit significantly from the presence of a German community. Almut Wurzbacher also tried to detach from the German community. She saw that this community had already adapted Canadian habits. One example she mentioned was that her three-year-old daughter was not allowed to run naked at the pool at the Concordia Club, which Almut perceived as prudish Canadian behaviour. In Germany, children that age were allowed to run naked at the beach. One female interviewee said that she needed the German community when she arrived in Canada and felt homesick, but later she did not attend the German clubs anymore because she did not feel the need to continue to celebrate her German identity — "wir deutschtümelten nicht mehr."[203]

Of course, the German-speaking community in Waterloo Region was never a complete replica of society as it existed in the German-speaking regions in Europe. Like any immigrant community, it is embedded within a wider social, cultural, and political context of the destination country that differs from that of the country of origin. While for many interviewees, the coethnic German-Canadian community could offer emotional and practical support during the settlement process, it also provided a connection to Canadian society. The members of the German-speaking community in the Waterloo Region have thus embraced to be both German and Canadian. Or, as described by Martin Giebel: "Deutsch-Kanadier sein, das bedeutet, zu versuchen sich das Beste aus beiden Welten auszusuchen."[204]

---

203 Translation: We no longer played-up being German.
204 Translation: To be German-Canadian means to try to choose the best of both worlds.

Earning a Living

Ryan Carroll and Grit Liebscher

A defining part of the migration experience is finding long-term work in the new country; the ability to support oneself and one's family is critical to a successful migration. For the German-speaking immigrants and their descendants in this book, adapting one's already acquired education and skills to the Canadian setting was a necessary step in making a living. The immigrants had to negotiate the work possibilities in a new economic landscape and assess which skills and training they already had and could use, and which they needed to acquire. Most of the immigrants knew that learning English was going to be a top priority. Although a lack of English proficiency did prove to be a hindrance to finding a job with a decent wage in some cases, the strength of the German-speaking community in the Region of Waterloo provided other immigrants with work opportunities in a predominantly German-speaking work setting or helped establish connections with other German speakers. Ultimately, it was flexibility and adaptability that allowed the immigrants interviewed for this book to earn a living and make the Region of Waterloo a permanent home. In this chapter, we look at the types of work that the interviewees mentioned, considering both the hourly jobs acquired in the initial years after their arrival in Canada, as well as their long-term careers. We will also discuss the education and training received, in addition to the disruptions in the interviewees' education and career. The education and training acquired by immigrants in their home country were not always easily transferred to the Canadian setting, meaning some had to consider re-training in Canada or starting a new line of work. For some interviewees, however, immigrating to Canada offered new opportunities, such as the chance to start their own business. This may have always been a goal, and Canada provided the necessary environment to achieve it.

In the years after World War II, which was the period of arrival in Canada for most interviewees, many Europeans were looking to rebuild or restart their lives, which had been disrupted by the chaos and horrors of the war. Jobs and education had been put on hold, but people desired to move their lives forward, to find opportunities to prosper, and to find the work in which they or their families had previously found success. Many began looking outside of their European home for the opportunities to support their families and their dreams. This holds especially true for the generation of immigrants who arrived in Canada in the 1950s and corresponds with the general picture of German immigrants coming to Canada.[205] One has to consider that German immigration to Canada immediately following the war was initially restricted to people from European countries other than Germany and

---

205 Andrea Koch-Kraft, Deutsche in Kanada – Einwanderung und Adaption: Mit einer Untersuchung zur Situation der Nachkriegsimmigration in Edmonton, Alberta. – Kanada-Studien. Bd. 7. (Bochum: Universitätsverlag Dr. N. Brockmeyer, 1990), 58.

Austria, as citizens of either were generally considered Enemy Aliens,[206] so it is not surprising that many of our interviewees came from German-speaking communities in Europe outside of the country of Germany. These immigration restrictions were removed by 1951, paving the way for higher numbers of Germans to immigrate to Canada: "Between 1951 and 1957, almost 220,000 German immigrants were admitted to Canada. Most of these settled in Ontario, a few in the West."[207]

When looking at long-term careers in which immigrants found the most success, five categories emerged from the interviews: construction and contracting, education and academia, food production and farming, engineering, and real estate and development. A broader category to which many German-speaking newcomers belong is that of an alternative and much more winding career path, which, in some cases, eventually led to a longer-term career. When they were just starting out in Canada, some of the interviewees report that they could not afford to be picky with their job, taking whatever work they could find. This meant that many of the initial jobs were hourly, manual-labour jobs in a factory, on a farm, or on a construction site. For some, these jobs gave them the opportunity to move up in position or start a long-term career, while for others they served primarily to earn money. However, they also provided opportunities for learning the culture and language before moving on to other jobs. Most of the interviewees were in their early twenties when they immigrated, and of these, many of the men arrived as skilled tradesmen, as many had completed a European-style specialized-trade apprenticeship, a *Lehre,* or a similar training in their home country. As evidenced in the interviews, this was a generation of immigrants who were prepared to work hard to make a living, an aspect that many of the interviewees emphasized when telling their personal stories.

Depending on when and where they arrived, the interviewees found different conditions when searching for a job. Most were prepared to do almost any kind of work that was available, even if it meant not continuing with their learned trade right away. Speaking about his professional training as a *Stuckateur* (ornamental plasterer), Tony Bergmeier described how his extensive professional experience in Germany, including completion of the *Meisterprüfung* (master craftsman examination) did not benefit him in Canada:

> "…ich hatte Gelegenheit [in Deutschland] meinen Beruf sehr gut zu
> erlernen. Das Bedauerliche am Ganzen ist es, dass [es] mir natürlich
> gar nicht half, als wir hier in Kanada ankamen. Ornamental
> plastering is not — ist nicht gefragt hier."[208]

It is noteworthy that this chapter represents more of the men's rather than the women's voices on experiences related to education and work. 40% of the

---

206 Koch-Kraft, Deutsche in Kanada, 39-40.
207 Rudolf A. Helling and Bernd Hamm, A Socio-Economic History of German-Canadians: They, Too, Founded Canada: A Research Report. (Vierteljahrschrift für Sozial- und Wirtschaftsgeschichte: Beihefte; Nr. 75. Wiesbaden: F. Steiner, 1984), 84.
208 Translation: I had the opportunity in Germany to really master my trade. The unfortunate part of it all is, that, of course, it did not help me at all, once we arrived here in Canada: ornamental plastering is not in demand here.

interviewees were women, but it was the men, more often than the women, who spoke at length about their work experiences in these interviews. Another reason may be the characteristics of the time. For example, some of the women interviewees immigrating in the 1950s and before, like Isa Schade, explicitly mentioned that they stayed at home with their children while their husbands went to work. However, when women like Helen Neumayer and Rosina Müehlberghuber talked about their work experiences in the interviews, it became clear that they worked as much as the men and faced the same difficulties when first starting out. Some women started their own businesses, as did Minnie Boese with her hair salon, but this was not very common amongst the women who immigrated in the 1950s. Of the women who did start or run their own businesses, most of them were born in the 1950s and immigrated in the 1980s, like Gisela Steckel or Almut Wurzbacher.

Education and Training

The level of education acquired before immigrating to Canada varied across the interviewees, but it did follow a general pattern, especially amongst those who immigrated in the 1950s. Reinhold Schuster is one of the many whose education had been disrupted by the war, and who were displaced from their homes and lived as refugees in a different European country. For those born in the 1930s, even their elementary and high school education was sometimes interrupted, since schools and teachers were not always available during and immediately after World War II, as was the case with Dieter Wolle, who, due to these circumstances, finished only up to Grade six in Germany. If the interviewees arrived in Canada as teenagers or school-age children, being placed in a Canadian school typically meant starting a few grades back until language proficiency improved enough to be placed in the appropriate grade, as was the case with Bill Kunsch, who had to attend pre-school kindergarten at the age of ten. Of those without any university studies, the vast majority had learned a trade in an apprenticeship in their home country, especially the men, as was the case with Wolfgang Wurzbacher. Of those who immigrated when they were in their late twenties or early thirties, like Manfred Richter and Alex Müntz, most had at least some university education. For other immigrants, the opportunity to go to college did not present itself until after retirement, which enabled some interviewees the chance to fulfil a long-deferred dream. Charles Hildebrandt, for example, came to Canada from Hamburg in the 1950s as a young man, but it was only after his children had grown up and he had retired that he was able to obtain his bachelor's degree in history from the University of Waterloo. Having completed an apprenticeship in their home country proved to be advantageous for interviewees like Kurt Boese and Herminio Schmidt, as it led to their success in the many construction and manufacturing jobs that were available in Canada at the time.

Often, previous training did not lead directly to a job, and papers were less important for hiring than recognizable skills. However, because of their trades, these immigrants were accustomed to manual labour, and consequently were willing to take on these sometimes arduous jobs. Some examples of these trades include plumbing, metal working, machine repair, plastering, and wood working. Many of the interviewees who had learned such trades, including Kurt Boese, continued to work in construction and manufacturing, with a few even starting their own businesses in Canada, as was the case with Tony Bergmeier and John Naas. A few of the food-related trades were butcher, the trade that Guenter Lotzmann learned in Germany and practised for many years in Canada, and miller, which Dieter Wolle learned in Germany, but did not practise in Canada. Although it was less common for female interviewees to have learned a trade, a few who had were Dagmar Schilha (stenography), Margarete Rowe (pottery maker), and Minnie Boese (hairdresser).

A few of the interviewees without prior university experience, such as Herminio Schmidt, made it a goal to attend university in Canada, as they felt this was crucial for a better career. In Ontario, it was necessary to pass the Grade 13 exams,[209] regardless of their past education. Many interviewees who arrived by their teenage years, such as Victor Rausch or Siegfried Schranz, were generally acclimated to the Canadian school setting by the time they reached Grade 13 and did not mention any difficulties with the exams. Herminio Schmidt and Siegfried Schranz were two interviewees who spoke about their experiences with the Grade 13 exams and getting into college in Ontario. Their stories describe how they found assistance through connections in the community, both from fellow immigrants and Canadians, as they both needed help navigating academic-oriented schoolwork and passing this type of exam, with which they were unfamiliar.

Due to familial obligations, Siegfried Schranz expected to start working straight out of high school. His uncle made him promise that he would support his mother financially, meaning he would need to start working after finishing high school, leaving him unable to continue his education. To better prepare himself for a job, he switched some of his courses from academic subjects, such as Latin, to more business-oriented ones, like typewriting. During an assembly near the end of Grade 12, he inquired how he could become a business teacher, which he said was "…a question just for the sake of asking a question. …That was the most important question of my whole life ever and ever will be." The principal took it seriously, and later called him into his office to discuss in earnest the next steps Siegfried Schranz should take. He was told he needed to improve his German grammar, to use this as a subject, and to improve his math skills, if he wanted to have a chance at passing the Grade 13 exam. Although the principal did not know German grammar, he used his grammar knowledge of other languages, such as Greek, Latin, and French, to tutor Siegfried. To improve his math, Siegfried turned to his optometrist to help him learn algebra. With their help, he was able to pass Grade 13 with a respectable average, despite some initial difficulties with English in the beginning of the year.

In retelling what it took for him to pass Grade 13, Siegfried Schranz reflected on the other times that community members assisted him in finding jobs or helping him

---

209 Grade 13 and its exams were unique to the province of Ontario. It was phased out in 1984 and became the Ontario Academic Credit (OAC), an optional fifth year intended for students pursuing post-secondary education. The OAC was eventually eliminated entirely in 2003, making the duration for Ontario High Schools the same four years as the rest of North America, see https://en.wikipedia.org/wiki/Ontario_Academic_Credit.

with his English. It was through a connection in the church congregation that he found a job with a family-owned hardware store, and in that job, he learned from a co-worker how to drive a truck. In 1957, through connections with the church's minister, he was able to get a scholarship to go to Waterloo Lutheran College (now Wilfrid Laurier University), where he finished with degrees in Business Administration and Secretarial Science. It was via this kind of community help, described in many of the interviewees' stories, that they advanced in their positions in school and work.

Herminio Schmidt's story begins a little differently, as he had already finished high school and had already been working for a few years when he made the decision to go back to university. Since his arrival in Canada in his early twenties, he had worked in several jobs, mostly as a welder, but he wanted something more. He considered going to college, but his education up until that point was only through Grade 9 in Germany. After seeking advice about how to get into a university in Canada, a friend sent him to a minister of a German-speaking church in Toronto, who was going to be the dean of a new university being established in Sudbury. With this minister's help, Herminio Schmidt was able to register for the Grade 13 exam. Since he had little high school education and had worked mostly as a tradesman for his adult life, Herminio Schmidt had no previous experience with this type of exam. Herminio Schmidt was able to fly through the section of the exam on German grammar but had to guess his way through some of the parts on literature. He finished sooner than most of the other students in the exam room and left feeling confident. That confidence was shattered when the results were finally published, as he had just missed the passing grade. However, through a bit of good fortune, many of the parents of the other students had complained about the difficulty of the exam that year, with the result being that any score close to 50% was deemed to be a pass. In the end Herminio Schmidt passed, and after applying to a handful of schools, he was accepted to Waterloo Lutheran College.

In general, college experience or a university degree was not mentioned by many of the interviewees, especially those who immigrated in the 1950s. Of those, many were able to work their way up in jobs without a college degree. In general, the later an immigrant was born and immigrated to Canada, the more likely it was that they had already studied in their home country or pursued a degree in Canada, as was the case for Alex Müntz and Manfred Richter. Their eventual jobs were more likely to be in fields such as engineering or education, rather than working as a tradesman, as was the case for those who immigrated earlier.

Adapting to New Career Paths

Many immigrants who arrived in the 1950s had already completed an apprenticeship in their home country, with some being highly skilled in their trade. This background proved advantageous for some, but others, including Helga Sarkar and Gisela Steckel, found that their qualifications were either not recognized, or that their profession did not exist in the same form in Canada. When this was the case, it meant either working to meet the qualifications and requirements of the profession in Canada or choosing a new career path. However, for some interviewees, it was not possible to continue with their previous jobs and training once they arrived in Canada, despite their best efforts. This was the case for Steve Schatz, who commented in his interview, "Beruf hatte ich, aber keinen Job."[210] Even though Steve came to Canada with professional training in locksmithing, metalworking, and machine repair, he was unable to find work in these trades when he first started out in Aylmer, Ontario. He had hoped to find work in nearby St. Thomas, where there was more work to be found in the automobile industry, but when he searched for work there, he was told his English first needed improvement. In Aylmer, he found work in a cemetery, in tobacco fields, and in apple orchards, but nothing in the way of his training. As it turned out, it was music that brought him to Kitchener, and eventually to a job there. His uncle knew that the Transylvania Club in Kitchener was looking for a lead trumpet player and encouraged him to inquire about the opening. Steve Schatz ended up being the conductor there for forty-five years, playing flugelhorn as well. Once he got his start in Kitchener, he was slowly able to find work in his area of training. In 1956, he started his own business in his garage, making iron furniture with a friend. In 1966, he ended that operation to start another business, Astron Specialty Metals, which has done quite well and is still in operation today. Another example of an interviewee who had attempted, but was ultimately unable, to continue with his job in Canada was Wolfgang Wurzbacher. He was trained and working as a nurse in Germany when he decided to come to Canada to be with his future wife, Almut Pfenning, who was already working on her parents' Pfenning Farms in New Hamburg, Ontario. Wolfgang had eight semesters of university studies in Germany, but only a quarter of these credits could be transferred to either the University of Waterloo or Wilfrid Laurier University, meaning that he would need to spend at least another two years at university in Canada. He ultimately decided that this was not worth the time, and eventually found himself working at his wife's family farm.

Dieter Wolle also had an indirect path towards his final career, which reflected the experiences of many other interviewees and was an example of the patience required to find a job. He arrived in Toronto in 1957 and hoped to use his previous training in the hotel industry to find a job. After trying for three months to find any kind of work in either a hotel or restaurant, he finally landed a position as a dishwasher. He wanted to improve his English, but Dieter Wolle found it difficult to go to night school, since his restaurant job required him to work evenings. At the time, however, he felt it was more important to hold on to steady work, rather than going to school. Looking back now, he wishes he could have gone to school to improve his English, but he knows he had to do what the circumstances required. He was able to put his hotel training to good use when he worked as a waiter at the Royal York Hotel in Toronto. Although hotel work treated him well, Dieter set his sights higher. Through a friend and co-worker, he was introduced to the business of real estate, a career in which other German-speaking immigrants, such as Willi Ristau and Joseph Piller, also found success. After working in real estate in Toronto

---

210 Translation: I had a profession, but no job.

for a few years, Dieter Wolle was offered a position in his company to start a new office in Kitchener, a place he knew nothing about. He knew he wanted to move up in his work to eventually become a manager, so he took the offer, despite he and his wife not wanting to leave Toronto for a city that he felt was rather sleepy at the time. Looking back, he said he had no regrets about making this move. In 1977, he was able to open his own real estate office and finally work for himself. By 2014, he had 65 real estate agents working in his office.

Others, like Joseph Piller, ended up taking a different career path, not necessarily by choice, but due to an illness that kept him from working his original job. He started out working on a farm and then in manufacturing, like many of the men who came over in the 1950s. He had been an apprentice in a factory in Austria until he immigrated to Canada in 1950, where his first job was working on a farm in Saskatchewan. Eventually, he made his way to Galt (now part of Cambridge), where a friend arranged housing for him, and got a job at Joy Manufacturing on his first day there. He was paid around $30 a week in 1951, which is the amount he said he earned in a month at the farm in Saskatchewan. At Joy Manufacturing, he was successful and worked his way up to a tool-and-die maker, until he was diagnosed with what was believed to be tuberculosis, for which he spent about a year in a sanatorium. Once Joseph was back in good health, he wanted to return to his job at Joy Manufacturing, which he said was secure and paid well. His wife felt that the risk to his health was too great if he went back to work right away in 1955, as tuberculosis had the potential to be deadly. Following a suggestion by his brother-in-law, Joseph Piller instead went into real estate. He was able to pass the exams, and that same year he began a 36-year career in real estate, starting his own office in 1963. He commented that, at first, he helped many immigrants buy farms in the area, which especially the Polish and German immigrants were seeking at the time. Later, he said, there were more Italian and Croatian immigrants, with the latter being especially good for his real estate business. Because he spoke Croatian, Joseph was recommended to many of these immigrants. As he reflected on this, he said, "I made a lot of money because I spoke Croatian." Despite his health problems and having to switch occupations, he said he felt really satisfied with his life in Canada.

It was uncommon for interviewees to take a direct path to their final career, although that did happen for some, as seen in the next section. For both men and women, it was often the case that they felt the need to work first, and only after they were more established could they start to plan a career. This often required patience on their part, but this indirect path presented them with other opportunities, such as making new friends, and acculturating themselves in the new country.

Support for Work Relationships

Often, immigrants coming to Canada had a connection to a person who was already established in the country. Sometimes it was an acquaintance, as was the case for Isa Schade and Herminio Schmidt, but mostly it was family, such as John Penteker's father or Hugo Schwengers's brother-in-law. These family members made finding work a little easier for newly arrived immigrants, and in a few cases, there was hardly any choice of what they would be doing to earn a living once they arrived. The friend or relative was often the connection that got them a job. Sometimes, it was this person's encouragement to come to Canada in the first place, often due to the job opportunities there. Such was the case for John Heffner Sr. who received a letter from his wife's grandfather in Canada urging John to come to Canada to open his own repair shop. These connections were critical for many of the immigrants, as they had little else when they arrived in Canada. The fortunate ones were able to get a job within a few days of arriving, such as Willi Ristau's brother lining up a job for him in construction, but even for them, work was not always steady or guaranteed. As Willi described, "it was a very simple life and we never worried about much. When I got laid off, which happened quite often, I just got another job."

For some interviewees, this connection was not necessarily somebody they already knew in Canada, but rather the promise of a job that would be waiting for them. Ingo Schoppel did not know anyone in Canada but arrived in Kitchener with a phone number and "good recommendations," which got him a job the very next day. It was rare that a job was already arranged before their arrival, and many interviewees stressed their willingness to do manual labour wherever they could find work.

Guenter Lotzmann was one interviewee who did have the promise of a job waiting for him in Canada. He had already worked as a butcher in Germany and knew he wanted to continue this work in Canada. His father was a butcher, and Guenter had apprenticed as a butcher with his uncle. However, the circumstances of living in East Germany meant it would be difficult to continue operating his father's butcher shop there. Guenter was able to move first to West Germany, but even there it was difficult to earn money. He had seen an advertisement seeking immigrants for Canada, where the economy was doing much better in the mid-1950s. He applied in Cologne to immigrate to Canada, and since he did not have any prior connections there, he told the immigration officials he just wanted to go where there was work. He ended up in Aylmer, Ontario, where his new boss picked him up from the train station in London, and he started work the following Monday. Later, as Guenter's spirit of entrepreneurship grew, he decided to make his own sausages. In 1975, he and a partner were able to open their own sausage factory, which is still operating today as Finest Sausage and Meat, Ltd. Guenter was able to bring his work experience and aspirations with him to Canada, and to continue what he had originally started in Germany, which was rather uncommon for most immigrants.

Once in the workplace, many immigrants made friends and established connections with Canadians or other immigrants who supported them in their efforts to learn their new duties, help them move up, to find better pay, or to just speak English with them. Helen Neumayer came to Canada in 1953 with her husband, arriving first in Winnipeg. She was 33 years old at the time. In Winnipeg, she found a large Ukrainian community, and it was there that she was able to find work, as she spoke Ukrainian and German. It was through a Ukrainian man, Don, that she got a job doing sewing work at Canadian Garments in Winnipeg. She was greatly assisted by a young Jewish man, Tscheya, with whom she could speak German. She recalled the first time he helped her at work by providing her with a pair of scissors. The foreman, Mr. Strauss, also spoke German, and Helen felt very welcome and accepted by him on the job. She told a humorous story, in which a young Ukrainian woman, who also worked in the factory, taught her some English, but it was mostly swear words and other foul expressions, which Helen repeated, not knowing what she was saying. She said the foreman was not happy with the women when he found out. She recalled that she was rather satisfied with the job and spoke especially fondly of the young man Tscheya and all he did to assist her.

Helen Neumayer's experience was like many of the other immigrants' work stories, in which they mention a particular person who acted as a mentor or guide, aiding the immigrants and getting them situated in the job. In Helen Neumayer's case, both Ukrainian- and German-speaking people came to her aid in both the process of finding work and then moving up in that job. With Tscheya's help again, Helen Neumayer was promoted to forewoman at Canadian Garments, and although she was able to speak German with two of the employees there, she had difficulties with the increased responsibility because she was not yet able to speak English well. Unfortunately, she ended up having to leave this job due to being overworked. She worked in a variety of other jobs including cutting grass in a cemetery, cleaning floors in a hospital, and working in a chocolate factory. She mentioned how much she worked throughout her time in Canada, especially during times when her husband could not find work. Helen Neumayer's work experience was typical for many immigrants, who were willing to work many types of jobs and often had little time left for themselves or leisure activities or let alone learn English in a classroom. Like many others, Helen used opportunities at work to acquire English, such as speaking with patients in the hospital where she was cleaning floors.

Overcoming Challenges

The interviewees also spoke about difficulties with finding a decent paying job when first starting out. The conditions were sometimes not great, but the interviewees wanted to prove to themselves, and to their families, that they could succeed in Canada. Kurt Boese arrived as a sheet metal worker and was able to find work but was unable to receive decent pay until his English improved. Because he wanted to support his wife, Minnie, and their daughter, he accepted the work he was able to get right away, even if the pay was low. He started out earning $50 per week in 1952 as a heating systems engineer. Kurt said he performed his job well, but despite his performance, he felt he was being taken advantage of. In Kitchener, he established a partnership with a man who ran a hardware store. While Kurt was the skilled handyman, his partner was skilled in the business side of things. He recalls a job for which his partner received $600 to install a new boiler, but Kurt was only paid $30 for a week's work, which he did by himself. After discovering this, he assumed it was because of his lack of English that he was paid so little. Commenting on the difficulty of starting out he said that "die ersten zwei Jahre waren furchtbar, weil man eben so ausgenutzt worden ist."[211]Minnie Boese recalled telling her mother about their first apartment in Clifford, Ontario, where they lived for their first two years in Canada. Upon hearing about the humble conditions in which they were living, her mother said she would have sent her money had she known. As migrants who had packed up and gone to another country, Minnie said no one wanted to embarrass themselves by admitting that they needed money. Reflecting on this difficult time, after which they had found success, it seemed easier to talk about this period, although the frustration was still palpable. Despite this difficult beginning, Kurt and Minnie Boese eventually found well-paid work. Kurt became a plumbing inspector for the City of Kitchener, working in this position for 22 years. Minnie, who had trained as a hairdresser in Germany but had to study to get licensed in Canada, eventually opened her own hair salon in Kitchener, which she ran until the year 2000.

The same pride in supporting oneself, rather than relying on other family members emanated from Victor Rausch's story. He came to Canada when he was nine years old, and saw his parents work hard in farm and factory jobs until they were able to become owners of a variety store. As a teenager, Victor was expected to work alongside his parents during some of the many hours they put in at the store. As a high school student, he set his mind on becoming a dentist, eventually being accepted to dental school in Toronto. To support himself rather than relying on his parents for money, he worked in tobacco fields in the summer and was employed by a family in Toronto to mentor their teenage son in his last year of high school. He also joined the Canadian Armed Forces to pay for his last few years of dental school, which meant a commitment of five years of service after he finished school. He practised dentistry during his service in the Canadian Army. The army setting allowed him a little more freedom in his practice, which gave him the leeway to bring his interest in hypnosis into play. His interest in hypnosis began at sixteen years of age, when he attended the show of a hypnotist in Kitchener. He found out that he was able to hypnotize a friend, who, in a hypnotized state, was unable to feel the sensation of Victor jabbing his hand with a needle. As an army dentist, he found a great degree of success in using hypnotism for pain management, a method he would not have been able to experiment with in a regular dental clinic. He eventually developed his own method of self-hypnotism, which he tested by using it on himself during abdominal surgery. Confident of its efficacy, he began teaching others and, at the time of interviewing, ran his own hypnotism training centre in Waterloo Region, Tri-Centric Hypnosis.

Most of the immigrants had difficulties when first starting out in Canada, but in most cases, these hard times were only temporary, and there was support to be found in family and in the surrounding immigrant community. There was a great sense of pride in finding work and supporting oneself, a pride that stayed with most of the immigrants as they moved up in their careers, or even started their own businesses, which most were not even thinking about when they first arrived in Canada.

---

211 Translation: The first two years were terrible, because you were just exploited.

Running Your Own Business

The dream of owning one's own business was the impetus for many immigrants to make their way to Canada. Even a decade after the end of World War II, many found it difficult to make that dream come true in Europe, especially those coming from the Soviet Bloc countries. Even in Canada, there were hurdles along the way to becoming an independent business owner, but in comparison to Europe, the Canadian setting seemed to be a more fertile place to start a business. Like many others, John Heffner Sr. started out working wherever he could, even though he came to Canada with both experience and the dream of running his own auto repair shop. He had worked in a repair shop in Hungary in the mid-1950s and oversaw 32 mechanics there. Although he enjoyed his work and earned a decent pay, he always had the goal of running his own shop. The political situation in Hungary that developed in the 1950s made him realize that this goal was going to be unattainable if he remained there. He was able to immigrate to Canada with his wife, whose family was already established there. As previously mentioned, it was through letters from his wife's grandfather that he was encouraged to immigrate. He was told that in Canada, he would be able to open his own shop and find ample work. John Heffner Sr. recalls that it was this encouragement that ultimately motivated him to immigrate, since he knew it would mean leaving behind a good job in Hungary. Upon their arrival in Kitchener in 1957, it only took John Heffner Sr. two days to find a job as an auto mechanic, although it did not take long before he lost the job to a licensed mechanic who was hired to take his place. It was apparent that proper certification was going to be necessary to find a more permanent position. In the meantime, he was able to get a job at Braun Manufacturing, which produced steel and welded parts. While working there he went to night school, and in April 1960, was able to pass the exam to get his mechanic's license. With his new license in hand, he went to car dealerships in the area looking for work but was consistently turned down because of his lack of experience in Canada. This circumstance motivated him to go ahead and open his own garage. He knew that there were many immigrants in the area, with many of them driving older cars that would need repairing. His language background worked to his advantage, as he was able to speak with the German and Hungarian immigrants, and his wife and father were able to speak Serbian. He opened his own garage in 1960, and by 1963 he already needed a bigger space to accommodate all the business. He was then able to begin selling cars, and after selling various English and European makes, he opened a Toyota dealership in 1976. A high point in his successful career was his award for being the best Toyota dealership in Canada. The reputation of his dealership led to a visit from the CEO of Toyota who was in Ontario reviewing locations for a new Toyota manufacturing plant, which began operation in 1988 in Cambridge, Ontario.

In many cases, earning a living meant continuing the family business. Jörg Stieber was not considering running his family's business, but he seemingly did not have much of a choice, since his father intended to hand over the Canadian company, Ontario Drive and Gear of New Hamburg, to one of his two sons. Jörg's brother, who was already in Canada at the time, had already refused to run the company. Jörg had wanted to go to

Australia at the time, but his brother's refusal meant that Jörg was going to Canada instead. After immigrating to Canada in 1983, he took over the company from his father in 1985. An engineer by training, he had little experience in the business side of things and had to learn quickly. Jörg ultimately found success in this position, and the company continued to flourish under his direction.

Other immigrants had family businesses on a smaller scale, such as a restaurant or convenience store. For a handful of the immigrants who arrived when they were teenagers or younger, it was expected that they would work in these businesses after school and on weekends. In the case of the Pfenning and Wurzbacher families, it was the parents' farm that helped spawn a natural food and organic produce store in St. Agatha. Barnhild Pfenning and her husband bought land and started an organic farm outside of Waterloo in 1981, which they grew from selling at farmers markets to eventually running their own packing and distribution. Their youngest daughter, Almut, worked on this farm as a teenager with her three siblings. Today, Almut and her husband Wolfgang Wurzbacher run their own organic food store, which started out selling produce from the Pfennings' farm, and is still thriving today as a family-run business.

Although some of the interviewees were able to start their own businesses, not all came to Canada with that intention. There were also a handful of the interviewees who tried their hand at running a business, but eventually left it in favour of other pursuits. For some, it was not even a thought in their mind until it was suggested to them by someone else. The Canadian environment seemed to encourage entrepreneurship, and some immigrants were very successful.

Special Work Conditions in Canada

In speaking about his work experience in Canada, John Naas highlighted a central aspect of the Canadian work environment that many of the other immigrants referred to in their own stories. This central aspect was the apparent freedom that these immigrants found when working in Canada. Many admitted that it was a difficult start and nothing was guaranteed, especially not a job. But they found that it was the quality of their work and their knowledge that was recognized, rather than their specific qualifications. John Naas experienced this soon after arriving, and it was a lesson that stuck with him throughout his working life in Canada. He grew up in Hungary where he attended a trade school and was trained in plaster work, both ornamental and repair. In 1956, shortly after turning 18, he immigrated to Canada. After arriving in Hamilton, he began looking for work, which he was unable to find in his area of expertise. Although he had paperwork documenting his training (*Lehrbrief*), he was told by an employer in the construction industry that all that mattered was what he could actually do, not what was on a piece of paper: "Mit meinem Lehrbrief...man hat mir gesagt dann, 'Papiere tut nichts, nur was du kannst'."[212] John realized that he would only get paid based on the work he actually performed, and not based on his qualifications. He also realized a positive corollary to this: although you might not find work in your area of expertise, you can still get paid for doing work for which you have no training. John Naas continued to work in construction over the next twenty years, greatly improving his knowledge of the industry; he worked on jobs doing both larger buildings and smaller ones, renovating government-built wartime houses constructed for Canadian soldiers coming home after World War II. During this project, a building inspector suggested to him that he should start a business himself. At the time, he felt that he did not know enough about running a business but decided to try it anyway. After receiving assistance from the building authority in Windsor, Ontario, he started his own business in 1978. He recalled that, with this business, he worked as a subcontractor with another building engineer, with whom he built 48 Zehrs grocery stores over 25 years in Ontario. Reflecting on the success he found with his company, John felt that the Canadian setting really made it possible. In Canada, he commented, "die bezahlen dich nicht oder du kriegst die Arbeit nicht wegen der Qualifikation, sondern das Endresultat muss richtig sein, und für mich war so 'was ausgezeichnet."[213] Overall, he expressed strong satisfaction with this Canadian way of working, for which you just need the knowledge and the ability, and then you can do the work and make a living from it, or even successfully start your own business.

In the mindset of most of the interviewees, their only option was to make their immigration successful. This mindset was influenced by various factors, such as not having the money to make the return trip, not wanting to be seen as a failure in the eyes of their families back home or having an obligation to support their families in Canada or to run a family business. Finding work was an absolute priority for them upon arrival, and they did whatever they needed to start earning money. Even if they could not find work in line with their previous training or area of expertise, they were resourceful in finding a job, be it seasonal work in a tobacco field or janitorial work in a hospital. Sometimes these jobs provided opportunities for them to improve their English, or to establish connections with other immigrants or Canadians, both of which would lead to other job opportunities in the future. For a few, staying in these hourly jobs was all they could do for the time being, as they had to balance earning money with taking care of their children, leaving little time for night school or other education that was needed to improve their job situation.

The period recounted most often by many of the interviewees was their first few years in Canada, when nothing was guaranteed. Rosina Müehlberghuber, for example, while speaking about the difficulties of trying to find work and taking care of children, said "das waren schwere Jahre."[214] The wages from a first job were needed both to survive in Canada and to pay back the money borrowed to get to

---

212 Translation: With my certificate of apprenticeship…I was told, 'papers don't mean anything, only what you can do'.
213 Translation: You didn't get paid or you didn't get a job because of qualifications; rather, the end result had to be correct, and that worked for me excellently.
214 Translation: Those were difficult years.

Canada in the first place, as Willi Ristau recalled. These first few years were difficult for many who arrived in the 1950s, as they had to scrape by and take whatever work they could find to support themselves and their families. Some even expressed the desire to go back to their home country, but the money was not available, as they had already spent all they had to get to Canada. Despite these difficulties, most of the interviewees recounted the positive aspects of those first years in Canada. The new-found freedom of Canada made these first few years wonderful and despite having little money, they enjoyed the adventure of it all, having left behind the worries of their home country.

In her interview, Helga Sarkar contrasts the extreme difficulties of her childhood in post-war Germany with the opportunities she experienced in Canada, saying that

> "the first two years in Canada provided me with what I never had in
> Germany. I lived a carefree time. Yes, I had to work and yes, I had to
> cope with various situations, but I wouldn't want to trade in those
> two years for anything."

Whether they found a job immediately upon arrival or had to take whatever job was available, work played a pivotal role in these interviewees' immigration experiences. Through their work in Canada, they were able to build a new existence and find new opportunities for themselves and their families.

Who Are We?

Alissa Melitzer, Nataša Nuhanovič, and Paul Malone

To what group of people does one belong when more than one country — for instance, Germany and Canada — constitute one's biography? This question raises a whole set of multi-layered and complex questions. In lines often attributed to Goethe it is said: "Zwei Dinge sollen Kinder von ihren Eltern bekommen: Wurzeln und Flügel."[215] The desire to have both roots and wings is consistent with many immigrants' descriptions of their own cultural identities, which are often difficult to define in such stark terms as I-am-German, or I-am-Canadian. Identity can only be defined through the relationship between the remembrance of the old and the experience of the new. For some, it is a balancing act between preserving their heritage and embracing a new way of life. Guenter Lotzmann, an immigrant who left from West Germany in 1958, expressed this dichotomy with an adage often repeated by members of the Kitchener Concordia Club: "Lass dir die Fremde zur Heimat, aber die Heimat nicht zur Fremde werden."[216] This chapter will focus on the nature of the sometimes complicated feelings of allegiance immigrants have for their country of origin, and the country in which they have chosen to make their home and raise their families. The stories of German immigrants living in the Region of Waterloo provide insight into the nature of having a blended cultural identity, and what this means in terms of their self-perceived acculturation in Canada. Are they Canadian? German? Both? Neither? Global citizen? A person is shaped by their roots — historical, social, political, cultural — and the branches of themselves which they create — individual personality, and emotional. When combined, these elements make up one's notion of self and allow for an integrated concept of identity. The first section of the chapter will focus on origin and heritage, the second on personal thoughts and feelings about identity, and the third on that which emerges in their coming together. In this third section, identity is determined by how one perceives the seemingly contradictory concepts of us and them, rootedness and mobility, and past and future.

The Roots: Political, Historical, and Cultural Layers

Acknowledging and maintaining a connection to one's roots is important for many people with German background now living in Waterloo Region. How individuals

---

215 Translation: Children should receive two things from their parents: roots and wings. The apocryphal nature of this saying is pointed out in "Zitatforschung" https://falschzitate.blogspot.com/ 2017/05/zwei-dinge-sollten-kinder-von-ihren.html, accessed May 18, 2019. In the English-speaking world this aphorism is equally popular, and frequently attributed to 19th-century clergyman and abolitionist Henry Ward Beecher, cf. "There Are Two Lasting Bequests" https://quoteinvestigator.com/2014/08/12/roots-wings/, accessed May 18, 2019. However, it seems to be traceable no farther back than a 1953 book by American journalist Hodding Carter, who credits it only to an unnamed "wise woman" (ibid.).

216 Translation: Let the foreign become home, but let your home never become foreign.

view their past inevitably influences how they choose to shape their future. The history of German immigration in Waterloo Region spans decades; and whether one arrived in the 1930s, 1940s, 1960s, 1980s, or in the digital age, plays a major role in the way people relate to their new home. Although the focus of this chapter is culture as a marker of perceived national identity, political and historical layers need to be at least briefly addressed and acknowledged as well. Neither of these exists in isolation; rather, they are integral pieces of the identity puzzle. On the political level, as sociologist Zygmunt Bauman has stated, our modern society has seen, if not a divorce, then at the very least a separation between the state and the nation.[217] A state is defined in geographical and political terms, while a nation is defined culturally and ethnically. In addition, birthplace and nation are often inescapably linked.[218] Thus, people who move from one country to another are potentially between two nations and two states. For example, Gisela Steckel, who arrived in 1988 at the age of 31, had to become a Canadian citizen to sponsor her parents, and lost her German citizenship "by accident." Recounting the story, she said, "that's what happened, and that has killed me many times already." Citizenship is an obvious measure of identity. However, despite having lost this piece of herself, Gisela Steckel continues to have a multi-national view of her own identity. She can draw from both the German and Canadian side of herself and, in her words, "pick the good things out of everything and make it a good life." Such a story shows that one may still feel rooted in a country in which one may no longer be recognized as a citizen.

The moment in time when one leaves the Old Country and when one arrives in the new country should not be overlooked. Many immigrants or their families have been recovering from such dehumanizing events as World War I, World War II, the construction of the Berlin Wall, or a generally difficult economic situation. For others, the situation in their home country may not be particularly extreme, yet the desire to rebuild one's own life, one's profession, or pursue a romantic relationship may inspire one to leave. Similarly, one may arrive in the new country during either a period of stagnation, or, as was the case in Canada from the 1940s to the 1960s, of prosperity. The reason someone chooses to leave can either increase receptivity to their new surroundings or, conversely, a deeper attachment to the ones they left behind.

Gerald Drews, for example, spoke of his parents never feeling comfortable in Germany in the post-war years. His parents, Germans who had been living in what became Poland, found it difficult to integrate into German culture.

> "They were resented because they had nothing, and the local people
> then had to end up supporting them. They didn't really feel like it
> [post-war Germany] was their country, and it wasn't."

They came to Canada because they wanted to create a new life, and they wanted to become Canadian while still retaining aspects of their connection to German

---

217 Zygmunt Bauman, Identity: Conversations with Benedetto Vecchi (Cambridge: Polity Press, 2004), 61.
218 Bauman, Identity, 19, 22.

culture. Tony Fieder similarly told of his parents' difficulties after the war and their escape to Austria:

> "They were very glad to be out of a country that had gone through a major war. They worked very hard, and they lost everything in the war when we were evicted from our house, and I think they were looking forward to rebuilding their home here in Canada."

When the history of one's country of origin becomes a burden due to such negative experiences, it can be preferable to reinvent oneself. In some cases, it is a necessary survival mechanism that allows someone to discard the weight of their past in favour of a more promising future.

At the same time, Canada's roots as a nation have hardly had time to grow so deeply as to impose an overbearing culture to which newcomers must assimilate. In that sense, even geographically, Canada's wide-open spaces reflect the potential of a less historically confined, less claustrophobic identity. Daniela Wolff touched on this point when she talks about her German homeland.

> "Compared to Germany, North America is a very huge continent. We are pretty crowded over there [in Germany], so I always just loved the idea of these open spaces."

The whole world might meet in Canada, as Ronny Horvath said.

Germany's attitude towards immigrants, Christopher Wolff asserted, is to force them to adapt to the — heavily debated — Leitkultur (dominant culture), whereas Canada prides itself in a discourse that promotes difference. The US, as Herwig Wandschneider observed, has adopted the "melting pot" philosophy, while, according to him, Canada has managed to remain international. Indeed, in comparison to other nations, Canada is seen as making it a simple matter for an individual to become someone else, giving him or her the freedom to pick and choose elements from various cultures — or to invent completely new ones. This brings us to the idea of acculturation.

In the preface to their book *Cross-Cultural Adaptation: Current Approaches*, Young Yun Kim and William B. Gudykunst write, "The flow of humans across national and cultural boundaries is more active than ever before."[219] The experience of so many individuals from a multiplicity of cultures, traditions, languages, value-systems, everyday lifestyles, oddities, norms, and the like results in interaction between these cultures, and interaction leads to change. The concept of acculturation captures this interaction.

Psychologist Vanessa Smith Castro describes the "Quadri-Modal Acculturation Model," which illustrates what happens when two or more cultures meet.[220] The two

---

219 Young Yun Kim and William B. Gudykunst (eds.), Cross-Cultural Adaptation: Current Approaches (Los Angeles: Sage Publications, 1987), 7.
220 Vanessa Smith Castro, Acculturation and Psychological Adaptation (London: Greenwood Press, 2003), 18.

basic components which this model evaluates are maintenance of one's cultural heritage and contact with and participation in the new. The four possible outcomes listed by Castro are integration (retaining some of both cultures); assimilation (attempting to disconnect from the old culture); separation (attempting to disconnect from the new culture); and marginalization (losing contact with both cultures).[221] In general, integration is now the most prevalent outcome, particularly for the digital-age generation. However, this integration takes place to varying degrees along a continuum, depending on an individual's personal circumstance, as we have seen with many of the interviewees.

Following tradition can mean celebrating Christmas either the German or the Canadian way. In Germany, many of the festivities, including putting up the tree and opening presents, take place on Christmas Eve, while Canadians often decorate their trees a month in advance, and wait until Christmas Day to exchange and open gifts. Often, families celebrate Christmas by taking elements from both cultures, and establishing new traditions. Tradition may also determine how one celebrates Oktoberfest, if at all. As Almut and Wolfgang Wurzbacher mentioned, sometimes there is liberation in drifting away from a broader cultural tradition and creating one's own family tradition.

> "Eigentlich versuchen wir so ein bisschen von den Traditionen, egal ob [das] jetzt deutsche sind oder kanadische, ein bisschen wegzukommen. Einfach, man muss nicht feiern, wenn alle feiern. Wir wollen nicht mehr so traditionell werden."[222]

For some German immigrants and their families, Christmas in Canada represents a unique blend with aspects taken from both cultures, and the opportunity to create new traditions of their own. For example, Bernd Brandt's children

> "always had two Christmases. Christmas at home on the twenty-fourth with my brother, and then on the twenty-fifth we went to my wife's family in Ingersoll [in Ontario] and they had Christmas again."

The feeling of belonging to a culture is often spoken about in terms of personal relationships, but it can also be inherently tied to the physical places themselves, as Michael Drescher described. Born in Hannover, Germany, he now lives in Canada with his wife in the area where she grew up.

> "I envy her sometimes because she knows every corner of the area where we live. She remembers how she was riding on horseback over these hills, and so she has this rootedness in that land, and I don't have that at all, and I miss that a lot."

---

221 Smith Castro, Acculturation, 18-20.

222 Translation: Actually, we're trying to move away a bit from the traditions, whether they're German or Canadian. It's simple, one doesn't have to celebrate, when everyone else celebrates. We no longer want to be so traditional.

Other times, less tangible things such as perceived differences in work ethic can serve as a reminder of the differences between the two cultures. In Ronny Horvath's view, in Germany the general approach is to "do it yesterday," while Canadians are more likely to say: "take your time to do it right."

There are many such ostensibly clear contrasts in attitude. Canadians are often perceived as polite yet distant, unwilling to state their opinion, while Germans are seen as outspoken and stubborn. As Christopher Wolff mentioned, he feels more German than Canadian, not because that is his intention, but rather because that is how his personality is inclined; he feels himself to be more straightforward than a "typical" Canadian.

In contrast to these perceived clear-cut differences, acculturation often means mixing and adjusting. The Oktoberfest in Kitchener can be seen as a facet of acculturation: an admixture of German form and Canadian attitude; many interviewees commented on Canadians' more conservative and reserved attitude towards alcohol. As Almut Wurzbacher pointed out, one cannot even stand on the tables...where is the fun in such an Oktoberfest? The Canadian attitude seems different and more complex, however, when it comes to nudity. As Christopher Wolff mentioned, people in Canada do not like to see naked people, and yet there are such huge gaps in many bathroom stalls that you can see people undress.

At the same time, interviewees also saw many positive aspects in the Canadian attitude. Many interviewees have found themselves warmly welcomed and accepted by Canadians, without being judged. This easygoing attitude is also reflected in Canadian styles of dress, as seen when one goes back to Germany and is suddenly told, "so kannst du doch hier in Deutschland nicht rumlaufen,"[223] as Herwig Wandschneider recalled. A picture of Canadians is created in which they are both less judgemental and differently aesthetically oriented.

Language, too, becomes a central factor in determining where one finds oneself on the continuum of acculturation. The topic of language is covered more thoroughly elsewhere in this book, but it must also be mentioned here as it relates to one's identity. The generations who arrived in Waterloo Region spoke a mother tongue other than English, which — even if it is no longer used regularly by many — cannot easily be forgotten. As Michael Eckardt mentioned, it can be so deeply embedded in one's being that with his second marriage to a German woman, his presumably lost German language returned: "(Es) ist erstaunlich wie stark die Muttersprache in einem drinsitzt."[224] In most cases, parents feel it is important to pass the heritage language on to their children, not only for preserving this heritage in its own right, but also because it increases their children's future possibilities; the more languages one speaks, the more opportunities one has to reinvent one's own life and identity. However, often one must choose between sending one's children to German school or to hockey practice. Manfred Strauss found himself facing this dilemma, having

---

223 Translation: You can't dress like that here in Germany.
224 Translation: It's amazing how deeply rooted one's native language resides within oneself.

already seen the difficulties in finding a balance between school and extra-curricular activities. "Ich meine, wenn andere Hockey gespielt haben, mussten die Samstagvormittag zur Schule gehen, und das hat vielen eben nicht so sehr gut gefallen."[225] He decided not to send his own children to German school, and instead taught them the language in other ways, such as reading German books to them.

No moment can be unlived; yet some people feel less need to hold on to their old identity, propelled forward by the seemingly endless possibilities for shaping a new one. While in this first section, we enumerated some of the elements that constitute one's sense of an identity as part of and influenced by a community, the next section focuses on the inner world of the individual. How does this inner world affect not only the relationship to the new place, but the way the immigrant experience is created and recreated, and the self is extended into the future, or held by the past? One of the primary impulses in a human being is the desire to belong.

Belonging: Being and Longing

The researchers Ukf Hedetoft and Mette Hjort make an interesting observation when they split belonging into be-longing, that is being and longing.[226] This distinction makes it clear that the idea of belonging has two sides. On the one hand it is cognitive, logical, and reasonable; and on the other affective, infused with irrationality, emotionality, and sentiment. Both sides of longing determine the self we wish ourselves to be or wish to become. We are generally born into a family unit, living in a specific town, in a specific dwelling. These are the first boundaries that define our world: our toy, our bed, our room, our house, our street — home. The boundaries of this place give us a sense of self in relation to the world around us. As we grow into adults, we form an increasing awareness of, and a connection to larger networks: extended social, professional, cultural, and political networks. If everything familiar around us were to suddenly disappear — the most extreme state — the result would be anxiety, sadness, and disorientation or at the very least a heightened awareness of our own existence. In the words of one interviewee, David Nötzold, one can see one's own culture better and simultaneously getting to know what other people think about one's culture, which provides an even broader perspective.

The value that our contemporary world places on constant change is also embedded in belonging and longing. It can, of course, be difficult to adjust to the initial change of leaving one's life and family behind, but the process of adapting does not cease after one has established a life in a new place. In some cases, the change is reflected in infrastructure and businesses, as Monika Hoedl observed:

---

225 Translation: I mean, when others played hockey, they had to go to school on Saturday mornings, and a lot of them didn't really like that.
226 Ulf Hedetoft and Mette Hjort (eds.), The Postnational Self (Minneapolis: University of Minnesota Press, 2002), ix.

"Nowadays, you know that part of King Street East has become, you know, more Asian. All the Asian stores are in there, and the German delicatessens, they're actually not around in this area."

The decrease in the prevalence of German culture and the number of German speakers in Kitchener-Waterloo is a change felt by many German immigrants, who found themselves in a much different environment upon their arrival in Canada. John Kreutzer recalled,

"When we arrived, I believe the majority of the people in the twin cities [Kitchener-Waterloo] here were of German origin and you could go downtown and speak German to practically anybody."

Perhaps the most drastic change is the one noticed by Harry Drung, who arrived in Canada as an infant in 1950. "I mean the biggest change is basically that, you know, people that came over here in the nineteen fifties and sixties are now slowly dying off."

Although there is an inherent stability in settling down in a community, it is an inevitable fact of life that the places, people, and customs which one has grown used to over the years will change. How one reacts to this change will determine to what extent one continues to grow and expand, on an individual level and within the community around them.

Beyond Us and Them

The combination of acknowledging one's German heritage, and the feeling of having established a life in Canada come together to form a blended version of the immigrant's self. This blended identity certainly has the potential to leave one trapped between two cultures, where it is difficult to feel any strong sense of inclusion on either side. In the case of Evelyn Guderian, she described it as the feeling of being somewhat of an outsider in both countries, although she considers Canada her home: "Now I feel German here and in America, but I feel Canadian in Germany." On the other hand, there is an opportunity to perceive oneself as more than simply German or Canadian, but rather as having an identity which transcends both citizenship and kinship, and is instead something wholly unique, individual, and all-encompassing. A frequent echo in the interviews is that one sees oneself as both Canadian and German, or even as not belonging to any nation or national concept. Often, interviewees preferred to think of themselves as global citizens, or simply as persons living here or there, but not belonging to a single country, nation, or culture. The heritage, traditions, and memories one grew up with are present, and so are the culture and everyday lifestyle in the new place. However, these are simply elements that contribute to a more holistic perception of oneself in the world. For many German immigrants, Canada represents an ideal place to construct this patchwork-like identity. Harry Drung noted more specifically the difference between Canada and the United States, in terms of preserving the integrity of the pieces which make up one's self:

"You have an ethnic background as opposed to the United States,
you know it's the big Schmelztiegel. You get, you know, mixed up.
In Canada we are more like the bunte Suppe, where you can still
identify the pieces, you know."[227]

Experiencing different cultures and locations may lead us to a more elevated consciousness and an understanding not only of ourselves, but of others as well and of how we are all interconnected. Dietrich Look, who was born in 1944 and arrived in Canada in the 1970s, described himself as primarily a citizen of this earth. After living in Germany, he also lived in South Africa; but he moved to Canada because he did not want his children to grow up in the system of apartheid. He stated that while he identifies with Canada, he feels a deep rootedness in his German history, and thus feels more German than Canadian. But he further asserted that his emphasis is not really on either-or, but rather on living peacefully with other people. Retaining one's heritage is not in opposition to breaking the confines or altogether confining one's identity to a country. However, as Dietrich stated, if Canada and Germany were playing in the World Cup, he would cheer for Germany.

Michael Drescher, who was born in 1972 and arrived in Canada after 2000, expressed a similar feeling. Having lived in the Netherlands, South Africa, South America, and France, it is perhaps not surprising that he said he feels little attachment to any specific place. He stated, "I don't feel like a citizen of anything. I just live where I live; I think I am a good citizen, but not of a [particular] country."

In her research paper "Cross-Cultural Adaptation and Perceptual Development," Muneo Jay Yoshikawa says that "successful cross-cultural adaptation is conceived as a result of the individual's transcendence of binary perception of the world."[228] This process of transcendence passes through five stages. In the first stage, contact, one encounters a different culture, but one's original worldview persists. In the second stage, disintegration, bewilderment and conflict occur due to the discrepant worldviews of the two cultures. In the third stage, reintegration, a solution is sought, and an identity crisis or search for belongingness occurs. In the fourth stage, autonomy, one begins to stand on one's own two feet and to gain a more flexible worldview. In the fifth and final stage, double-swing, one is fully able to accept and draw nourishment from both similarities and differences in the two cultures.[229] One is free to experience and explore the paradox of human diversity and unity. The last stage is a change from the binary mode of experiencing the world as either old or new to seeing these categories as complementary and in constant interaction.

Acknowledging one's own and other's cultural experiences can have a positive effect on accepting both oneself and others simply as human beings, moving away from the us-versus-them mentality, which can cause tension and division. Gerald

227 Translation: Schmelztiegel: melting pot; bunte Suppe: colourful soup
228 Muneo Jay Yoshikawa, "Cross-Cultural Adaptation and Perceptual Development", in Cross-Cultural Adaptation: Current Approaches, edited by Young Yun Kim and William B. Gudykunst (Los Angeles: Sage Publications, 1988) 140.
229 Yoshikawa, "Cross-Cultural Adaptation," 141-3.

Drews, for example, said in his interview that he does not consider himself a "hyphenated Canadian," but rather a Canadian with German roots. Having experienced a mixture of cultures has given him perspective on what other immigrants have gone through and what they have to offer. He went on to say:

> "Probably a lot of immigrants and kids of immigrants like myself
> continue to value new immigrants coming into the country as well,
> wherever in the world they may be from."

Peter Wiese's advice would be to "look at all cultures" from their own point of view. He stated that he believes that by embracing other languages and cultures, one can extend beyond belonging to one place: "Then you're a citizen of the world and can live life to the fullest."

Between Rootedness and Mobility

Among the interviewees, some people were more attached to their original roots; some found it easier to let down new roots; and some had difficulty letting down any roots at all and rather spread their wings and fly around the globe. The metaphor of roots and wings has been woven into this chapter. However, the concepts of rootedness and mobility have changed over time; what does this mean in our contemporary world of globalization and the digital age? For immigrants who came earlier, leaving their home and emerging into the wider world was a much different experience from that of someone leaving their home in the age of globalization. Helene Schramek's mother and father arrived in 1948. Her mother worked in the shirt factory in town, and her father started his own business in 1949. Their social network consisted of family members already in Canada and the German clubs. Leaving Germany in the 1940s, as Schramek states, meant never knowing whether you would see the people you were leaving behind again.

This concern is less present in our digital world, where a buzz in one's pocket can mean a picture or a message from a nearby family member or friend thousands of kilometres away. Hendrik Walther, who arrived in 2010 with his best friend to pursue research at the University of Waterloo in optometry, faced a much different reality from that of Helene's parents. Walter mentioned being in contact with his family through WhatsApp on his smartphone every single day; he and his friends have a group in which they all see messages from each other. In the digital age, our roots have become more flexible: they can stretch and bend over space and time so that we no longer feel that there has been a major break. Clearly, a text message cannot replace our being immersed in the everyday reality that we once had, but it keeps us just enough in touch to ease the pain of separation.

Increased mobility has a similar effect. In the 1930s, 1940s, or 1950s, unless one was particularly wealthy, it was much less feasible to create a life with bases in two countries, to say nothing of two continents. It was necessary to choose one or the other. Nowadays, however, leaving one place is increasingly no longer seen as leaving anything behind, but rather adding another base. Hendrik Walther, for example, shared that he would like to live in both Germany and Canada, travelling back and forth between the two. Even in today's world, however, the possibility of becoming a true global citizen is limited to those privileged with enough time and money to be able to transcend a purely local life by living in multiple places, rather than merely by participating in the digital world. One's roots can thus be stretched across national and cultural boundaries.

So, if we stretch our view of the world, the way we experience time — the past, present, and future — may also leave us with a better understanding of ourselves. We are all aware of time passing, of the brevity of mortal life. This sense of temporality can be the cause of anxiety and a feeling of fragmentation and separation; yet it can also provide the opportunity to set goals and to celebrate goals achieved. Herwig Wandschneider said that he has always lived mostly in the present or in the future, and that he is not old enough to live in the past.

Manfred Strauss, born in 1946, noted that when people get older, their thinking reverts into their past and into their childhood. As we pass from one country to another and change our lives, we become more aware of the transience of things around us and of life itself. We become more aware of death; as Manfred Strauss states, we will all at some point hopefully ask ourselves the question, "War das jetzt das Leben?"[230]

Some people focus more on the past; others more on the present and the future, such as those who have more traumatic memories, or those who simply wish to make the transition easier. Michael Drescher stated that holding on to his old identity would make him feel more aware of the loss he experienced. His solution is to balance this sense of great loss with gaining a global perspective. Gisela Steckel, having lived 19 years in Germany, 11 years in Serbia, and almost 30 years in Canada, said that she experiences herself as mostly Canadian. Yet she still feels at home when she goes to Germany. She also stated that the more time she has to think, the more she misses home.

So, then, how Canadian do Germans in Waterloo Region perceive themselves to be? The world has changed since the 1930s, in Canada and abroad, from a slower and hardly connected world to a faster-paced, globalized, connected, and digital reality; but what has not changed is the human being's innate need to belong. Some immigrants have chosen consciously to keep their old traditions, heritage, language, and everyday routines, while others have decided to focus chiefly on the new life that they have embarked upon, whether due to a sense of adventure or out of necessity for survival. None of them believe that our past does not matter and has not contributed to making us who we are now, as well as to the new environment that we are creating for ourselves. Customs, cultures, and lifestyles from our past combine with the present and with our heritage to create a continuous interplay.

Some interviewees see themselves as more German when it comes to missing good food, having pedestrian zones, being more outspoken, or simply missing friends

---

230 Translation: Was that life already?

and family. Some see themselves as more Canadian when it comes to new friends and family, liking the open space and nature, enjoying the feeling of being accepted, and appreciating that Canada seems to allow everybody more latitude to be who they want to be. What transpires from the interviews is the common idea that when we have achieved distance from previous familiar surroundings and the familiar self, we may have the opportunity to see more globally. Being somebody who has lived in different countries has to do with the ability to understand one another, relate to one another, and see unity in duality. Experiencing different cultures and different ways of seeing oneself can be a great opportunity to recognize our common humanity and increase our sense of empathy. As we have seen at the beginning, a popular aphorism attributed to Goethe points out the human being's need for both roots and wings.

The more conscious one is of one's surroundings, the more the capacity for openness, sensitivity, and responsiveness grows; but openness leads in turn to increased vulnerability. Clearly, we cannot escape the culture we live in, nor is the erasure of all differences the goal. We can, however, strive towards a perceptual maturity, in which the middle way is seen less as a compromise and more as a recognition of the opposing poles and the dynamic of their interaction; and one can experience life moment to moment, unrestricted by prearranged social and cultural realities.

How to Build a Canadian Bird
with Feathers from Across the Sea

Melanie Weiß [231]

The majority of those interviewed for the Oral History Project regarded the preservation of their culture and heritage as crucially important. Mathias Schulze put it like this in his interview: "Tradition bewahren heißt nicht, die Asche aufzuheben, sondern das Feuer am Leben zu halten."[232] This chapter focuses on the aspects of culture, religion, and leisure from the homeland that immigrants of Waterloo Region left behind, and on those aspects that travelled with them, and that played a formative role in the immigrants' experiences. Shared elements across interviewees' experiences include preserved cultural traditions centred on religion and church membership, and leisure activities that emerged from active participation in cultural, social, and religious institutions. The chapter also discusses interviewees' encounters with new cultural events and conventions, such as Halloween, and dress codes, and explores what they miss from their home countries. At times, the interviewees reflect on their own prejudice and the ways in which their experience of stereotypes changed over the years as they made their way into being part of a new, sometimes unknown culture.[233] Most of those interviewed will never forget their first impressions of Canada or their first intercultural encounters, especially since most did not know what to expect in a country so new to them.[234]

Knocking on Canada's Doors

When he first arrived in Toronto, Martin Giebel said he became colour-blind because, as he and many others pointed out, in Canada there are many people from many different countries, and cultural background does not seem to matter a great deal. Andrea von Weyhe referred to the common assumption that "Canada is a melting pot." Most of the immigrants, even while seeking to preserve their cultural heritage, wanted to adapt from the very beginning. "People wanted to embrace the Canadian culture pretty quickly," explained Marga Weigel. "It also had to do with the post-war era." One of the female interviewees who did not want to be identified said,

---

231 Melanie Weiß and the editors acknowledge Ann Marie Rasmussen's help with this chapter.
232 Translation: Preserving tradition doesn't mean to keep the ashes but to keep the fire alive. Mathias Schulze paraphrased a well-known proverb that has been attributed to Ricarda Huch, Benjamin Franklin, and Thomas Moore, among others. "Asche" https://falschzitate.blogspot.com/search?q=asche, accessed May 18, 2019.
233 For more information on prejudice and stereotyping, see John F. Dovidio (ed.), The SAGE Handbook of Prejudice, Stereotyping and Discrimination (London: SAGE, 2010).
234 For more information about the European history preceding the time after World War II and for more details about Canadian history, see Paul Hayes (ed.), Themes in Modern European History, 1890-1945 (London; New York: Routledge, 1992) and Canadian History: A Reader's Guide. Toronto: University of Toronto Press, 1994. 2 vols. (Vol. 1: Beginnings to Confederation. M. Brook Taylor, ed.; Vol. 2: Confederation to the Present. Doug Owram, ed.)

"I am proud of being Canadian." She originally came from Romania, and she was very anxious when she arrived because she knew nothing about Canada and its culture. However, she explained that she felt as though she had found a new home when she was welcomed with open hearts and shown lots of support. The warm welcome received in Canada was mentioned by many of those interviewed, who also remarked that Canadians were not judgemental. Wolfgang Pfenning said that, growing up in Germany, he learned never to tell anyone that his parents were organic farmers because they were looked down on and criticized, and so they were surprised that in Canada it was different from the very beginning. "We [Canadians] are laid back people," suggested Herwig Wandschneider. The first destination for Michael Drescher was Guelph, Ontario, in the 2000s. "Everybody raved about Guelph," he said. For the locals, Guelph is one of the region's most historical cities. But Michael had lived in the Netherlands, where many cities go back two thousand years to Roman times, and he misses this historical depth of ancient history. Hans Kahlen said he also misses the historical German cities with their old buildings, and the German countryside with its ample opportunities for hiking and walking, and its rustic yet cozy guest houses. Dietrich Look admits that "I miss walking over a bridge that was started in 1400." Many recognize that Canada is still a young country with young cities. Mathias Schulze and Hendrik Walther explain that German cities feature a city centre and pedestrian zones where people meet and relax, where there is always something to experience and somebody to meet. In Canada, on the other hand, such central civic squares and marketplaces are uncommon, and urban development makes it likely that there will be multiple, smaller civic centres, as Mathias Schulze pointed out. Still, there are some historical particularities in Waterloo Region. Willi Ristau, for example, was involved in setting up a plaque where the Kaiser Wilhelm bust in Victoria Park had been.[235] He enjoys telling the story that, after the death of the British Queen Victoria, the statue that was erected of her "had to be bigger than the one of Wilhelm." As a matter of fact, they were placed so that they gazed upon one another.[236]

Local customs and cultural practices in Canada also made an immediate impression on new immigrants. Brigitte and Tony Bergmeier as well as Alan Nanders realized soon that no one locked their front door because there was no fear of theft. As Alan further explained, "wenn man eine Zeitung kaufte, warf man seine Fünf-Cent-Münze…in einen Kasten ein und man nahm sich eine Zeitung raus,"[237] even though you could have taken more, this is what one would call the honour system. Ernst Friedel and John Naas talked about the milk boxes that existed about fifty years ago, and that they were basically holes in the outer wall of every house where people left money to get milk in exchange. Apart from milk boxes, drinking age is also one of the cultural differences nearly everyone mentioned. It was a small culture shock

---

235 English and McLaughlin. Kitchener, p. 83. See also the discussion of this event in the present book, in the chapter "The History of Waterloo Region".
236 See English and McLaughlin, Kitchener. 91, 117, for more about the statues and Victoria Park.
237 Translation: When you bought a newspaper, you threw a five-cent coin into the box and then just took a paper.

for Tony Bergmeier, when he had to show his ID everywhere in Canada to buy beer; in Germany, no one would have asked. Even his wife, who as they like to recall was already showing pregnancy at the time, had to show her ID when buying beer. His worst experience, he told with a smile, was when they wanted to purchase beer and accidentally got root beer instead. Not knowing what it was, and it being so dark and so different in taste to what they had expected, they were not able to finish it. Dieter Conrad laughed when he remembered how he and his late wife moved into their new home in Kitchener. It was a very hot day and so he sat on his front porch having a cold beer. When his brother came by and, somewhat embarrassed, told him that doing this was illegal in Canada, Dieter Conrad called his wife and told her to pack things because they were going back to Germany, which, of course, they did not do.

New holiday experiences also form important first impressions. Anneliese Kraehling will never forget her first day of Grade one at King Edward School in Kitchener, on Valentine's Day, after immigrating only one week earlier from southern Germany. Her classmates knew she was the new girl, and so they also prepared cards for her. To Anneliese, however, Valentine's Day and its traditions felt odd because back then no one in Germany knew about it or celebrated it. Bernd Brandt recalled how as a child he felt embarrassed during his first Halloween trick or treat. At the suggestion of his friends, who knew that he did not have a costume, he had put his coat on backwards. Laughing, Bernd told in his interview that he never participated in Halloween again because he felt as though he was begging; the traditional meaning of Halloween was unknown to him. In contrast to these experiences, most immigrant families quickly began celebrating Canadian Thanksgiving. Since the year 2000, Ontario has celebrated German Pioneers Day on the Tuesday after Thanksgiving,[238] a day on which the Burgund family enjoys remembering their origin and traditions.

Liberty or Freedom — or Both?

Beyond first impressions and on a more abstract and emotional level, many of those interviewed recollect complicated feelings connected with their arrival in Canada. According to Herminio Schmidt, one key difference he observed is that in Germany, freedom means political freedom; in Canada, it means feeling free because of the vastness of the natural world. Martin Giebel shared this feeling. For him and for Ursel Wandschneider, owning a cottage is a symbol of personal freedom that they see as a difference to Germany. Many interviewees own cottages. With a wink, Hugo Schwengers said: "If you have a cottage in Point Charlie, never bring your mistress — there are too many people from Kitchener." Many people connect the feeling of freedom to the space offered by Canada's geographical vastness. Astrid Braun explained how in 2009, she vacationed in Füssen, Germany, with her granddaughter. She loved the vivid place amidst the mountains that, though small, contained everything so that she had no urge to go anywhere else. But thinking about the

---

238 "German Pioneers Day Act, 2000, S.O. 2000, c. 7", accessed May 18, 2019, https://www.ontario.ca/laws/statute/00g07

German landscape, she emphasized the vastness of the space in Canada as compared with Germany; everything in Canada seems so beautifully ample. The Griebenows became so accustomed to these vast distances that, once on a visit in Germany, they spontaneously decided to drive two hours from Leipzig to Jena and back again because Gerhard Griebenow had accidentally purchased tickets for the wrong opera. Most Germans, he said, would never have undertaken the drive, but for him the distance was no obstacle. Bernd Brandt mentioned how easy it is to travel by car in Canada. In comparison, he felt that traffic in his home country, Poland, was chaotic and dangerous because Polish people seemed to drive how ever they wanted, when he visited in 2005. Alan Nanders remembered realizing for the first time that there was a kind of thoroughness and diligence anchored in his cultural background, when he and his mother arrived for his first day at school, bringing with them all their documents and certificates, which had been translated by the British embassy. As Alan recalled, it was the first time the principal had seen something like this and did not know quite how to react. Ursel Wandschneider described a similar experience. When she arrived in Canada, she applied for jobs and was astonished how quickly and spontaneously she was invited for a job interview. She took all her certificates, officially translated by the Embassy, with her in a bag to the interviews, yet no one ever asked to see them. "Once you start working here, we'll figure out if you're qualified or not," was the only reaction to her neatly translated certificates.

Waving the Flag and Germanness

Immigrants are often asked if they are proud of their home country. The interviewees often mentioned being proud of German soccer. When it comes to soccer customs, the second generation often appeared to take up interests related to their parents' home country. Harry Drung's oldest son, Thomas, though born in Canada, became a fan of the German Bundesliga,[239] with Bayern Munich being his favourite. Gisela Steckel has always been a fan of the German soccer team BVB Dortmund. Gerald Drews recalled being astonished when visiting relatives in Germany during the 2014 World Cup, and noting that apart from his wife and himself, no one wore a German team jersey, not even for the finals. His cousin explained that there had been no nationalism, and no waving of flags or the like until 2006, the year Germany hosted the World Cup for the second time. For most of those interviewed, there were also inner characteristics typical of being German. When asked what kinds of German behaviour immigrants might have retained, Martin Giebel responds that he has kept his "deutsche Sturheit."[240] He described how he sometimes feels that Germans behave like "Elefanten in einem Porzellanladen"[241] because they tend to complain too much. Although David Nötzold would consider himself to be diplomatic, German directness, or in his own words "to bring [one's] point across", is a very important part of his culture. On the other hand, interviewees explained that Canadians are not

---

239 Translation: top-tier professional soccer league in Germany.
240 Translation: German stubbornness.
241 Translation: bull in a china shop (literally: elephants in a china shop).

judgemental, and they would accept people making small mistakes based on one's original cultural background, or on poor knowledge of the language.

When thinking about Germanness, many interviewees also reflected on the upbringing of their children, and how they managed their households. The Bergmeiers and the Kahlens believed that they raised their children in a German fashion, which to them means being strict but loving with their children. Though born in Canada, Christine Burow looked upon the austere rules, the focus on cleanliness, and even the way the dog was treated in her parents' household as German. Katy Pfeiffer remembered that when she was still a young girl, pyjama parties and sleepovers were common in Canada. But her family did not know of this practice, and so she was not allowed to stay at her friend's place like the other girls but had to come home before returning to the party the next morning. Sue Stein remembers the *Struwwelpeter*[242] quite well; a collection of illustrated short stories about children who do not behave, always with "a morbid ending," as she put it. Because she sucked her thumb as a child, her mother read to her the *Struwwelpeter* story about a boy who did not want to stop sucking his thumbs, so one day a tailor entered the house, cut off the boy's thumbs, and ran away. Almut and Wolfgang Wurzbacher remembered an essential piece from their southern German home: a TV figure in the form of a small kobold called Pumuckl. He lives together with an old carpenter named Meister Eder and carries out all kind of pranks on him.

Schnitzel, Roulade, Bread, & Co.

Food traditions are crucial when talking about customs that shape identities.[243] For many readers, it will not come as a surprise that many of the interviewees explained that they still prepare Schnitzel, Spätzle, Klöße, Rouladen, or Sauerbraten with red cabbage, and occasionally serve Sauerkraut.[244] For Annika Nicholson, the red cabbage one purchases in a jar, as in Germany, tastes best. One of the interviewees told that she still makes Sauerkraut herself for at least three families, and that she always has some home-made jam for her husband. Bernd Brandt's family cooks eastern-European food, even though his mother started to adopt French cuisine due to the influence of Bernd's wife, who lived in France. He explained that after World War II, it was not possible to plan the foods to prepare, but rather you had to use what was on hand. Most of the interviewees referred to all kinds of homemade soup, such as lettuce soup from Siebenbürgen or Borschtsch[245] from Ukraine, as being European. Dietrich Look said that he still prepares Labskaus for his family, which

---

242 See "Struwwelpeter", https://en.wikipedia.org/wiki/Struwwelpeter, accessed May 18, 2019. The stories have the Struwwelpeter (messy-haired Peter) as the central fictional character.
243 Eva Lavric and Carmen Konzett (eds.), Food and Language: Sprache und Essen. InnTrans, Bd. 2. (Frankfurt am Main: P. Lang, 2009).
244 Spätzle are a special kind of pasta made with eggs; Klöße are dumplings made with bread and potatoes; Rouladen (engl. roulades) are beef rolls with pickles, onion, mustard, and spices; Sauerbraten is beef marinated in vinegar, cloves, and onions; Sauerkraut is cabbage cut fine and allowed to ferment in a brine made of its own juice with salt.
245 Borschtsch (engl. borsch) is a soup made with beetroot.

looks "ugly" to him because all the ingredients are mashed up, but it tastes delicious.[246] Willi Huber explained that he and his wife brought diverse ways of preparing meat and sausages into the regional culture of Kitchener-Waterloo through their meat-processing company. According to Guenter Lotzmann, Germany is the "Wurstmacherland" (land of sausage makers). But there are also different kinds of traditions within Germany, and there are people living in Waterloo Region from diverse German backgrounds. So, whereas Rosina Müehlberghuber's first memory of unfamiliar food was cutlets with applesauce served in a restaurant on King Street, others considered this exact meal to be typically southern German. Even though Brigitte and Tony Bergmeier would consider themselves a German household, over the years their cooking has changed, and nowadays it is a mix of both cultures, something that applies to most of the interviewees. Bernd Brandt said that he would never get used to the white bread in Canada that he calls Wabbelbrot (flabby bread). Isa Schade calls it Knatschbrot (munch bread). Most interviewees reported that they miss the culture around German bakeries. For David Nötzold, it was common in Germany to get up early in the morning, leave the house in your pyjamas and a jacket to line up at a bakery for buns for the whole family. Monika Hoedl remembered that children from her school always made fun of her because she was the only one who brought dark rye bread for lunch. Evelyn Guderian explained that her first boss always ate long sandwiches she had never seen before, and that his Austrian wife baked fresh Apfelstrudel (apple strudel) for them. For her, being incapable of throwing away leftover food is typically German, maybe because of the hunger common during and after World War II, she guessed. Brigitte Schmidt spoke about how she still grinds her own flour; she uses it for all the food she cooks or bakes. She buys the kernels at an organic farm in Tavistock (near New Hamburg) and has a mill at home.

For many interviewees, certain homemade cakes are still part of a birthday celebration, for example Linzertorte, Krümeltorte, Pflaumenkuchen, Schwarzwälder Kirsch and many more.[247] In Harry Drung's family, his "oldest one," as he said, bakes excellent cheesecake and Schwarzwälder Kirsch. Christine Burow's favourite tradition is having coffee and cake in the afternoon, especially with yeast cakes. Irmgard Burow explained that her neighbours still are amazed when her family does not have coffee after lunch but at 4 pm. A tradition some keep alive is a Kaffeeklatsch (coffee party) with close friends; whenever they meet, each brings some cake. To purchase ingredients for typical German baked goods, the Burows, Margarete Rowe, and many others used to shop at Fiedler's Delicatessen, a store on King Street in Kitchener that sold groceries, baked goods, and household items with which Germans were familiar. Rita Schirm said that, when they moved here, her family found German food at Fiedler's store, and that shopping for groceries there

---

246 Labskaus is mashed potatoes with minced meat and beetroot.
247 Linzertorte is a cake that is typical for southern Germany and Austria, made with cinnamon, nuts and redcurrant jelly; Krümeltorte is a fruit crumble cake, often also with a soft cheese filling; Pflaumenkuchen is a plum cake; Schwarzwälder Kirsch is Black Forest cake.

from time-to-time helped them when they felt homesick. When the Heffners began establishing their automobile business in Kitchener-Waterloo, their grandmother prepared Kipferl[248] once a year for the whole company for the annual Christmas party, until the number of staff grew too large. The food in Gerda Wolf's home was always more Austrian; her mother prepared Kaiserschmarrn and Pflaumenknödel.[249] Gerda Wolf always admired how her mother grew as much food in her own garden as possible, even though they lived in the city; she explained that her mother did so not to save money but so that they would have fresh food. Mathias Wolf also recalled harvesting fruits, such as plums and cherries from his own trees, and making soup with beans from his garden.

Answering the question of other culinary traditions from her parents, Christine Burow explained that they eat bread and cold cuts for breakfast, have dinner on Sundays at noon, and make hamburgers outside on a little campfire. With a laugh, she explained that everything her mother cooks must start with bacon. John and Willy Heffner remembered that their grandmother always made typical Hungarian goulash, lecsó,[250] and red peppers stuffed with ground meat. They explained that sometimes the art of cooking was to make a meal out of whatever could be found because there were times when there was not much to eat in the house.

Faith and Church: Start-Ups for a New Life

Alongside individual experiences in encountering a new culture and new traditions, many people sought support in their faith and in their church. Alice Bromberg remembered that the first place to which her family went after arriving in Regina, Saskatchewan, was church; it was the one institution they knew welcomed people regardless of their ethnic background. Many immigrants with similar histories met at church, and so church became a cultural meeting point. Nelly Kilianski explained that church was a safe place for all of them. Alice Bromberg remembered that many families decided to send their children to the German school, the Ida Pruefer German Language School at Bethel Lutheran Church. German school was taught once a week by volunteer teachers such as Willi Ristau and his wife. Werner Bromberg and many others attended German school as soon as they arrived in Kitchener. Church was a "focal point" for Harry Drung, and he ended up being a chairperson there for more than twenty years. Anneliese Kraehling talked about her father having a very beautiful encounter at Bethel Lutheran Church. He had spent five years as a prisoner of war in Russia before restarting his life in southern Germany and then later emigrating to Canada. At the church he was reunited with his godfather's daughter, whom he had not seen since they were expelled from their village in Yugoslavia during the war. When Bethel Lutheran Church organised a day for all immigrants

---

248 Kipferl are a kind of vanilla cookies.
249 Kaiserschmarrn are shredded pancakes; Pflaumenknödel: sweet dumplings filled with plums.
250 Lecsó is a typical Hungarian, Polish, Czech, and Slovak stew based on bell peppers, tomatoes, and onions, sautéed with lard or bacon.

who had come to Canada on the Beaverbrae,[251] a transport ship that brought Displaced Persons from Bremerhaven to Canada, Danuta Grigaitis was asked to recite one of her poems. She chose *Thoughts on the Beaverbrae,* and recited it during her interview:

Farewell our precious homeland,
This ship is sailing out to sea.
Toward a very new beginning,
Yet unknown life's destiny.
Deep the waves, as our longing
For peaceful sunsets soon somewhere
United with our sisters, brothers,
Life's endeavour now to share.
May tomorrow's days be guided
By God's grace and loving hand,
As we sail the deep, wild ocean
To a very distant land.
Canada.

I'm Going Home for Christmas

Religion plays a major role in the life of most immigrants and their children since it is closely linked to cultural customs. The main custom kept by most of those interviewed is celebrating Christmas on the night of December 24. According to Michael Heitmann and Paul Schulze, the advantage for a child in this custom was that you always received your gifts before your Canadian friends. Most of the interviewees still prefer buying a living Christmas tree instead of an artificial one, setting it up on the morning of December 24 and keeping it up until Epiphany, January 6. Some explained that getting together with family and baking typical German cookies such as Spritzgebäck, Lebkuchen, Kipferl, moon cookies, Christstollen, and Honigkuchen is a very important and joyful time.[252] For many, marzipan, made of almond paste, is a traditional German Christmas candy. Heiderose Brandt-Butscher and her husband, as other families, celebrate both Canadian and German Christmas because their children have grown up in Canadian surroundings. For Astrid Braun and for the Burgund family, having lights on the Christmas tree that look like candles, manifests another difference to their Canadian counterparts. The Griebenows still use real candles on real trees to create an authentic Christmas

---

251 The ship was originally named Huascaran, built in 1938 by Blohm & Voss in Hamburg, and had capacity for thirty-two passengers. First being used as a submarine depot ship, she was captured by the allies in 1945 and brought to Montréal as a cargo liner. There, she was renamed Beaverbrae. After a refit, there was accommodation for more than seven hundred passengers, and after 1947 she sailed regularly from Bremerhaven to Canada to transfer Displaced Persons. See "Beaverbrae", accessed May 21, 2019, https://www.theshipslist.com/ships/descriptions/ShipsB.shtml#beav

252 Spritzgebäck are butter biscuits made with an icing bag; Lebkuchen is a gingerbread cookie; Kipferl are vanilla cookies; Christstollen is a fruit bread for Christmas; Honigkuchen is a kind of gingerbread with honey.

ambience. Many people still love to have an advent wreath and advent calendars. Christine Burow remembers that as a child, she was very aware that their house looked different from others because it was decorated in a German fashion, including decorations like "the guys where you pull the string and the arms would go out," referring to the Hampelmann (jumping jack). One of the interviewees reported that she misses special things from their traditional Romanian Christmas a lot. She remembered going from house-to-house on Christmas Eve, collecting ingredients for cookies, getting together in front of the church, and baking together with all villagers. It was all very solemn, she said, and sometimes also a bit sad. When the church bells began to ring, everyone stood next to the graves of those they had lost. After mass, the fathers hurried home before the others, so that when the rest of the family arrived, the candles on the Christmas tree were lit already. Steve Schatz shared a memory from Siebenbürgen, where they did not have much, and he lived with eight people in one room. It was similar when they found refuge in Austria. For lack of space, the tree they cut for themselves in the woods stayed in the yard, where they lit candles and spoke prayers together. Afterwards everyone cried, and there was a long moment of silence, until Steve's family and the Austrian hosts went inside and sang Christmas songs together.

Theresia Burgund explained that there was a time in Waterloo Region when the entire family attended service at Bethel Church on Christmas Eve. Meanwhile, a student who rented a room in their house prepared dinner and put the gifts under the tree. When the family returned home, the children thought that the Christkind (Christ Child) had visited, and laid gifts under the tree while they had been to church. Herminio Schmidt told his children that they had to search for the Christmas Star, so he took them out, sometimes even in the car, while another adult family member put the gifts under the tree, pretending it was the Christkind who brought them.

Many people, Michael Heitmann among them, still put out their cleaned boots on December 6, the night St Nicholas comes and fills the boots with treats for the children who behaved well throughout the year. Anna Kreischer remembered how during their childhood in Romania, her father's friend came during the night of December 5 dressed as the Krampus, and made noises to scare the children, which was a reminder to behave well in the future. When John Heffner was young, his father played Knecht Ruprecht.[253] He would come into the apartment and ask the children whether they had been good the past year. The children were afraid that if Ruprecht found out about something bad, they would get "a couple of wackies on the Popos."[254] Regina Karschti and Anna Kreischer told of a similar Romanian tradition on New Year's Eve, when people put linen sheets over their heads. They always went after the badly-behaved kids and pretended to push them into a well.

---

253 Knecht Ruprecht, as well as another mythological figure known as Krampus, are counterparts of St. Nicholas, as they punish naughty children. As companions of St. Nicholas, they were invented later in time, especially in Germany and surrounding countries to the South. Whereas Ruprecht is a single person, Krampusse can show up in a group.
254 Translation: a few spanks.

The Anchors of Cultural Heritage

The history of European immigrants in Waterloo Region goes back to the early 1800s. There have been, and still are, many clubs and associations focussing on the preservation of cultural heritage, and on the support of business and handicrafts. This chapter only discusses some of the many clubs and associations that had a great influence on regional culture. The German-Canadian Business and Professional Association was established in 1967 by bicultural business and academic professionals, as well as by consultants and entrepreneurs. Its purpose was to promote business and professional interests and relations, to help immigrants become settled Canadian citizens, to actively support networking, and to preserve the German cultural heritage.[255] Harry Drung, Willi Ristau, Tony Bergmeier, and Marga Weigel all were presidents of the association. Many other interviewees were members — Werner Bromberg, for example, for more than thirty-five years. Harry Drung recalls how he met many important politicians through the Association. At one event, he met Peter Boehm, Canada's ambassador to Germany at that time.[256] The Association had been organizing a German language contest for high school students and named it after the first Honorary Consul of the Federal Republic of Germany in Kitchener, Wilfrid L. Bitzer. During the Bitzer event, prizes for the winners of the German contest, and awards for outstanding high school and university students are presented to promote the learning of the German language and a better understanding of German culture. Wilfried Bitzer once organised a tour through Europe with a youth dance group, and they visited sixteen cities in two weeks. Willy Heffner was then part of a small music group that accompanied the dancers and played (French-) Canadian songs at interludes.

Participation in local clubs has been very important to many interviewees. Most clubs depend on their volunteers and on donations, and most of those interviewed participate in more than one club to keep their cultural heritage alive, and to support the other clubs as well. The umbrella organization for most of the German clubs and associations in Ontario was the Trans-Canada Alliance[257] of which Heinz Kreitzer has been the president. People share many stories about their experiences in clubs. The oldest and biggest club in the region is the Concordia Club, which was founded in 1873 for "the preservation of the German language, German customs and traditions" by Germans who mainly came from central and northern Germany.[258]

---

255 German-Canadian Business & Professional Association, accessed May 21, 2019, https://www.germancanadianbusiness.com/
256 Peter Boehm was born in Kitchener and served from 2008 to 2012 as Ambassador in Berlin, Germany. Afterwards, he worked in the Ministry of Foreign Affairs in Ottawa, Canada.
257 The Trans-Canada Alliance of German Canadians was incorporated in 1952 to serve as an umbrella organization for German organizations across Canada. It grew out of the Canadian Society for German Relief and the co-operative effort by German Canadians to extend aid to war-devastated Austria and Germany after the war (see "Trans-Canada Alliance," Trans-Canada Alliance of German Canadians, accessed December 8, 2015, https://data2.archives.ca/pdf/pdf001/p000000076.pdf).
258 See "Concordia Club Facts", Concordia Club, accessed December 9, 2015, https://www.concordiaclub.ca/about-the-club/interesting-facts

In the year 2012, Ronny Horvath became one of the youngest directors of the Concordia Club. Minnie and Kurt Boese have been members of the Concordia Club for more than fifty years, and highly recommend the Schnitzel Day that takes place every Thursday, which features exceptionally large schnitzels prepared by a German chef from Kiel. One of the female interviewees said that she, like many other women, worked in the club's kitchen as a volunteer for many years. For one event, she and her friends prepared an unbelievable 380 schnitzels.

Many of those interviewed were part of the club's choir. Michael Heitmann was president of the male Concordia Choir in Ottawa during his time there. Every Wednesday after rehearsal, he recalled, they went to the Stammtisch (table reserved for regular guests) for a few beers and kept on singing German songs there. Together with fifteen other choirs, it is now part of the German-Canadian Choir Association. They participate in exchanges with other member choirs. Many people also joined the choir of the local Lutheran church. Minnie Boese was part of it for more than fifty years. Others were active in local choirs. Reinhold Schuster auditioned for the Kitchener-Waterloo Bach choir under the direction of Howard Dyck. He has had highly successful baritone solos of Bach's Magnificat and the Fauré Requiem as well as solo roles in the Messiah. In later years, Reinhold joined the board of the Philharmonic Choir to raise money to sustain this world-class local community choir, now known as the Grand Philharmonic Choir. Before coming to Kitchener-Waterloo, Dieter Conrad lived in Manitoba where he was head of one of the biggest German choirs in Canada, which had 94 active members.

Another German-heritage club is the Alpine Club. It was founded in 1953 by the Gottscheers,[259] more specifically by Wilhelm Hoegler. It now has more than 200 members. The Transylvania Club is also well-known. It was founded in 1951 by Michael Kiertscher, Fred Schuller, Michael Stierl, John Melzer, and George Schuster.[260] While some of the younger generation is still involved in the clubs, traditions are changing. Therese Burgund described a very joyful tradition that is now disappearing, in which people would dress in traditional clothing for special events. The members of the Transylvania Club would usually wear very colourful dresses. Therese Burgund recalled that the Donauschwaben show a very different style of traditional dress.

Like the Brombergs, many people are members of the Schwaben Club; John Heffner told us that he has been a member since 1964. The Schwaben Club was founded in 1931 under Wilhelm Goss as its first president. Willy Heffner described how he once attended one of the club's dance marathons that went from 6 pm on Saturday until 6 am on Sunday morning. Willy was a member of the dance group, and they raised money for an upcoming trip to Germany. Heidi Peller-Oliver

---

259 The founders of the Alpine Club have been descendants of the Gottscheers. This is an ethnic group of originally German settlers in Kočevje (Gottschee), a region in Slovenia, and Gottscheerish is said to be a Bavarian dialect. (see "History of the Gottscheers," Alpine Club, accessed December 7, 2015, https://alpineclub.ca/our-story/history-of-the-gottscheers/).
260 "History," Transylvania Club, last accessed December 8, 2015, https://transylvaniaclub.com/about/history/

explained that there are twenty Donauschwaben Clubs in the US with more than 2,000 members, and that these club members of North America meet annually — in 2015, for example, in Los Angeles. "We all get together and celebrate the heritage of our culture together," Heidi said; no matter their age, everyone parties and dances together. The clubs were so popular in former times, Hans Kroisenbrunner explained, that you had to be waiting at the door of the Alpine Club before 7:30 pm, because afterwards it would be full, and no one else was admitted. Rita Schirm recalled that you could only become a member of a club if someone vouched for you.

Many people made friends for life or met their future partners at the four big clubs. Regina Karschti described how she met her future husband during a dance at the Transylvania Club when she was only sixteen years old. She remembered how her father considered her too young to go out, so she sneaked out to meet her friend at the club. When she returned home late, and realized the front door was locked, she stayed in the car of her sister Anna's husband until early morning, when her mother let her in. Her father, she said, never found out. Michael Heitmann met a young lady who wanted to learn dancing with him, so they borrowed a tape from the library that teaches foxtrot and started dancing at the Transylvania Club; they also did some folk dancing at the Schwaben Club.

Feasting and Festing

In every culture, there are a vast variety of customs connected to seasons, days, or events, in which people love to participate and wish to keep alive. Werner Kuehlenborg remembered one of his favourite traditions, Klootscheeten. It is a winter game from north Germany that is played with a group of people, two balls, and a lot of schnapps. The two teams go for a long walk, and each group tries to throw a ball farther than the other group. When the game is over, they usually go to a restaurant and eat Grünkohl und Pinkel.[261] Another famous tradition is the Christmas market. Tony Bergmeier, who was president of the German-Canadian Business and Professional Association, founded the Christkindl Market. As Tony explained, he felt obligated to represent and support his German heritage. He saw an opportunity when Valerie Chipon, then Head of the Industrial Development Department of Kitchener, wanted to renew downtown Kitchener, and asked the German-Canadian Business and Professional Association for support. Tony believed that the Christkindl Market might be an event that children would enjoy and that would benefit the city. He began raising funds, worked with the carpenters at Conestoga College to build booths, and persuaded vendors to participate. He wanted the Christkindl Market to have a real tree, so he attended City Council meetings to convince the representatives to have a real Christmas tree. He dealt with things such as insurance, decorations for the vendors and so on, an incredible amount of volunteer work that, he said, was worth every second. His own children and grandchildren were supportive during all those years, for example, by volunteering to appear as Mary and Joseph in the

---

261 Translation: kale and sausage.

nativity scene. Danuta Grigaitis remembered with a smile that as the Concordia Club Choir began singing 'Leise rieselt der Schnee',[262] and the children were skating on the rink, then it really started snowing. As Gerhard Griebenow pointed out, the Christkindl Market has provided an opportunity for German immigrants to participate and keep their traditions alive. Gerhard works on the committee and plays Knecht Ruprecht. The German Language School, where he worked, has distributed gingerbread men to the students at Christmas every year.

Most interviewees love participating in the Oktoberfest.[263] Traditionally the women wear a Dirndl, and the men Lederhosen.[264] Many of those interviewed still enjoy wearing their traditional dress, be it from Bavaria, Transylvania, or Siebenbürgen. Many have participated in the Oktoberfest for years. Gerhard Griebenow's membership in the Oktoberfest committee started one year when he was volunteering at the bar for a friend. Monika Hoedl remembered that one year, she and the Ladies Group of the Schwaben Club prepared 2,280 cabbage rolls to be sold at the fest. Heidi Peller-Oliver explained that it is crucial to keep the Oktoberfest alive; not only is it very popular but it is one last German tradition that connects everyone, no matter their background. Katy Pfeiffer remembered that in the 1970s, when you went to the Oktoberfest with your membership card from the dance group, you received a special mug with the year and your club's name on it. Andre Schilha recalled that the Oktoberfest seemed even bigger in the 1970s and 1980s than it is now: they invited all the beauty queens from the US, paid for their stay in Kitchener, and had one big pageant. Mathias Wolf and his Hofbräu Band have played for the fest for sixty-three years and he said he hopes that they will go on doing so for as long as possible.

Leisure Activities

Apart from living their culture in rituals, be these traditional or religious, most of those interviewed consider their leisure activities as either being typical for a certain culture or as being very important for their cultural encounters with others. When asked how he likes to spend his leisure time, Alan Nanders quoted: "Gerettet ist das edle Glied Der Geisterwelt vom Bösen, Wer immer strebend sich bemüht, Den können wir erlösen."[265]

---

262 This is a well-known German Christmas song. Its title loosely translates as 'The snow is falling silently'. Also see https://en.wikipedia.org/wiki/Leise_rieselt_der_Schnee

263 First held in 1967 at the Concordia Club, the German clubs met in 1969 to make this event bigger. Ever since, every first week in October, the German clubs offer everything that can be found in the original fest as well: traditional music, clothes, events like runs and Miss Oktoberfest contests, and sausages and beer served in big Festhallen. Among the founders were Richard Hermansen, Owen Lackenbauer, and Darwin Clay. Meanwhile, it attracts more than one million people annually. See "Welcome", Oktoberfest, accessed December 8, 2015, https://www.oktoberfest.ca/#welcome

264 A Dirndl is a woman's folk dress; Lederhosen are leather shorts, traditional men's folk attire.

265 This quote is from Goethe's Faust. Der Tragödie Zweiter Teil. (Akt Bergschluchten, Engel.), see Goethe, Johann Wolfgang von. Goethe's Faust. Translated and with an introduction by Walter Kaufman (Doubleday/Anchor Books: New York, 1961/1962), 492–3.

Alan stated that he is very moved by these words, because even if he were to die tomorrow, he would always try to do his best, and accomplish as much as he can. He said he was an active volunteer in many organizations. In 2008, he received the Canadian Forces Decoration to honour his service, and in 2013, the Queen's Diamond Jubilee Medal for distinguished volunteer work. Margarete and Michael Rowe received the Mayor's Award for outstanding volunteering at the German clubs.[266] Some of those interviewed refer to traditional German poetry when thinking of something typical for the German culture, some like Manfred Richter enjoy attending live theatre performances of plays that are of German origin. Some appreciated theatre in Canada. In this context, Stratford and seeing Shakespeare's plays was mentioned often. Many of those interviewed are dedicated to classical German culture, and especially to classical music.

Danuta Grigaitis has an extraordinary hobby: she writes poetry and has printed her autobiography.[267] It was an incredible honour for her, she recounted, when the police choir from Dortmund came to Kitchener, and surprised her by singing her song *Please Let There Be Peace* at the Concordia Club:

> Into the garden one morning I walked
> To gaze at the flowers and trees.
> A beautiful longing my heart overwhelmed,
> Please let there be peace.
> Far then I went, wandering by the brook
> That danced in the breeze.
> It seemed that it murmured that very thought:
> Let there be peace.
> Butterflies freely danced through the air,
> Surrounded by birds and bees.
> And I thought to myself how lovely they are,
> Please let there be peace.
> A little child with innocent eyes
> Her face smudged funny with grease,
> Skipped carefree by,
> and I thought "dear God,
> Please let there be peace."
> For the sake of that little innocent child,
> For the sake of the flowers and trees,
> For the sake of all beauty that touches our soul,
> Please let there be peace.

Translation: Saved is the spirit kingdom's flower / From evil and the grave: / Who ever strives with all his power, / We are allowed to save.

266 Michael received his award from former Waterloo Mayor Lynne Woolstencroft, and Margarete from former Waterloo Mayor Brenda Halloran.

267 Danuta Grigaitis. To Whom It May Concern: Poetry and Autobiography in 2 Parts. Kitchener, Ontario: Danuta Grigaitis, 2010.

John Heffner Sr. also published a book.[268] It is his biography, from his first years in Hungary, where food was sometimes at a premium and one cooked whatever one could find, to becoming a well-known car dealer in Waterloo Region. The father of Waldemar Scholtes also wrote poems, and through his strong link to the Transylvania Choir transformed most of them into songs. He collected his father's poems for a book which will be published soon, as he explained.

For many of those interviewed, cultural background is strongly connected to music. In the case of John and Willy Heffner, their mother made them play the accordion for many years; they consider this instrument to be the most German of all. Steve Schatz played in six bands in Canada. With the Transylvania Band, he played in local clubs and taught people how to dance the polka and waltz. They were even shown occasionally on local television and composed songs themselves. Steve and the band toured many European countries, such as Germany and Austria, where they played a concert of which a DVD was made. John Kreutzer and his brother founded their own five-man band in which John played the accordion, and his brother the saxophone and the clarinet. They played German dance music, toured all over Canada, and went to the US and Jamaica. Heinz Kreitzer recalled that, before he came to Canada, his brother-in-law asked him to bring along a saxophone. His brother-in-law founded a band "during a time when the clubs were still flourishing," and Heinz became the band's drummer for 24 years.

Among those interviewed, many were very successful in sports. For example, Kurt Boese was a wrestler, and participated in the Olympics once as an athlete and twice as a coach. He explained how he started at the age of nine in Germany, won the Canadian championship six times, participated in the Commonwealth Games in 1958, and won bronze during the Pan-American Games in Brazil. Gerhard Griebenow's alma mater is the University of Tübingen, and so he participated annually in the famous punt race on the river Neckar.[269] Four times in a row, he and his team of fraternity friends won the race because of their perfected paddling skills and his excellent punting technique, as he explained. There are many successful sportspeople amongst those interviewed. Ronny Horvath, for example, participated in the world championship for the Canadian ice stock team (or "Bavarian Curling") in 2012. Since this is not a common sport in Germany, his former employer took him to the Concordia Club to learn how to play and discovered that Ronny was a "natural."

Others developed uncommon interests in their new surroundings. Victor Rausch referred to himself as having been the "black sheep" when he was younger because of his interest in hypnosis. When he was sixteen, he attended a show, and afterwards purchased a book about hypnosis. He remembered trying it on his friend and realized that he somehow caused absentmindedness in his friend. As a test, Victor started

268 John Heffner and Ulrich Frisse, From Hungary to Canada: The Building of My Dream. (Kitchener: Transatlantic Publishing, 2009).
269 "Stocherkahnrennen", accessed May 21, 2019 https://de.wikipedia.org/wiki/Stocherkahnrennen. This race is famous amongst students of south Germany. It takes place in Tübingen every year, and participants are sometimes quite creative with styles and utensils.

poking his friend with a needle, even sticking it through his hand, and his friend never remembered anything. At this point, they began a career as hypnotists, appearing at parties and small events. During his time at university, Joerg Stieber joined something like a fraternity club, but with "less drinking and more building," as he pointed out. They constructed their own gliders together. In Canada, Jörg kept his love for aviation going. Henry Malon, because he does not attend the clubs and their events anymore, has spent most of his leisure time writing books. He has already published over 30 books in German and in English. In terms of uncommon hobbies, Kaethie Pfeifle's late husband did something quite entertaining in his leisure time: he bred and trained German shepherds. His dogs had an appearance in the film *Wolf Dog*, which was filmed in Markdale, Ontario, in 1957 and came out in 1958.[270]

Many of the leisure activities of the interviewees have a strong connection with German customs and traditions and with a German way of life. In parts, this is rooted in a strong connection with the Old Country.

---

270 See "Wolf Dog" https://www.imdb.com/title/tt0052401/ for details, accessed Oct 8, 2020.

Connecting with the Old Country
Lisa M. Rosen and James M. Skidmore

What does it mean to belong, to feel like you belong to a group, a community, a nation? Can an immigrant belong to two societies, the sending society and the receiving society? Belonging has become a central concept in research on migration. It speaks to the importance of understanding a migrating individual's perceptions and experiences, as she or he crosses borders to permanently move from one country to another. These reflections are the subject of the interviews being analyzed in this chapter. We wish to better understand the expatriates' experiences with migration and its impact on their feelings of belonging, not just to their new society (Canada), but also to the societies and cultures they left behind. Before we do so, we will turn to some previous research and theoretical frameworks to pick up central concepts and categories of belonging. By then relating these ideas to what we found to be stories of the Old Country, we will demonstrate that belonging can be a dynamic concept that encompasses the many identities to which immigrants may relate in different ways. Finally, this chapter exhibits some of the patterns and experiences as to how the interviewees in this project are connected to old and new, as well as to the in-between of the place of origin (German-speaking parts of Europe) and place of settlement (Waterloo Region in southern Ontario). The attention that academic scholarship in general has paid in recent years to the trend of globalization has convinced many that national borders have become more porous in the globalized age. This is based on the observation of the freer flow of capital, commerce, and communications. Sociologist Peggy Levitt's work points out that, in order to reflect on the broad and general effects of migration, we first need to approach the experience of simultaneity: the parallel impact of ties with the sending <u>and</u> the receiving culture.[271] As researchers recognize, the fact that immigrants maintain ties to their originating societies can be highly relevant to their migration experiences. Today, scholarly interest has moved away from the ability of immigrants to settle in and assimilate to a new culture, towards understanding immigrants as participants in plural cultures. Migration scholarship has adopted the term transnationalism to capture the spectrum of contact that immigrants have with their sending and receiving societies.[272]

As sociologist David Fitzgerald and others have pointed out, researchers now often reject the dichotomy of immigrants having been once there and now here, in favour of the notion known as "third space." This concept helps to reflect the reality that immigrants live in, namely an experience of both places that is often fluid and present to varying degrees throughout their lives.

---

271 Peggy Levitt, "Transnational Migration: Taking Stock and Future Directions", Global Networks 1, no. 3 (July 1, 2001): 195.
272 Levitt, "Transnational Migration" (Ibid.).

According to Fitzgerald,

> "those who move abroad are not definitively immigrants or
> emigrants, but rather people whose lives span international borders.
> …Their experiences cannot be understood from the perspective of
> the destination country alone."[273]

Marco Antonsich, among others, calls this transnational belonging. The term does not stand for:

> "de-territorialisation of belonging, but for increasingly plural,
> multiple forms of belonging 'here' (the receiving society) and 'there'
> (the place left behind in the process of migration)."[274]

Antonsich contends that belonging is a mix of "movement (or becoming)," and "attachment and rootedness."[275]

Anthropologist Pnina Werbner points out that

> "in a world of transnational migrations and blurred borders,
> immigrant cultures cannot therefore be neatly packaged in fixed
> multicultural policies or subjected to loyalty tests devised by
> politicians in a futile attempt to create order out of ambiguity and
> flux."[276]

Werbner and Fitzgerald both argue that immigrants' cultural identities challenge conventional, or standard, cultural identities, such as German or Canadian. Instead, they inhabit the conceptual third space, a subjectively perceived state of mind in which different spaces of belonging are constantly rearranged.

The scholarly literature also refers to the concept of multiple belonging as hybridity. Yet even hybrid groupings (e.g., German-Canadian) run the risk of being understood as culturally consistent communities. That is why third space is preferable; it does not define a cultural category, but rather establishes a conceptual space wherein immigrants can negotiate multiple identities. Focus turns to the individual's experience of migration and reminds us that immigrant experiences are by no means homogenous.

Another way of thinking about third space is to view it as a transnational social space. The study of immigration from the perspective of transnational social relations raises some interesting questions for scholars.

---

273 David Scott Fitzgerald, "The Sociology of International Migration", in Migration Theory. Talking Across Disciplines, ed. Caroline B. Brettell and James F. Hollifield, Third Edition (New York; London: Routledge, 2015), 132.

274 Marco Antonsich, "Searching for Belonging — An Analytical Framework", Geography Compass 4, no. 6 (June 1, 2010): 651-652.

275 Antonsich, "Searching for Belonging", 652, cf. also Anne-Marie Fortier, "Migrant belongings. Memory, Space, Identity" (2000: New York, London: Berg).

276 Pnina Werbner, "Migration and Culture", in The Oxford Handbook of the Politics of International Migration, ed. Marc R. Rosenblum and Daniel J. Tichenor, Oxford Handbooks (New York: Oxford University Press, 2012), 236.

Levitt states that

> "those who live within transnational social fields are exposed to a set of social expectations, cultural values, and patterns of human interaction are shaped by more than one social, economic, and political system."[277]

The thickness of the transnational social field — the depth, longevity, and intensity of the migrants' social and cultural connection lines and relationships to sending and receiving cultures — is dependent on the structures, methods and tools available to them. Some of these connections might be institutional and formal in nature, for example, the ability to have dual citizenship, allowing individuals to participate in the political life of both countries. Others can be more informal, for example, contact with family and friends. In any event, as sociologists Peggy Levitt and Nadya Jaworsky point out,

> "Most scholars now recognize that many contemporary migrants and their predecessors maintained a variety of ties to their home countries while they became incorporated into the countries where they settled. Migration has never been a one-way process of assimilation into a melting pot or a multicultural salad bowl but one in which migrants, to varying degrees, are simultaneously embedded in the multiple sites and layers of the transnational social fields in which they live."[278]

Turning now to the interviews, we can ask: What methods and tools do the interviewees employ to maintain their contacts across this space? Do they express a belonging to two places or societies at once, or does time take its toll on one of these ties? These questions can be addressed by looking at how the interviewees reflect on and understand belonging in a general sense. It should be noted that the interviewees come from a variety of Old Countries in Europe (e.g., Germany, Romania, the former Yugoslavia, modern-day Poland) and it is for this reason that we use the German word Heimat, which can mean home, homeland, or native country, among other things, to refer to the general idea of the Old Country. We acknowledge that, in the German Studies context, the word Heimat can be burdened with meanings. We are using it here simply to indicate the interviewees' German-speaking homelands or places of origin, just as the interviewees used the term frequently and without bias.

Overall, the comments of many of the interviewees indicate their experience of a third space even if they are unfamiliar with the concept. This becomes evident when we consider how their relationship to Heimat developed over time and how they began to see themselves inhabiting a space of personal memory and identity that acknowledged and valued multiple belonging. This space had Canadian features such as the adoption of English and the adaptation to the customs and demands of the

---

277 Levitt, "Transnational Migration", 197.
278 Peggy Levitt and B. Nadya Jaworsky, "Transnational Migration Studies: Past Developments and Future Trends", Annual Review of Sociology 33, no. 1 (July 18, 2007), 130.

labour market, but there were also several traditions, commodities, and personal possessions of the original country that were almost universally and intentionally retained.

The motivations that prompted migration also played a considerable role in defining the respondents' relationships to both the old and the new Heimat. For some, the decision to go to Canada was the result of rejection or disappointment they experienced in their country of origin. Whether of an economic or social nature, this experience has a significant impact on the way the Old Country is remembered by the interviewees. For example, many who were born in the 1930s came to Canada seeking refuge from specific personal experiences of World War II. Others, born in the decade following World War II, often had economic or social motivations. Finally, the youngest generation of interviewees was most often motivated by curiosity and wanderlust (longing for traveling). As Christine Burow, Minnie and Kurt Boese, Ekkehard and Irmgard Burow, Annika Nicholson, and many others mentioned in their interviews, the fact that their departure was not traumatic made return visits to the place of departure relatively easy.

Despite this variety of individual experiences, some general trends and similarities exist among the interviewees' replies. We have grouped the responses according to two broad themes: (1) physical contact with the Heimat, either by visiting the Old Country or having visitors from there; (2) virtual contact with the Heimat via a variety of media.

Connecting with the Heimat

One of the most significant aspects of transnationalism is that it can render state borders meaningless, although natural borders such as oceans and mountains remain. One might think that the idea of a nation could lose its meaning for immigrants, but in practice that was hardly the case for the Germans of Waterloo Region, especially those who pursued Canadian citizenship. Instead of rejecting national belonging, some immigrants depicted how they came to see themselves as intercultural bridge builders between societies, with their transnational experiences serving as a starting point for exchange. But difficulties connecting to the Heimat can also provoke homesickness and nostalgia. Especially those interviewees who came to Canada in the mid-20th century experienced many technological and financial barriers that hindered connections with the home country. For some, these barriers were the reason the image of the country they left behind became locked in time. For those who were expelled from lands to which they could no longer return due to geopolitical changes, such as moving borders, the experience of separation and loss could be overwhelming. As many point out, homesickness was especially painful in times of crisis, such as the death of a loved one left behind.

A key strategy to maintain connections, even over a long period of time, is the objectification of Heimat. This can be achieved by keeping relics such as food recipes with a regional flavour, like Streuselkuchen (streusel cake) and Dresdner Christstollen (stollen), as Irmgard Burow explained. She kept her German cookbooks to bake Spritzgebäck (butter cookies) for Christmas every year. On a similar note, Gerda Wolf preserved some of her mother's Austrian cuisine, and Heinz and Hilde Kreitzer said that they still have Schwarzbrot (dark rye bread) at Christmas as on every other day.

Preserving customs and celebrations is another way immigrants retain their connections to Heimat. A traditional German Christmas is important for interviewees such as Werner Schnittke, Theresia and Franz-Josef Burgund, Alice and Werner Bromberg, David Nötzold, Heiderose Brandt-Butscher, Guenter Lotzmann, and others. Many interviewees, for example Paul Schulze, Alex Müntz, and Helene Schramek, would schedule their journeys back to Europe to coincide with Christmas. With the influx of German-speaking immigrants in Canada, some Lutheran and Catholic churches were able to hold services in German at Christmas or Easter, as Johann Wolf reports. For other families, New Year's Eve (or Silvester, as it is known in German), was favoured over Christmas. The fact that New Year's Eve was the date of the arrival of Elisabeth O'Reilly in Preston (today part of the city of Cambridge in Canada) underscored this date's symbolic value for her and others.

Overall, retaining connections and a sense of cultural community prove easier when whole families or groups emigrated. This was mentioned by Katy Pfeiffer, who felt that being in the same situation with others made it easier to maintain traditions and customs. In Katy's case, this manifested itself in participating in social communities such as her dancing group, the Kitchener Oktoberfest marketing committee, and the Schwaben Club in Kitchener.

Going Back: Occasions and Opportunities

The habit of returning for limited periods of time illustrates an important feature of inhabiting a third space. Most of the Germans in Waterloo Region can afford to travel back to their place of departure frequently, and most of them feel comfortable rejoining the old living environment for a couple of weeks. Pauline and Hans Schmidt have returned more than fifty times since coming to Canada in the 1950s. However, as they and many others remarked, it is exactly the time limitation, the status as visitors, which enables them to regard Germany from a more relaxed and rather positive perspective. In the interviews, this was brought up by Christiane and Hans Peter Kahlen, Katy Pfeiffer, Theresia and Franz-Josef Burgund, and Barnhild and Wolfgang Pfenning. Still, the difficulties of travel have kept some of the older interviewees from making the journey more often. A common occasion for return visits is to reunite with families, classmates, or friends. Christiane and Hans Peter Kahlen arranged biennial family reunions in various German cities; and Marga Weigel's family reunions at Lake Constance, Lake Starnberg, and in Italy have drawn her back multiple times. The great pleasure of showing new Canadian friends or family around one's place of origin, as was the case for Horst Wiesner, who is originally from Breslau (today's Wrocław), is mentioned frequently. Klassentreffen (school reunions) were also important opportunities for Dagmar Schilha, Theresia and Franz-Josef Burgund, Heiderose Brandt-Butscher, Dieter Conrad, Margarete

Rowe, and Gerhard Griebenow to socialize with old friends. The anniversary of Werner Schnittke's confirmation class even made it into the German press, attracting participants from Canada and the USA. Some interviewees vividly depicted the communication around scheduling of reunion events in Germany, which required intricate planning to accommodate anniversary dates and summer holidays. As Manfred Strauss states, "Da kommen [wir] dann mal an Geburtstagen."[279] When his parents celebrated their golden wedding anniversary, however, they postponed the party by three months, so that he and his family could attend. Transylvanian Saxons in Canada mentioned that the annual Siebenbürger Heimattagtreffen[280] was also a welcome excuse to return.

Christmas and summer are the times that most visits take place. For Ingrid Hann, a Christmas card sent by a friend containing a warm invitation to Germany became the occasion for the family to dare to take the journey and reminisce about school experiences. It also gave her father the chance to attend to some family matters in Romania. Monika Hoedl, who only visited Germany once, ten years after her departure, picked Christmas as the occasion for this unique experience.

Beyond family reunions, some interviewees have been able to maintain connections through business or other social contacts. For instance, Dietrich Look has had reason to visit Germany in his capacity as Chairman of the VW Canadian Dealer Advisory Council. Marga Weigel, who worked as a property manager and realtor, traveled to Munich twice a year with her partner, and Manfred Conrad is often in Germany on business as well. Other reasons to visit Europe involve cultural exchange activities, such as John and Willy Heffner travelling to Germany to give performances with their dance club, while Danuta Grigaitis, Waldemar Scholtes, and Andre Schilha and his wife Andrea undertook several choir tours.

The effort needed to plan these trips indicates an openness to German and European culture. While borders may not have disappeared, the ability to travel back with relative ease to countries of origin indicates that national borders have become easier to cross in the globalized age. But despite the desire to see old friends and families, barriers remain. The cost of airfare, especially around Christmas, is often reported as a hindrance for frequent travel, as noted by Ronny Horvath and Hendrik Walther. It was only in the 1990s, after forty years in Canada, that John Penteker could afford the journey, and meet a school friend from Romania. For John Naas and his wife, flight costs encouraged them to come up with a five-year-plan to afford regular travel back to Europe.

Another, less commonly mentioned, obstacle is a sense of alienation from the Heimat. Christine Lindner, since leaving with her husband for Canada in 1983, reported hearing very little from her brother. As she pointed out, some of her friends and family resisted her emigration plans, and this led to a refusal by them to accept her decision to emigrate. Strikingly, it became one of the greater challenges of the

---

279 Translation: We go there for birthdays occasionally.
280 Translation: Transylvanian Heimat Day Reunion.

emigration process for many of the interviewees to prove to people back home that they hadn't changed all that much. Several interviewees, including Irmgard Burow and Anne and Hans Kroisenbrunner, related that they had to convince those they left behind that moving to Canada did not mean leaving the civilized world. In contrast, Martin Giebel said that his friends largely acknowledged his courage and spirit of adventure when he decided to move to Canada, and that they even contended that it might be the more pleasant place to live.

The experience of hosting visiting family members, most often parents, in the new Canadian home was often considered emotionally challenging according to Brigitte and Tony Bergmeier as well as Minnie and Kurt Boese. Helga Sarkar recalled a moment of happiness when she took photos of her grandfather and her two children in the stroller in front of Niagara Falls. Other immigrants had to wait several years for their families or friends to visit or follow. Sometimes political reasons had prevented them from travelling, other times relationships just had to stand the test of time, as in the case of Julianne and Willi Huber: as they say today, the fact that Willi had to wait a long time for Julianne to arrive after they had decided she would follow him to Canada strengthened and deepened their relationship and continues to make them passionate about travelling together.

The Second Generation Discovers Its Heritage

Even though air travel can be expensive, it has become more accessible over time. The opportunity to cross the Atlantic Ocean on an airplane — and not, as many had on their first journey, on a ship — made it much easier for the interviewees to maintain personal contact with their home countries. In a noticeable number of cases, this chance has been seized not just by members of the emigration generation but by succeeding generations as well. It turns out that members of the second generation appear to be particularly adept at maintaining contact with their parents' Heimat and developing new friendships, as we learned when Dieter Conrad, Barnhild and Wolfgang Pfenning, and Manfred Strauss spoke of their children. For instance, Manfred Strauss's second son rejected his father's plan to send him to German Saturday school; instead, he read German children's books daily, and while at university spent a year studying science in Stuttgart. Manfred's first son finished his theological education at the same seminary in Germany that his father had once attended. Helene Schramek's daughter went to Germany to take a course, and another interviewee's son met his future wife when he was on a trip to Romania with his mother. After the woman had visited him in Canada for a couple of weeks, he followed her back to Germany to start a family, which now receives frequent visits from Canadian friends. John Penteker's daughter went to German Saturday school and later to Aalen near Stuttgart on a school exchange. Similarly, the daughter of Elizabeth Reuss, Jackie, who went to Saturday school for several years, goes frequently to Germany now with her own son to meet her grandma. Jackie's brother Stephen went to Germany for one term during his co-op studies at the University of Waterloo, and Pauline and Hans Schmidt's daughter went to Germany to study, later working for some time as an office clerk in Munich. Dorothea Snell's daughter

Eleonore used a newspaper delivery job and a scholarship to pay her way to Germany as an eleven-year-old. Mrs. Snell was impressed by how comfortable she was in German: "und ja, sie ist besser in Deutsch als ich."[281]

However, not all members of the second generation feel the desire to visit their parents' birthplaces. Manfred Conrad, for example, said that his children exhibit little interest in establishing personal bonds with the Saarland area in Germany, despite Manfred having taught them much about the language and history of the area.

Destination Heimat?

Most interviewees indicated that the first place they want to visit when returning to Europe is the place where they grew up. Nevertheless, travelling to different places to see loved ones is also popular among the community members. For example, Gisela Steckel went on a backpacking trip to meet her friends; Henry Malon was inspired to travel to places that are associated with his favourite German authors, such as Riedlingen, the birthplace of Ernst Jünger. John Naas first went to Marburg, where his daughter was studying, and then went on to Osnabrück to meet his wife's sister. Margarete Rowe, apart from seeing her hometown, went to Helgoland many times to meet a German friend. Mathias Wolf, who came to Canada from Romania, went with his choir to Germany, and then made a round trip visiting several places where Transylvanian Saxons had settled. John Schultheiss and Annika Nicholson said that they appreciate Germany's compactness and the ease with which one can travel there. In general, it is worth noting how often interviewees refer to Germany's bustling city life as a community characteristic, which they miss in Canada — a sentiment noted by Mathias Schulze. The stories and experiences told in the interviews raise some questions. What impact does Heimat have on the emigrants' identities? To what extent, or in what way, does the place of birth exert a claim for the third space? The experience of Paul Stagl is instructive in this regard. Born in the 1950s in Canada to a Danube Swabian father, who had been displaced by the war, Paul was called a DP[282] by some of his peers in early grade school. However, he found a lot of support in the German-speaking community in Canada. Through his involvement in the Schwabenclub and its dance group, partaking in accordion and German lessons, he turned German culture into an integral part of his childhood. It was only when Paul was in his teens that he visited Europe to meet with his extended family or, in his words, people who "looked like him." One of Paul's greatest challenges was keeping alive the memory of his German family, of which he was only told by his parents when he was old enough to travel there and meet them in person. For people like Paul, travelling back to live and work there for a short period of time was a way of discovering his own roots, making this journey a personally meaningful one. In his case, it involved finding German documents which enabled him to trace back his Danube Swabian, Habsburg, and German roots to the 1600s. The discovery provided him with a sense of his family's heritage that helped him resolve conflicts and reflect

---

281 Translation: And she is better in German than I am.
282 Displaced Person, an official label that became a pejorative word in the 1950s.

upon the anti-German sentiment he had encountered before. His experience of growing up being called a DP in Canada was shared by others, for instance, by John Schultheiss. For both, experiencing exclusion reinforced a pronounced desire for Heimat — a place where they would not feel like strangers.

Other respondents reported having a partly negative image of Germany, especially those who experienced hunger, intimidation, and pain before their departure. The experience of the Third Reich has left a mark on their memories and a bad taste in their mouths; some said that they have never been able to lose completely a sense of foreboding associated with that period of history. Nelly Kilianski, for example, lived in Poland before she came to Germany, suffering hunger and mistreatment, which is why she returned to the European continent from Canada only once. But post-war developments in Germany also had an impact on respondents who returned to visit. When Johann Leinweber returned to East Germany, the authoritarian nature of the state reminded him of the Nazi regime. Helga Sarkar's grandfather was one of a small number of East German citizens who were permitted to leave the country to visit his granddaughter in Canada, which she acknowledges today with great gratitude. Elizabeth Schilling mentioned that she has only been to Germany twice since emigrating and found everything to be very different compared to the time of departure. For respondents with no memory of their birthplace, the experience was naturally different. Gerda Wolf left Austria with her parents when she was eight months old. Returning to Austria and Romania, her parents' original homeland, as a teenager was intense and very exciting, but worrisome, too, as she explained, since Romania was part of the Warsaw Pact[283] at that time.

It can be noted that those respondents who emigrated recently see less difference between Canada and Europe than those who left much earlier; technology and globalization have played their part in changes in both countries. Although they appreciate the culture of their Old Country, more recent immigrants to Waterloo Region also acknowledged the difference in perspective their move afforded them. As David Nötzold explained,

> "the best thing I ever did was moving out of my culture, out of my comfort zone, out of my surroundings. I think that I can recommend that to any young person. And I am recommending it to whoever I can. Because you get challenged in your view."

---

283 The Warsaw Treaty Organization, officially the Treaty of Friendship, Cooperation and Mutual Assistance and commonly known as the Warsaw Pact, was a collective defence treaty signed in Warsaw, Poland, between the Soviet Union and seven other Eastern Bloc socialist republics of Central and Eastern Europe in May 1955, during the Cold War. In 1991, the Warsaw Pact was declared disbanded. (See https://en.wikipedia.org/wiki/Warsaw_Pact)

Christa Streicher stated:

> "Ich genieße die Weltoffenheit. Ich fühle mich auch eher mehr als Weltbürger. Richtig typisch deutsch oder so bin ich nicht. Aber Deutschland ist meine Heimat nach wie vor."[284]

With regard to Germans being able and willing to adapt to a new culture, Sue Stein talked about them as being prone to assimilation, possibly more so than Portuguese or Greek immigrants.

Changing Borderlines, Changing Memories

The return to the Heimat leaves imprints in the memories of immigrants. Many of the interviews contained observations on the political changes in central Europe over the past eighty years. Even the members of the younger generation of immigrants acknowledged that life in their former Heimat had changed significantly since their departure. The most obvious change is the shifting of borders. John Penteker's birthplace was part of Romania when he was born, then later became part of the Hungarian state, and then reverted to Romania. Even if not explicitly stated, some transformations also became evident in the stories of the generation that arrived in Canada in the 1970s and 1980s: they clearly distinguished East and West Germany when stating their place of birth. For them, the image of a divided country still seemed very present. Some interviewees discovered that the place they left behind had changed due to subtle political or social developments. Some, like David Nötzold and Alex Müntz, originally from Transylvania, recounted how their ties with the Heimat are also shaped by the recognition that their friends and family had moved on. Elisabeth O'Reilly and Anneliese Kraehling referred to the transformation of their parents' lives since emigrating. With her (modern) Yugoslavian roots, Anneliese highlighted that she would be referred to as Danube Swabian today. When Helene Schramek's father visited the Old Country — the former Yugoslavia — in 2002, he and his daughters realized that the area had been devastated by the war in the Balkans in the early 1990s, making the visit a troubling experience. Martin Giebel experienced a similar shock after returning to Poland. Since all the buildings in the area had been torn down, and the landscape and view had changed completely, Martin was unable to find his paternal grandfather's farm. Quite a different change was experienced by Waldemar Scholtes; he recalled that the school where his father taught in Romania had been governed by different states despite never changing its location. Yet the lure of the Old Country transcended generations as Waldemar's mother, who was born in the United States in a Transylvanian immigrant community, returned to Transylvania, where she met Waldemar's father.

---

284 Translation: I enjoy the openness. I feel more cosmopolitan. I'm not really a typical German. But Germany is still my Heimat.

At the same time, as Martin Giebel pointed out, visiting Europe held a special meaning and provided him with positive energy:

> "Es gibt so viele Plätze, die ich besuchen kann, wo ich weiß, die haben Jahrhunderte Geschichte, die man sehen kann. Die mir bewusst ist. Das gibt mir ein anderes Gefühl. Das ist Heimat."[285]

For those born in the 1960s or later, things did not change too much since their departure, something they viewed positively. Many explained that they feel delight when things they used to like about the Old Country still existed in some form. As an example, Gerda Wolf had poignant experiences with restaurant menus in Austria that contained the same dishes as back in the day. This rediscovery of familiar sites seems to bring comfort to German expatriates in search of a transnational identity that fully embraces both the old and new countries. For many of these more recent immigrants, personal contact with the Old Country along with fast reintegration during visits are very important. Before moving to Canada, Jörg and Renate Stieber had joined a student fraternity called Akaflieg München, in which the members build gliders and fly them. They reported that, after years of living in Canada, they are still in regular contact with that group, that fellow members visit them, and that they see them when they visit Germany.

Connecting with the Heimat: Virtually, through Mail, or by Phone

As a result of the rapid developments in communication technology at the end of the 20th century, email, telephone, and video calls have become the preferred means of communication. Mathias Schulze related a story about his elderly mother in Germany installing Skype on her computer so that they could talk every Sunday and see each other during the conversation. The ability to bridge space and time virtually through near-instantaneous contact has had a remarkable impact on emigration, making the process of leaving the original homeland easier, as not all bridges are burnt. Even though many interviewees mentioned their appreciation for handwritten letters, most of them, even those born before 1960, have embraced internet technology for staying in touch with the Old Country. Before Facebook, Skype, WhatsApp and other applications helped to virtually shrink the distance between Europe and North America significantly, and phone calls became relatively inexpensive, postal mail used to be the most effective and popular means of communication, and sometimes the only one. As Christine Burow explained, her father proposed to her mother by letter after meeting his future wife during vacations in Germany. Despite the immediacy afforded by electronic communication, especially elderly interviewees like Steven Schatz felt that letters to family and friends remain important, especially around Christmas. One year, Steve wrote 70 Christmas cards. As Henry Malon put it, people still write letters because they appreciate the effort that goes into written

---

285 Translation: There are so many places that I can visit, where I know they have hundreds of years of history that you can see, that I am aware of. That gives me a different feeling. That's Heimat.

communication, such as his correspondence with his best friends Jupp, Bernie, and Rudi. A more recent immigrant like Alan Nanders sent letters — in his case, to his former school friend — to share his first impressions of the new country. To maintain a penpal correspondence with friends from school comforted Dagmar Schilha and many others when they felt homesick.

Making overseas telephone calls in the 1950s was generally described as very complicated. The connection was often poor and would not allow for proper conversations, as Johann Wolf and Werner Bromberg explained. In addition to phoning her mother and stepfather, Rita Schirm would make voice recordings for them. Rita also reported that the calls often had to be arranged in advance to make sure all family members could gather around the telephone. The high cost of long-distance telephone calls made them rarer, as Rosina Müehlberghuber explained. As a result of the technological and financial hurdles, in addition to the time difference, the frequency of phone calls was significantly lower than today, which, some interviewees felt, resulted in more excited, intense conversations.

During the 1950s, 1960s, and 1970s, newcomers to Waterloo Region were able to buy German magazines or newspapers at local delicatessen stores. Manfred Conrad frequented Fiedler's store in Kitchener, where a range of magazines was available, though they arrived about three months after they had appeared in Germany. Yet despite the time lag, these publications were attractive to him. They offered an authentic insight into German life, allowing him to stay in touch with current events while also helping him keep up his German. Similarly, Siegfried Schranz made an effort to maintain his German language by reading *Der Spiegel* daily. Marga Weigel, Werner Schnittke (who has a particular interest in sports results), and Ingo Schoppel mentioned that they regularly read the German papers. Gerda Wolf said that she learned German by watching movies and television soap operas, benefitting from the actors' slow and clear pronunciation. At the same time, it was not just the German-language media that contributed to the well-being and personal comfort of the immigrants. Some of the interviewees, for example Siegfried Schranz, remarked that English-language media proved to be of great support in learning English quickly. Siegfried, a self-declared 'bookworm', read all his English books more than once — turning him into a living dictionary, with unique translation skills. As the tone of his statement suggested, he considered this an advantage and enjoyed the comfort of being able to communicate fluently in two languages.

In some cases, the use of media is directly impacted by the political situation. The case of Herminio Schmidt is telling in this regard. Herminio's father, who was from Spain, ran a news agency for Latin American newspapers in Berlin, until he had to flee from the Gestapo in 1939. The family had a Grundig short-wave radio which received broadcasts from around the world. During Hitler's seizure of power and the institution of Gleichschaltung (establishing Nazi totalitarian control of all aspects of society), the Grundig radio was replaced by a smaller Volksempfänger (People's Radio) which would only receive Nazi-government propaganda. Later, when he stayed with a host family in German-occupied Poland, Herminio wondered why everyone seemed to be glued to their Volksempfänger, only to realize that they were trying to hear news from the battlefields. Herminio's father had to flee Germany, leaving his wife and two children behind. With the help of a teacher and the Red Cross, Herminio was able to reunite with his father after a long and strenuous process. His father taught him some aspects of journalism and critical investigation.

Changing with the Times: From Television and Radio to the Internet

The availability of German media, such as *Deutsche Welle TV*, other broadcasters, and German newspapers, via the World Wide Web has relegated print and other subscriptions to the past, and this has had an impact on the third-space existence. For example, Martin Giebel and Dietrich Look said they now make frequent use of the *Deutsche Welle TV* channel but gave up their subscriptions to printed newspapers in favour of the more immediate access afforded by online resources. Martin used to order *Der Spiegel* as a print magazine, but said he prefers to read it online today, among various other magazines and online newspapers. As Alan Nanders, Manfred Conrad, Andrea and Holger von Weyhe, Julianne and Willi Huber, Dagmar Schilha, Christa Streicher, and others confirmed, *Deutsche Welle TV* was especially popular thanks to its focus on serving Germans living abroad. Interviewees between the ages of twenty and forty — for example David Nötzold — mentioned that this almost unlimited online access has enabled them to be better informed about politics in Germany and the European Union than about current affairs in Canada, their country of residence. Many older interviewees said they like to read a German print newspaper, magazine, or book if they come across it. Those who came to Canada before the 1960s, like Gerhard Griebenow and Waldemar Scholtes, enjoyed reading *Das Echo*, a German-language newspaper from Toronto, or the *Deutsche Presse,* another Canadian publication which has now ceased publication, both of which tended to be available at German delicatessens and other stores as well as at the German clubs. Others used to read publications connected to their specific cultural community, for example Saxons from Transylvania, who could obtain such magazines published in Canada.

In addition to making available magazines and newspapers from Germany, the internet has facilitated access to radio and TV stations from Germany and Austria. Since they can usually be watched or listened to from almost any device, and often for free, they supplement the local radio and television cultural programming. Werner Kuehlenborg as well as Andrea and Holger von Weyhe reported that they enjoyed listening to German radio. Rita Schirm noted that she particularly enjoys the songs of a chantey choir being played on the radio, because her cousin used to be a member of such choir. Asked about their favourite features of the programs, John Kreutzer remarked that they like to maintain a connection to the language, while also getting the most recent information on daily affairs. Reinhold Schuster explained that he has an emotional connection to the medium of radio since it was the *Heimkehrerbericht* (Returnee Report) that told him about his father's release from Soviet custody when Reinhold was eleven years old.

Overall, the interest in German media and news demonstrates a desire to keep up to date with the Heimat. By maintaining this nostalgic routine, immigrants can preserve a connection with the Heimat. Doing so fosters in them a cultural duality, a hybridity that is the hyphen between German and Canadian.

Connecting through Music, Cinema, and Literature

We also found it significant how the interviewees cherished music, cinema, and literature from the Old Country, and how these art forms provide the immigrant community with opportunities to reflect on their transnational lifestyle. Several interviewees referred to German literature as "high culture," "the best of Germany." Dorothea Snell mentioned the work of Ursula Hegi, a German-born American writer, as instructive about North American immigrants' ways of dealing with their dual heritage. Gisela Steckel recommended *Ans dunkle Ufer*, a work of German fiction by Alfred E. Johann, based on the experiences of a Mennonite family in Canada. Reading the novel prompted Gisela to draw connections between places and traditions she is familiar with, such as the Joseph Schneider Haus in Kitchener. Also, music enjoys great popularity as a memory-keeper; it can be replayed at any time and instantly brings back the spirit of old times. Elizabeth Reuss, for example, said she still has a lot of CDs by Freddy Quinn, an Austrian singer and actor; Steve Schatz mentioned his large selection of classical German music for easy listening; and Dagmar Schilha shared that listening to the farewell concert of the Flippers, a German Schlager band, used to cheer her up after a bad day.

The transnational experience and the location also influence the language-specific type of media that interviewees tend to choose. As Gerda Wolf and Renate and Jörg Stieber explained, when in Canada, they prefer English-speaking media — magazines, films, books, but choose to read something in German when visiting their former homeland. Similarly, other interviewees like Dieter Wolle regarded it as integral part of their adaptation to the new adopted country to stick with the North American newspapers.

Transnational memory is maintained by access to German resources in Canada. For those seeking to read German fiction, the first point of contact was usually the German section at the public libraries. Among the books, they could also find publications by local authors, such as a volume of poetry, which Danuta Grigaitis self-published[286] to capture her own immigration experiences. However, for many interviewees, like Helene Schramek, who was born in Canada, living in an English-speaking environment for decades has made it difficult to read German. Other German language pastimes, such as Rätselhefte (puzzle magazines) and Kreuzworträtsel (crosswords), are found to be rarely available in Canada, much to the regret of Andrea and Holger von Weyhe. They added that they also miss the Bertelsmann Book Club and the Quelle shopping catalogues, items they consider uniquely German.

---

286 Danuta Grigaitis. To Whom It May Concern: Poetry and Autobiography in 2 Parts. Kitchener, Ontario: Danuta Grigaitis, 2010.

German? Canadian? Blended!

This chapter has shed some light on the transnational nature of the interviewees' lives. While it seems inappropriate to generalize their experiences, the strategies employed by the immigrants to come to terms with their third space illustrate that belonging is not a fixed point, it is a multitude of fixed points that outline a spectrum of experiences. Many German immigrants regard not only their own identities, but also those of their children, as being very much rooted in the Old Country. For some, this causes concern and pain due to the country's history, but others are filled with pride when recalling their origins. One of the female interviewees used to advise her children:

> "Vergesst nicht meine lieben Kinder, von wo ihr gekommen seid.
> Seid froh und seid stolz, was ich in meinem Leben geschafft hab:
> euch eine freie Welt zu geben. Jetzt könnt ihr machen was ihr wollt.
> Ihr seid frei. Ihr könnt euch euer Leben schön machen. Aber ihr
> könnt auch fallen. Es ist euer Entschluss. Aber vergesst nie, wo ihr
> geboren seid und was [der] *background* ist, den ihr habt. Und ihr
> könnt es wem-immer erzählen. Und bestimmt hören sie euch zu."[287]

Others described their sense of belonging explicitly as a blend of two ingredients. Hans Peter Kahlen and his wife referred to Germany as their Heimat but to Canada as their Zuhause.[288] This sentiment is likely shared by many German-Canadians, illustrating succinctly the theory that immigrants inhabit a third space where they continually negotiate their identities between two or more worlds. The interviewees feel they belong to Canada, their Wahlheimat (chosen homeland) and therefore the Canadian way of life makes its presence felt in everyday activities. At the same time, the sense of belonging to the Heimat does not cease, thanks to both physical and virtual contact with the country of origin. Instead, it has become an integral part of their special and unique story, which they deliberately wish to see incorporated into the new surroundings.

Regardless of the circumstances initiating the move to Canada, the life-changing experience of migration becomes an essential component of the personal biography, placing the immigrant in the third space that is often simply described as being German-Canadian. It is in fact much more complex than that.

---

287 Translation: Never forget, my dear children, from where you came. Be happy and proud of what I have accomplished in my life: we gave you a free world. Now you can do as you please. You can have a beautiful life. But you could also fall. So, it is up to you. But never forget where you came from and what background you have. You can always talk about it and, undoubtedly, others will listen.

288 Translation: home — the precise place where you live.

Speaking the Language

Wes Lindinger and Grit Liebscher

When immigrants arrive in a new land, they bring not only their cultural traditions, education, and life experiences with them, but also their language. This chapter will explore the stories of immigrants to Waterloo Region and their experiences arriving in a community where they could encounter others speaking their home languages. In her interview, Alice Bromberg spoke of her very first experience with English in Canada:

> "We landed in Regina on Sunday morning, and everybody was at the station. And from there we went to church [that] had a German service and [one in] English. The minister came with us for lunch and…there was a dog lying around and the dog came. He says: 'Ah, now what do you call that?' He knew German. 'Ein Hund. Well, auf Englisch this is dog.' So that was my first word: dog."

While this exchange with the minister took place in Saskatchewan prior to Alice's arriving in Waterloo, others may have encountered similar experiences in Waterloo Region. The German language, while not as widely spoken as Canada's official languages, English and French, has had a strong presence in many parts of Canada, particularly in Waterloo Region, especially in the town of Berlin, Ontario, known since 1916 as Kitchener. Shortly before the outbreak of World War I, the 1911 Canadian Census recorded approximately 36,000 German speakers in Waterloo County, a number which one hundred years later amounted to 16,515.[289] While census data provide us with some background on the scope of German-speaking presence in the area, the stories told in the narratives of the people interviewed add to this picture in depth and complexity. These include stories about the difficulties of arriving in a country with a different language and the journeys of learning English. They also include narratives about the role German and other immigrant languages have continued to play in individual lives, and in the community at large, including the intertwining role individuals' languages have played in their lives and the lives of their children. Interviewees also recounted experiences of mixing languages or of having difficulties remembering parts of one's first language, a process commonly referred to as attrition.[290] The commonality of these experiences after immigration

---

289 Government of Canada. "Census of Canada, 1911." Library and Archives Canada, accessed May 21, 2019, https://www.bac-lac.gc.ca/eng/census/1911/Pages/about-census.aspx. The results were found using the search engine for the 1911 census to find German speakers and combining the numbers for Waterloo North (District 130) and Waterloo South (District 131). Region of Waterloo. "2011 Census Bulletin 6: Language." Region of Waterloo, accessed Oct 9, 2020, https://www.regionofwaterloo.ca/en/resources/Census/2011_Census_Bulletin_6_Language_singles.pdf
290 Michael Clyne, Dynamics of Language Contact (Cambridge: Cambridge University Press, 2003): 208.

has been attested across the globe, including in other German-language communities such as the one in the Czech Republic.[291] We will illustrate and discuss these common experiences in this chapter.

Arriving in a German-language Region

As described by many in the interviews, the German language was, and to some extent still is, alive in Waterloo Region in public spaces, such as churches, stores, and clubs, as well as private spaces such as homes and family gatherings. As we saw in the story told by Alice Bromberg, interviewees may have felt fortunate to arrive in a place in Canada where their language was still widely spoken, enabling their transition to their new home. Comments such as the following by Werner and Alice Bromberg attest to the overall presence of German in the area: "Ja, damals da war viel Deutsch, das war alles Deutsch in Kitchener. Überall wo du hinkamst konn'ste Deutsch sprechen."[292] Astrid Braun also recalled that her mother was able to use German in Waterloo Region. Her mother only started to learn English when she moved from Waterloo Region to Montréal. Astrid said: "My mother did not learn to speak English in Kitchener. Everybody spoke German, especially the people that you'd get to know." Similar experiences with German being used in Kitchener were also mentioned by Dieter Conrad, whose mother did not speak English even after many years in Canada, "weil hier in Kitchener zur damaligen Zeit, ob das jetzt beim Metzger oder beim Bäcker war, die haben alle Deutsch gesprochen."[293] As is often the case in immigrant situations, the presence and use of German was connected to certain activities or places — linguists call them domains.[294] Not surprisingly, the home has remained one of the strongest domains of the use of German. This is hardly exclusive to the German-speaking immigrants in Waterloo Region.[295] The home, where language of the parents is used with the children, is often the strongest bastion of a family's heritage language. Some interviewees like Willi Huber, who has been living in Canada for over fifty years, reported that they still speak German at home and make use of new technologies to tune in to German-language media. Willi also mentioned reading German newspapers, as well as watching the Deutsche Welle TV channel. This situation, however, was different for their children, who through their schooling and socialization were often much more in contact with English than their parents. To keep German as the household language, some parents commented on a policy of only speaking German at home. For example, Brigitte and Tony Bergmeier, who arrived in Canada in 1957, stated that:

---

291 Jiří Václav Neustupný and Jiří Nekvapil, "Language Management in the Czech Republic", Current Issues in Language Planning 4 (2003): 194.

292 Translation: Yes, at that time there was a lot of German, it was all German in Kitchener; everywhere you went you could speak German.

293 Translation: Because here in Kitchener at that time, whether at the butcher or the bakery, they all spoke German.

294 Liebscher and Dailey-O'Cain. Language, Space, and Identity in Migration (Palgrave Macmillan: Basingstoke, 2013): 1

295 Calvin Veltman, Language Shift in the United States (Berlin: Mouton Publishers, 1983).

> "Wir sind ein deutscher Haushalt. Das haben wir beibehalten. Unsere
> Kinder, die durften nur Deutsch sprechen im Haus. Und draußen
> natürlich haben sie dann Englisch gesprochen."[296]

This kind of arrangement was not uncommon among immigrants and their families, making the home a domain where German is spoken, and public spaces an English-dominant domain. This separation, however, was not always so clear cut, and mixing languages did indeed occur, as discussed further below.

Being a community with a strong German presence, the German language was, of course, not only restricted to the home, but also present in other parts of daily life in Waterloo Region. The church was one such location where the German language remained strong for many decades. Indeed, despite their ability to speak English, German was still preferred as the language of worship by many of the families during the latter half of the 20th century, as was the case for Heiderose Brandt-Butscher who recalled: "The church was in German. It had English service as well, but we chose to go to the German service." Churches where German was spoken also served as one of the providers of language education in the community, where some of the children of the immigrants learned German. The Bethel Evangelical Lutheran Church in Kitchener was one such church, where, as Gerald Drews recalled, services, confirmations, and school were all held in German. Gerald Drews described it as an "integrated German-language school with confirmation," where students learned the language while receiving religious education leading up to the confirmation ceremony in Grade eight, which was held in German as well. The school met every Saturday, and Gerald Drews started attending it from Grade one or two. The Bethel Evangelical Lutheran Church continues to hold weekly services in German on Sundays following the English-language service, and while other churches have since discontinued their services in German, some continue to offer Sunday services and Bible study in German, such as the Gospel Church in Waterloo and Pilgrim Evangelical Lutheran Church in Kitchener. The role of German schooling, however, has continued until today through the so-called Saturday School, the Concordia German Language School, which was attended by many of the participants in the Oral History Project, as well as by their children and grandchildren.

Learning English

Despite the strong presence of German in the region, learning English was still very much a necessary step for German-speaking immigrants, especially if they wanted to succeed in a profession. For example, Kurt Boese, who arrived in 1952, felt that not knowing English made him an "Ausländer...Man konnte die Sprache nicht. Und bis ich mal genug Englisch sprechen konnte, dann hab ich Geld verdient."[297] Many arrived with little knowledge of English, instead speaking standard German or a

---

296 Translation: We are a German household. We have kept that up. Our children were only allowed to speak German in the house. And outside, they spoke English, of course.
297 Translation: A foreigner: You couldn't speak the language. And only after I could speak enough English, I earned money.

German dialect, but also other languages like Hungarian, Serbo-Croatian, and Polish, depending on where they had lived. Stories of experiences with English include those of learning the new language in the first months after arrival. For some who migrated as adults this meant attending evening schools, such as Minnie and Kurt Boese, but for those who arrived as children, English was acquired through their schooling and interactions with English speakers. Depending on their age, this may have taken different forms. Those who arrived quite young reported very few difficulties with learning English, acquiring it much as children learn their mother tongue.

While some interviewees arrived in Canada with little or no knowledge of English, others had some previous experience with English in their education. Tony Bergmeier, for example, described the English he came with when arriving in Canada as "Schulenglisch"[298] and called it a "bisschen erbärmlich, aber man konnte sich verständigen."[299] Others echoed a similar opinion about the English they had learned in school prior to leaving for Canada. This English was far from fluent, but nevertheless provided newcomers with a good foundation upon their arrival in Canada. For others, such as Heiderose Brandt-Butscher, English was learned through free English courses offered to new Canadians at the local high schools.

For those children who were somewhat older when they arrived, the path to learning was still remembered as being relatively painless, though, of course, filled with its own challenges, and sometimes amusing moments. Bernd Brandt, who came to Canada in the 1950s as a teenager, recalled arriving in Canada without speaking any English. Since he arrived close to the end of the school year in May, his family did not register him for school for that year and hence, he didn't learn any English in the first few months. He went on to describe how his teacher helped him with the transition when he started school in the fall: "I didn't know much English but…we had a very good teacher. …He was a very understanding fellow. He allowed me to do my work in German." Bernd recalled an amusing moment in a Canadian-history class when he wrote his report about Champlain's explorations around Lake Ontario in German and "because it was long enough, they felt that I knew. So, I got a pretty good mark." Bernd Brandt told another curious incident describing how he was made to represent his seventh grade at a spelling bee within his first year of schooling in Canada, but he didn't get one word right in the school-wide final contest which was broadcast over the school's public announcement system. Within three months, he was able to go from speaking practically no English to being fluent through his immersion in school, and this was indeed the case for many young immigrants. For some, however, this process was not easy to describe. For example, John Heffner only remembered that he went to kindergarten where "he got a rudimentary understanding of the language and then it just kind of developed from that point forward."

Astrid Braun, who also arrived in Canada in her early teens, had a slightly different experience in learning English in school; she was briefly held back to

298 Translation: The kind of English learned in school in Germany.
299 Translation: A little pitiful but one could make oneself understood.

improve her English and was to join her same-aged classmates later. In recounting this experience she said:

> "So there I was at twelve years old in Grade two. I could just pick up the English. So that first year I did [grades] two, four, and five in one year."

Under the current curriculum in Ontario schools for English as a second language education, this would not have occurred since students today are placed in a classroom at the grade level appropriate for their age and receive English-language support, throughout the day and across all subject areas, from the classroom teacher and/or the ESL/ELD teacher.[300]

One particularly interesting and unique example of learning English was recalled by Gerald Drews. While his mother did not speak English prior to arriving in Canada, his father had learned some English while in a prisoner-of-war camp in Colorado. When the family came to Canada, his father mostly spoke English with him rather than the Low German spoken in the area of present-day Poland where they came from, and his father had explicitly told him "he wanted to practise his English through his kids."

The ease of learning English is often attributed by the immigrants to the immersion situation in which they found themselves. Some also reported on the close linguistic relationship between German and English, though this West Germanic connection was viewed slightly differently by immigrants depending on the type of German they spoke. Minnie Boese, for example, stated that English was easier for her, since she speaks Hochdeutsch, or Standard German. Her husband, Kurt Boese, made a case for speakers of Low German having a definitive advantage in learning English, and he provided an example: "das ist die Tür auf Hochdeutsch…de Döör in Low German. In English [it] is a door."[301]

Mixing Languages

It is common for speakers of more than one language to mix languages when they talk.[302] The reasons for these mixes or code-switches from one language into another are manifold. They may include adjusting to different conversational partners who may not speak the language currently used or giving additional meaning to parts of one's speech (e.g., marking a quote or a summary). Peter Auer calls these code-switches "participant-related" and "discourse-related," respectively.[303] Examples of mixing show that multilingual speakers simply draw on their different language

---

300 Ministry of Education. "English as a Second Language and English Literacy Development: A Resource Guide." (Government of Ontario, 2001). accessed May 21, 2019, http://www.edu.gov.on.ca/eng/document/curricul/esl18.pdf
301 Translation: That is die Tür in Standard German…the Döör in Low German. In English it is door.
302 Peter Auer, "Bilingual Conversation Revisited", in Code-switching in Conversation: Language, Interaction, and Identity. ed. Peter Auer (New York; London: Routledge, 1998): 1-24.
303 Auer, "Bilingual Conversation Revisited", 8.

resources. A typical example of mixing occurred in the interview with Kurt Boese who inserts the English "pronounced" instead of the German ausgesprochen into his German speech: "in Englisch viele Sachen werden ja nur anders pronounced."[304] This mixing of English and German was described by many interviewees, including Franz-Josef Burgund, who states that what they spoke at home was "Kauderwelsch, einmal Englisch einmal Deutsch."[305] While Kauderwelsch is a common everyday German word meaning language use that is non-standard, such as mixing German and English, it is often not meant positively. A similar word for this phenomenon would be Denglisch (Deutsch + Englisch), which is a portmanteau like Franglais (français + anglais), a word heard often in Canada. However, mixing generally occurs with some degree of regularity,[306] and it is a functionally specific resource of a multilingual speaker. Several different reasons have been identified for this kind of mixing, from drawing attention to a particular part of the conversation (e.g., quoted speech) to speaker preference that is often due to changes in the living environment due to immigration, as in Kurt Boese's example above. Other interviewees recounted the reasons for this mixing as a result of contact between the two languages. For example, due to the presence of the English-language work environment in most of the immigrants' lives, some German words found themselves replaced by an English counterpart even at home, as Franz-Josef Burgund described: "Da gebraucht man die Ausdrücke, die man im Beruf gebraucht."[307] His wife, Theresia Burgund, recalled a funny incident, in which visitors from Germany started to adopt the mixed language at their Canadian home, using garbage can instead of the German word for it, Abfalleimer. For the generation who did their education and professional training in Canada, the use of English professional terminology when speaking German is a common phenomenon, such as Kurt Boese who discussed his work for the City of Kitchener: "Die haben [einen] plumbing inspector gebraucht...da war ich chief plumbing inspector." [308] In another example, Michael Eckardt said: "Es gibt technische Situationen, wo mir im Deutschen dann die technischen Worte [fehlen], habe ich nie gelernt."[309] He went on to make reference to one of the machines produced at his work, skid steer vehicles, and while also referring to the machine in German as a Schleifkettenfahrzeug, he stated that skid steer for him was the "real term".

Another common story highlighting this German-English mixing is connected to the interactions between the immigrants and their children. While German was spoken at home, the children growing up in Canada spent much of their time in the English language, whether at school or with their friends. As a result, although the children were able to speak and understand German, they would use more English even at home with their German-speaking parents. Christine Burow described such a

304 Translation: In English, many things are just pronounced differently.
305 Translation: Gibberish, one instance English, another instance German.
306 Clyne, Dynamics of Language Contact. 103-58.
307 Translation: [At home,] one employs the [same] expressions used at work.
308 Translation: They needed a plumbing inspector...there I became the chief plumbing inspector.
309 Translation: There are technical situations, where I don't have the words in German, I never learned them.

situation where her parents, who are both German speakers, would speak German to them at home, and they would respond in English "because our lives as kids — we were immersed in English."

Travel with the family and a connection to German-speaking Europe also has an impact on switching languages. Tony Bergmeier recalled his daughters' readjustment to speaking English after a trip to Germany:

> "Als sie zurückkamen, sprachen sie natürlich nur noch Deutsch mit den anderen. ...Die haben sie bloß dumm angeguckt, bis sie merkten, sie müssen sich wieder umstellen."[310]

These kinds of adjustments and reorientation were certainly not exclusive to the Bergmeier family and are likely a familiar phenomenon for many multilingual individuals.

German-language Education

For many parents, it was important that the German language be passed on to their children, resulting in them searching for ways to give their children German-language education such as German-language school at churches or the German Saturday School, as many still call the Concordia German Language School. One of the early German-language schools was run by Peter Quiring and his wife Magdalena at the St. Mary's Roman Catholic Church in Kitchener, where Peter was the organist. Peter and Magdalena became well known in the community for the private German Language and Music School, which they founded and operated until their retirement in 1983, having taught over 2,500 students over the years. Helene Schramek, Margarete Rowe, Rosina Müehlberghuber, Gerda Wolf, Pauline and Hans Schmidt, Anne Kroisenbrunner, John Heffner, and Katy Pfeiffer talked about their various experiences with the Quirings as their German or music teachers or as their chaperones on trips to Germany and Austria.

The formation of the Concordia German Language School was an important event for the German-speaking community in Waterloo Region. The school itself was formed through the churches, each of which had their own school; this system grew into the Kitchener-Waterloo German School that received its current name, Concordia German Language School, with sponsorship from the Concordia Club in 1971. With the acquisition of his teaching certificate, Peter Wiese became the first principal of this new German school with its founding in 1965, a school which his children also attended. The school became a success in the community and was integrated into the Waterloo County Board of Education in 1973 by the Ontario Ministry of Education.[311] In 1978, only thirteen years after its founding, the school had reached an enrolment of over 800 students.

---

310 Translation: When they returned, they only spoke German with others...[and when] the others merely looked at them uncomprehending, they realized, they had to readjust.
311 Ministry of Education. "English as a Second Language".

Peter Wiese was succeeded in 1970 by Herminio Schmidt, who took on the job after being recommended by his professor of German at Wilfrid Laurier University, and being encouraged by other people, even though he had self-doubts. He said in his interview:

> "I was very grateful that people thought I could do it. It gave me confidence, so I met the former principal and he said…we need a teacher. So, I became a teacher first for a year."

Herminio Schmidt told about the learning curve as a teacher, and the strenuous times for him in this job. Despite a rocky start teaching, Herminio later rose to the challenge of running the school, which at this time only consisted of five teachers and around sixty-five students. In trying to increase the popularity of the school and to bring up enrolment, he organized an advertising campaign with the help of a university student who told him: "you need something special." The result was a photo with a boy and a German Schultüte that appeared in the local paper. The Schultüte, a colourfully decorated paper cone filled with candy and small school utensils, was a particularly clever idea, since it highlighted the German-speaking element of the Saturday School and was a nice teaser for potential students. It turned out that a father of another boy at the school could provide every child at the school with a Schultüte. With some support from a local Zehrs grocery store and the media, the campaign turned out to be a massive success, and enrolment began to soar. Herminio recalled:

> "The kids came with their Schultüte [on their] first day. Instead of sixty-five students, a hundred and fifty students came. …The next year we had four hundred and fifty students. …And [in] the following years we had more than nine hundred students."

Facing Challenges and Keeping the Language

Since German immigrants in the area could often be recognized through their language and culture, they sometimes faced being mocked or denigrated as German, particularly following World War II. This included teasing for cultural aspects, such as wearing Lederhosen or eating German sandwiches, but also teasing about language or accent, and being called something in association with one's German heritage. Monika Hoedl, who completed only Grades one and two in Germany before coming to Canada at a young age, recalled a story from her high school years, when she was in her Grade nine history class discussing World War II. Some of the students called her a Nazi, an experience she found very upsetting and confusing, and she had to ask her father to explain it to her. "I'll never forget it," she said of the incident. These stories present a much less positive aspect of life in Waterloo Region for the German-speaking immigrant; yet as Monika pointed out, these comments were coming from children who likely did not know better. While this does not excuse these prejudices, she believed that the adage that children can be cruel is valid, and if they can find some reason to pick on someone, they will. The expression of these prejudices was not, however, only based on elements of German-speaking cultures, such as wearing Tracht, a traditional costume, or German history, but also sometimes on the language itself, or perhaps more precisely, on the presence of a German accent in English revealing the speaker's language background. Theresia Burgund told of an incident during her time as a substitute teacher in the 1970s, when "antideutsche Gefühle waren schon noch zu spüren."[312] The result of this was that students were calling "Hitler, Hitler, Hitler" behind her back, when she was filling in as a substitute teacher. Michael Eckardt also told of such an encounter and attributed it directly to the presence of a German accent in his English. When dealing with a difficult client who was not paying his bills on time, he was accused of using "Nazitaktiken."[313] "Das hat mich dann doch total tief getroffen. Ich habe nicht gewusst, was ich sagen soll,"[314] he said looking back on the incident, which he believed was the result of the client targeting him for his German accent in English, since his "deutscher Akzent war immer da."[315] Overall, such incidents were few and far between, and stand in contrast to the overall positive experiences the interviewees spoke of regarding their time in Waterloo Region, and the promotion and celebration of their language and culture in the schools, churches, German clubs, and the region in general.

Despite the strength of the German language and culture in Waterloo Region, however, the number of German speakers has diminished over time, which is not dissimilar to other German-speaking communities outside of Germany, e.g., in Australia.[316] As cited at the beginning of this chapter, German speakers in the Waterloo Region amounted to 16,515 people in 2011, less than half of the number a century prior. Yet arguably more significant than the absolute number is the proportion of German speakers relative to both the still-growing population of the region and to the presence of other minority languages. While German remained the second most spoken mother tongue after English in Waterloo according to the national census in 2011, the number is declining, having dropped 12% between 2006 and 2011, while other languages such as Arabic and Chinese are on the rise.[317] This reflects new trends in immigration and the presence of new groups in Waterloo Region. German also, in comparison to languages such as Mandarin, Arabic, Serbo-Croatian, Spanish, and Portuguese, tends to be maintained by the older generation. Consequently, the use of German in the community has receded progressively with each successive generation, despite the efforts of some parents to keep German alive in their family. In addition, while cultural events are still taking place in the community and clubs, they are more often occurring in English.

Herminio Schmidt described this trend, and how it occurred in his family, when asked if he spoke English or German with his children. When the children were

---

312 Translation: Anti-German sentiments could still be felt.
313 Translation: Nazi tactics.
314 Translation: That hurt me very deeply. I didn't know what to say.
315 Translation: His German accent was always there.
316 Clyne, Dynamics of language contact, 20-69.
317 Region of Waterloo. "2011 Census Bulletin 6: Language," accessed May 21, 2019, https://www.regionofwaterloo.ca/en/resources/Census/2011_Census_Bulletin_6_Language_singles.pdf

younger, the Schmidt family spoke German at home, and Herminio said this was no problem until his children were around nine or ten, and then they started to answer back in English instead of German due to living in an English-language environment. He also noticed this in the German school, where sometimes the first child in a family maintained their German, while the second child would still understand everything but had difficulty speaking, and by the third child the German language was generally gone. A similar process often takes place over three generations. This process is known as language shift[318] — in our case a shift from German to English in families and social groups and communities. For example, Calvin Veltman discovered in his research with multilinguals in the United States that the process of language shift in immigrant communities took place over the course of decades, most often over three generations.[319] In his model, the first generation maintains their ancestral language, with the second being able to communicate in both languages, and the third most often having lost most of their heritage language and primarily, or exclusively, using the majority language of their new home. The process of reversing a language shift is an arduous one, and one which has little historical precedent of successful attempts outside of the revitalization of the Hebrew language.[320] Nevertheless, German remains spoken in Waterloo Region in families, German schools and clubs, and universities.

Conclusion

The German language retains an important and active role in the life of many people in Waterloo Region. While it is less often heard these days, one can still come across German at the market, and, of course, at the various German clubs and cultural events. The Concordia German Language School and some high schools offer students the chance to learn the language, something of particular interest to the many residents of the region with German heritage but to others as well. Two local universities — the University of Waterloo and Wilfrid Laurier University — also offer students the opportunity to study the language, where young people of German descent may gravitate towards the language and rediscover their roots. The language has been ever-present in the community, from the first settlements in the early 1800s, to the arrival of the people interviewed for this project, and still to this day.

---

318 Clyne, Dynamics of Language contact, 20-69.
319 Veltman, Language Shift, 213.
320 Joshua Fishman, "Language maintenance, language shift, and reversing language shift" (Oxford: Blackwell, 2006).

Family and Children

Friederike Schlein and Linda Warley

The women and men interviewed in the Oral History Project have narrated part of their life stories both as a gift to others and for themselves. Like other autobiographers, they wish to make sense of their experiences, to put their memories in some meaningful order, and to validate their own sense of where they have come from, and who they are — both in Europe and in the various places they lived before and after they emigrated. However, the interviewees are also motivated by the desire to pass on their memories and stories to others, including subsequent generations in their own families. While it might not be posterity they are looking for, since many of the interviewees think of themselves as ordinary people, these stories tell of difficult circumstances overcome, choices made, and recount how their lives as immigrants to Canada unfolded. The interviewees pass on more than their experiences — they pass on their wisdom. While much of this book has focused on the experiences of the interviewees themselves, in this last chapter we turn our attention to what they have to say about and to their children and grandchildren. Throughout their narratives the interviewees often mention how their identities as German immigrants to Waterloo Region partly shape the identities of the next generations as well. They communicate historical and cultural knowledge, re-tell family stories, maintain traditional practices, and encourage the use of the German language. In the Oral History Project scenario, the semi-structured interviews functioned as a "coaxer,"[321] in that the questions the interviewer asked, and the interjections he or she made, inform the stories told and the answers given. Of particular interest in this chapter is the final interview question. The interviewees were specifically asked if they had some message that they would like to pass on to the next generations. However, there are also other topics that touch on the theme of family and children, to which we draw attention here. These include the following: how parents or young couples expecting children made the journey to Canada; how they were supported by family members in Canada and by Canadian society; the challenges and opportunities that awaited their families in Canada; what elements of German culture and identity they keep alive in the family, and what traditions have been adapted to the new country.

Arriving as a Family

A ship often marked the beginning of a family's journey to a new continent and a new country. Although travelling by airplane became more common in the late 1950s and onwards, thus resulting in the decline of the number of people who emigrated by boat, journeys by ship figure prominently in the oral narratives. This is not surprising given that about eight million emigrants left Europe through the port of Bremerhaven

---

321 Sidonie Smith and Julia Watson. Reading Autobiography: A Guide for Interpreting Life Narratives. 2nd edition. (Minneapolis: U of Minnesota Press, 2010). 64-69.

in Germany between 1832 and 1974.[322] Joe Piller left in December 1950, and he remembered, "I was in Bremerhaven for, I think, fourteen days it was. [At] the time the Beaverbrae was the ship that I came over with." Simone Blaschka-Eick illustrates in her book *In die Neue Welt! Deutsche Auswanderer in drei Jahrhunderten* how emigrants from all over Germany entered a ship full of hope for a better life in the new country, but also feeling trepidation because of the unknown future and possible difficulties they may face: "Und man vertraute auf die gleiche Chance, die Verwandte oder Freunde in Amerika erhalten hatten."[323] Families with small children who boarded the ship were also concerned about the wellbeing of their youngest family members on the long voyage. Blaschka-Eick tells the story of Louise and her little daughter:

> "Man durfte nun an Bord. Panik überfiel Louise: Was, wenn die
> älteste Tochter in die Lücke zwischen Schiff und Kaje ins Wasser
> fiel? Sie war doch noch so klein."[324]

Parents' loving care for their children shone through in the interviews. For example, Minnie and Kurt Boese travelled eleven days by ship, and had their two-year-old daughter Christa with them. Minnie Boese explains: "sie ist schon auf dem Schiff rumgelaufen. Ich musste so aufpassen."[325] Brigitte and Tony Bergmeier were newlywed when they started their sea voyage from Germany to Canada, and they did not yet have children. However, the crossing was turbulent, and Brigitte was quite sick. A steward who took care of the couple told them "Ich bin Familienvater. Sie sind nicht seekrank, Sie sind schwanger."[326] This turned out to be true. Even unborn children could be a worry for parents, particularly mothers.

Having family in Canada already and finding a job were two major reasons for their coming. Influenced by Canadian government incentives, most of them arrived here to build a better life for their families and themselves.[327] In 1956, Brigitte Bergmeier's brother, who had emigrated to Canada in 1950, visited her and her husband Tony in Germany. He convinced them to emigrate to Canada as well and start a new life abroad. At first, Brigitte and Tony remained sceptical about the idea of leaving Germany, because it was not clear whether they would be able to finance the endeavour. Brigitte's brother finally convinced them by explaining the financial support they would receive from the Canadian government if they emigrated to

---

322 "Deutsche Auswanderer-Datenbank", accessed May 21, 2019, https://www.deutsche-auswanderer-datenbank.de/index.php?id=532

323 Simone Blaschka-Eick, In die Neue Welt! Deutsche Auswanderer in drei Jahrhunderten (Reinbek: Rowohlt, 2010), 106. [Translation: And we relied on the same chance that relatives and friends had had in America.]

324 Blaschka-Eick, In die Neue Welt!, 108. [Translation: We were allowed to board the ship. Louise panicked: What would happen if her eldest daughter fell into the water through the gap between the ship and the quay? She was so small.]

325 Translation: She already was running around on the ship. I had to be so careful.

326 Translation: I am a father of a family. You are not seasick, you are pregnant.

327 Schmalz, Ronald E. Former Enemies Come to Canada: Ottawa and the Postwar German Immigration Boom, 1951-1957. (Ottawa: National Library of Canada = Bibliothèque Nationale du Canada, 2001).

Canada. The money they received covered the costs of their sea passage. They were able to pay off their debts after three months, and to build a new home for their family. Brigitte Bergmeier's brother already lived in Waterloo Region and became a first contact person for the couple. Their first child was born in Canada soon after their arrival, followed by their second child a year later. At first, Brigitte and Tony travelled to Canada with the intention of leaving the country again after a one-year stay. But because their family had increased through the birth of their second child, they decided to stay in Canada. They wanted to raise their Canadian-born children in their new home country.

Not all immigrants came as families. Immigrants also often had a desire for adventure. Minnie and Kurt Boese came to Canada in 1952 because Kurt wanted to see the world. Minnie followed him, although at first husband and wife did not want to leave Germany permanently. A distant relative had asked the couple if they wanted to immigrate to Canada, and if Kurt wanted to earn a living as a plumber. The relative promised that he would then bring the Boese family to Canada. Both agreed to leave Germany, but initially they wanted to go abroad only for a limited time. As Minnie remarked, "und weil wir die Welt sehen wollten, haben wir gedacht, ach wir kommen mal gucken."[328] They got an advance payment that was sponsored by the Canadian government, and that they had to pay back as soon as they settled down in Canada.

There are many immigrants who came alone. They often received help from friends rather than family. Hans Kroisenbrunner immigrated in 1957 as an eighteen-year-old young adult. The teenager travelled nine days by ship and was all by himself. When he arrived in Canada, he had one suitcase, twenty-five dollars in his pocket, and a piece of paper with a friend's name on it. After he had finally found his friend Josef Francisc in Barrie, Ontario, Hans Kroisenbrunner got a job on a farm with his friend's help.

Previous family experience in Canada could also be a factor in the decision to emigrate. One of the female interviewees who asked to stay anonymous arrived in Canada by airplane in 1995 with her daughter, who was a baby at the time. Her husband had been born to German parents in Canada and had Canadian citizenship. During his childhood, he and his parents had moved back to Germany. Later, he met his wife there. The young family were encouraged by the husband's older brother who already lived in Toronto and told them that now would be the time to move to Canada.

Family Dynamics

In coming to a new country, families seized opportunities and took on challenges. One such challenge was social isolation. Having left their extended families, friends, and co-workers behind, the immigrants had to establish a new circle of friends and build a social life in Canada. On the other hand, they strove to maintain the German

---

328 Translation: And because we wanted to see the world, we thought let's have a look.

language and specific cultural traditions. Retaining the German language for themselves and for their families was a priority for many. It was also important to establish an environment that supported the children's learning of German — whether the children were willing or not. An interviewee from a farm in a small village in Germany recalled how overwhelmed she was by her first impressions of Canada. She had not been abroad except for a school trip and a four-week language course. So, she was nervous about what she was facing when she arrived in Toronto. She remembered that, when they were driving on towards Square One in Mississauga, she saw all these high rises. She could not see anything but the big high rises and thought "I'm not going to live here. I'm not gonna make it." Suddenly she came to the full realization that she had left behind her extended family, friends, and all that was familiar about her life in rural Germany. The huge responsibility, not only for herself but also for her baby girl, shocked her. She said during the interview: "And all of a sudden you cannot imagine raising these children in a strange world." The young family lived on the sixth floor of a high-rise building. She still vividly recalled the number of people living in a comparatively tight space, when she said, "on every floor there were three times as many people as lived in my little village. On every floor. I counted." She was also afraid of driving in this unfamiliar environment and explained, "I mean, countryside in Germany and then five lanes, six lanes, eight lanes." Years later, when her parents came for a visit, her father admired how she was navigating the lanes on highway 401.

It takes courage to overcome your own fears and take on challenges. Her courage in overcoming such challenges provided her daughter with a strong role model. Even when her daughter was still tiny, she helped her mother along. Her little daughter was the reason she got dressed in the morning and signed up for story time at the library that had a German section. The loneliness and homesickness she faced were the reasons she watched out for a German-speaking person to come and take out a book in the library's German section. During such encounters she had a chance to speak German while her daughter was playing in the children's section.

Coming to a new country and learning English as their second language, the interviewees also strove to maintain their mother tongue in the family. Their goal, right from the start, was to establish an environment that provided their children the opportunity to learn German. Several interviewees mentioned that they found out about the Concordia German Language School; and families moved to Kitchener because of the large German-Canadian community in Waterloo Region. That way, they could raise their children to be bilingual. The interviewee also talked about her wish to support other children who wanted to learn the language. This made her go to Conestoga College to obtain certification to teach German on Saturdays.

Elizabeth Reuss also taught at the Concordia German Language School and took her children along with her for five years. The family spoke German at home when the children were small, but not so much after that. She wanted to ensure that the children would be able to converse with her husband's family in Germany. However, when her daughter went to kindergarten, the family felt that she was behind because her English language skills were not strong enough, and from then on there was more

English spoken in the household. Her daughter Jackie continued to learn German in high school. Elizabeth Reuss remarked that her older son Stephen "is still very good with languages and...he kept his German...the best." Nevertheless, she added, her daughter Jackie "has the more proper German, only she's afraid to make mistakes." Learning German enabled the Canadian children to communicate with their grandparents who lived in Germany. Elizabeth Reuss proudly said that her daughter Jackie still "goes back to visit her Oma (granny) in Germany on her own now or with her little son." And with a wink she added, "I mean she's got to keep it up you know."

John Kreutzer's three daughters all got married and started families of their own. When they were children, they were always encouraged to speak German with their parents at home and they also attended German school. He proudly reported in the interview that today all his daughters use German in their work as a teacher, a nurse, and a travel agent.

On the one hand, families often did everything possible to maintain a German identity and to pass it on to the next generation. On the other hand, keeping up the German language also caused conflicts between parents and children, and even grandchildren. German school started early in the morning on Saturdays and was an additional school day with extra homework on the weekend. Not all children were keen on spending half of the weekend at German school. It got even more complicated when the children became teenagers and young adults, because Saturday school made it less likely for them to go out with friends on Fridays when they would come home late at night. Astrid Braun — with a certain irony in her tone — talked about sending her daughter and son to German school:

> "I ruined their lives by making them go to German school on
> Saturday mornings. ...They sure didn't like going to school on a
> Saturday morning to learn German."

Nevertheless, Astrid proudly added that her daughter and her son are "quite good in German." Astrid recalled that when her granddaughter Kayla was old enough to attend German school, Kayla's mother said: "I am not making her do this." Having the best of intentions for her grandchild and driven by the desire to pass on her mother tongue to Kayla, Astrid decided, "And so for two years I picked her up every Saturday and took her to German school." Kayla never stopped complaining. She was very shy and felt very uncomfortable. After two years, her grandmother finally made a decision: "I've been through this once before. I'm not doing this again." Kayla stopped attending German school. Astrid mused: "We didn't even try with Quinton," her grandson. However, Astrid stated that her grandchildren are good listeners and are able to pick up German very quickly: "you can always learn if you really want to, but...you can't force them to...learn a language."

Passing on Culture and Family History through Stories

Emigrants often leave things behind. They do not come to the new country laden with furniture, clothing, household goods, or books. But what they do come with are stories. German identity, German culture, a particular family history — these can be passed on to the next generation through stories. As Katie Funk Wiebe perceptively remarks in her book *The Store-Keeper's Daughter*: Immigrants have only language by which to pass on what is important to them. The past is gone, often along with family heirlooms and other artefacts. The territory in the new land is new. Immigrants have only memories, a value system, and hope for the future. The only way to pass on the values inherent in their past and to explain the reason for making a break with it is through stories.[329]

Family stories, as well as more general cultural and historical knowledge, are often the trigger, and they can be renewed through return trips by the immigrants to their original homeland. Sometimes returnees take their children with them. Tony Fieder went back to his hometown in Serbia with his wife, daughter, and son-in-law, after they had urged him to go for some time. They all flew to Belgrade and drove to the little village that was his original home. Although Tony did not remember a lot from those early days of his life, he enjoyed finding the church he was baptised in, he met with the priest, and he was able to look at his birth and baptismal certificates. Seeing the house his parents had owned helped him to resurrect memories of his distant past and enabled him to pass these memories on to those accompanying him.

Another travel story was that of John Kreutzer who went to Germany, Romania, and Italy together with his middle daughter Krista and her husband. John experienced Germany as "very busy," with "a lot of people compared to here [in Canada]" and he concluded, "but the time we spent there was very nice."

Pauline Schmidt specifically spoke of her grandchildren while passing on her family story. Pauline was born and raised in Yugoslavia. She remembered how she and her cousin tried very hard to find something to eat, when she, her two-year-old sister, her mother, and her cousin were imprisoned in three different camps over two years after 1945. Two of the camps were called Jabuka and Rudolfsgnad (today Knićanin); the latter was remembered by Pauline particularly because of its cruelty and size. When they were able to find a handful of seeds in the attic, they ground them in a pig's trough, added some water, and baked little breads to appease their hunger for a while. Pauline revealed that she still has some of these seeds tied to a frame of a family picture. She showed the family picture as well as the symbolic seeds during the interview and said: "Das hab ich dahin getan. Das ist von denen der Samen, dass ich es den Enkelkindern zeigen kann, wie klein der Samen ist."[330] The seeds can be seen as a symbol of the pain and deprivation her family had suffered, but also as a symbol of hope for their future and that of their children and grand-children. All four — Pauline, her sister, mother, and cousin — survived the camps.

Besides stories of extreme hardship, German cultural traditions are also an important legacy imparted to the next generation. Many interviewees talked in detail about how they passed on their German Christmas traditions and customs to their

---

329 Katie Funk Wiebe, The Storekeeper's Daughter: A Memoir (Scottdale: Herald, 1997), p. 10.
330 Translation: I put it there. These are some remnants of the seeds. I have kept them so that I am able to show the grandchildren how small these seeds are.

children. Minnie and Kurt Boese celebrated Christmas on Christmas Eve, "am heiligen Abend." The children received their presents under the Christmas tree after they had recited poems by heart. The Boese family sang Christmas songs, experienced togetherness, and a shared identity through music within their family. Heiderose Brandt-Butscher's children and grandchildren still celebrate both German and Canadian Christmas on the 24th and the 25th of December. Astrid Braun's Christmas takes place on the 24th of December. A real fir tree, candle lights, and lots of tinsel are important to her. She keeps up the German tradition of having an Advent wreath and an Advent calendar. Her own children were always able to enjoy the fun of having an Advent calendar, and she regularly gave one to the children of their Canadian friends as well. Astrid said she has continued to be involved with the Christkindl Market in Kitchener through her twenty years of volunteer work. From her point of view, the next generation should cherish their German traditions, but also respect and embrace other traditions.

To Helga Sarkar Christmas has always been very special.

> "I've always made sure we had a real Christmas tree. We went out into the bush and cut our own tree. The children were little and would come with us, and it had to be just the right tree. And for the first couple of years, we even used real candles [on the tree]."

Helga always baked German Christmas cookies by the end of November and shared them with her family. They liked celebrating Advent, which included lighting four candles, one each for the four Sundays during Advent, and singing songs and reading scripture with their children. Elizabeth Schilling also talked about celebrating Christmas on Christmas Eve and remaining faithful to this German tradition, but she also stressed that celebrating on Christmas Day, the way Canadians celebrate Christmas, is as important to her as the German Christmas. She recognized that it is "sehr schön, dass man beides verbinden kann."[331]

Food is of great significance for the families because the lovingly prepared meals convey memories from one generation to the next. Food is a conveyor of both culture and memory, for stories of the past are often evoked by food (even the smell of food), and stories are often told over meals. For example, traditional German cookie recipes and Sauerkraut und Würstchen[332], one of the traditional German Christmas dinners, have been passed on to the next generation, as in the case of Ingo Schoppel and his children, as well as his grandchildren. Ingo recounted their experience of the family get-together after church service as "a wonderful time…that is a very highly concentrated family occasion." Elizabeth Reuss also talked about eating sausages and sauerkraut with her family on Christmas Eve, not turkey, as is common in other families. Elizabeth Schilling talked about her traditional way of making chicken goulash like her mother used to cook for her back in Hungary. While her daughter and her son-in-law especially enjoy her chicken goulash, her grandchildren love her

---

331 Translation: wonderful that one can combine both.
332 Translation: sauerkraut and sausage.

home-baked Kipferl, a crescent-shaped biscuit. Elizabeth's passion is so strong that she and her cooking club wrote a recipe book, which included some of her own traditional family recipes. Its intended readers include members of future generations.

The German clubs in Waterloo Region — for example the Concordia Club, the Schwaben Club, the Transylvania Club, and the Alpine Club — have played an important role for some interviewees in maintaining as well as passing on German traditions and German culture to the next generation. The clubs offered get-togethers, dance events with music, choirs, and regular group meetings where common interests were shared and familiar German food was eaten, and all with the possibility to speak German with other club members. John Kreutzer explained that the Transylvania Club

"has [still] a very strong youth group base. …I'm happy about that. And it's been strong for many years. Now my grandchildren are starting to get involved with it and they are having a lot of fun with it. …It seems like they develop lifetime friendships in the club."

Nevertheless, some German clubs have difficulties finding young people who want to join, and members struggle to include children and grandchildren in the club's social life. Gerhardt Griebenow was elected into the Vorstand der Arbeitsgemeinschaft der Deutsch-Kanadischen Clubs [333] by the German club presidents. In his interview, he talked about the problems they address: "die Sache mit der alternden Gemeinde, die Sache mit den Chören, die immer kleiner werden und so weiter und so weiter."[334]

Messages to the Next Generation

The interviewees' loving concern for the next generation's wellbeing as well as their desire to share their own intercultural experiences, are two recurring themes in the interviews. This includes sharing the intercultural competence they have acquired over the years, their awareness that different culturally specific communication styles exist, and being able to use this knowledge productively in intercultural encounters.[335] This goes along with the realization that culture is of particular importance in shaping thinking, experience, and action. From the perspective of the interviewees, Canada is experienced multiculturally; people move here from all over the world. This interculturality includes the family goal, voiced by Andre Schilha, that the next generation should learn about other countries and their cultures, to be open towards other people. Multilingualism as a family goal is also valued. Many of the interviewees stressed that the next generation should learn several languages and, as Peter Wiese said, "look at cultures from their own point of view [through the

---

333 Translation: Cooperative Council of German Canadian Clubs.
334 Translation: the issue of the aging community, the issue with the choirs that are getting smaller and so on and so forth
335 Astrid Erll and Marion Gymnich, Interkulturelle Kompetenzen: Erfolgreich kommunizieren zwischen den Kulturen (Stuttgart: Klett, 2013).

language] rather than somebody's pre-digested point of view." Interviewees also appealed to the next generation "die deutsche Sprache der Eltern zu pflegen und nicht zu vergessen."[336] Ursel Wandschneider stressed that speaking German at home with the children and attending German Language School on Saturdays might be a decisive advantage for retaining the German language and offers great advantages in one's working life as well. Waldemar Scholtes expressed his belief that children learning two or more languages and becoming bilingual benefit, "because the exercise of the brain transfers to so many other activities." Isa Schade emphasized that being bilingual is "ein unbezahlbares Gut, was man den Kindern mitgeben kann." This may include different kinds of bilingualism ranging from having a similar and excellent command of the first and the second language to being able to speak the second language to a much lesser extent.[337]

Another important message to the next generation is that they should reflect on their Austrian family background and family history as part of their own identities. Anne and Hans Kroisenbrunner recommended: "man soll seine Vergangenheit schätzen und ehren."[338] Similarly, with respect to family roots, Pauline and Hans Schmidt appealed to the next generation: "du sollst das bleiben, was du bist und verleugne nicht deine Heimat und die Herkunft."[339] Renate and Jörg Stieber noted: "man muss vorwärts schauen und aus der Vergangenheit lernen."[340] Coming to terms with the German past, Paul Schulze described his concerns that people often just focus on the period of World War II when thinking of German history. Therefore, he asked the next generation "to get the whole picture and look at all of history."

Passing on their German background in the form of cultural activities is relevant to most of the interviewees. For example, Steve Schatz encouraged his children to participate in musical and theatrical activities in the German-Canadian community. German traditions and knowledge about them were described as of value by Andrea and Holger von Weyhe. They asserted that cultural exchange and a relationship with Germany and other German-speaking countries should be maintained. Reinhold Schuster clearly affirmed that the next generation should "hang on to their cultural background as long as they can." Elizabeth Reuss stated: "don't be afraid to be proud of your culture and to open up about it."

Life advice for the next generation, as well as different values and beliefs, can be found in the interviews. One strong message is that it takes endurance and courage to succeed in life. For Helene Schramek, this means "stand up for yourself, and basically really anything is possible." Children should follow their interests and do what they really enjoy doing, for example turning their hobbies into their professions, said Almut and Wolfgang Wurzbacher. Gisela Steckel encouraged everyone to "go and look and try and that's the only way to find what you really like." Nelly Kilianski

---

336 Translation: To foster the German language of their parents and not to forget it.
337 Dietmar Rösler, Deutsch als Fremdsprache: Eine Einführung (Stuttgart: Metzler, 2012).
338 Translation: One needs to value and honour one's past.
339 Translation: You need to stay who you are and don't deny where you come from nor your background.
340 Translation: One must look forward and learn from the past.

advised: "never give up." In case someone does not reach their goals, children should not think of themselves as having failed, but rather realize the potential to learn from mistakes and emerge strengthened from a crisis, argued Herminio Schmidt. Flexibility in adjusting to situations is another piece of advice shared with the next generation. Marga Weigel mentioned in her interview that it is important "to be flexible and to roll with it."

The interviewees expressed their thoughts and feelings by sharing them with the next generation in different ways. They all have in common that they provided their advice with passion and empathy. Helga Sarkar asked for respect when she stated:

> "We have worked hard and prepared the way for our children and
> our grandchildren. A legacy that needs to be respected."

Hendrik Walther concluded that, if someone follows their dreams and wants to immigrate to Canada, they should try to do so, because they will be welcomed in Canada with openness and friendliness.

This chapter has focused on the lives of families and children. The interviewees often talked about their children and grandchildren. They explained how their identities as German immigrants to Waterloo Region partly shape the identities of the next generation as well. We also noted how the family life was shaped by overcoming challenges and seizing opportunities. Stories play an immense role in passing on German identity, culture, and family history to children and grandchildren. Some interviewees included a diary, a journal, or a book to which they referred during the interview, and they stressed how important it is for them to pass on their experience and family history to the next generation.

Helen Neumayer was the oldest interviewee in the Oral History Project wearing a sweater with a heart on its front during the interview, which included all the names of her children and grandchildren. The 94-year-old lady held on to her diary for the first twenty minutes of her interview, to remember every single detail of her often traumatic experience. Since 1944, she has been trying to overcome her memories of World War II and of leaving behind her hometown in the Batschka in Yugoslavia. She survived the physical hard work in a labour camp while witnessing inhumane suffering. Her story needed to be told and meant so much to her because she wanted to let it go as soon as she was able to pass on her experience to the next generation. She was not afraid anymore of all the horror she had to face in her life. Helen Neumayer passed away in 2015.

Hans Schmidt handed over a copy of his self-published book *The Lost Homeland* after the interview had come to an end.[341] Both Pauline and Hans Schmidt were in tears at the end of their interview because so many valuable but also sad memories were brought to light. Both also talked about their children and grandchildren with pride and deep affection.

---

341 John (Hans) Schmidt, The Lost Homeland [Die verlorene Heimat] (2002). Waterloo: Self-published.

The interviewees' strong attachment to their children and grandchildren were a key part in their autobiographical narratives. Often it was not easy for interviewees to share their painful memories with an interviewer sitting opposite them whom they did not know. However, passing on their wisdom and experience to the next generation, to their loved ones, was a strong motive for remembering past challenges as well as happy and sad memories of their lives. It took courage to face old memories, reveal them, and make them accessible to the public. Above all, the interviewees' courage deserves respect and recognition for their strong commitment and openness in support of the Oral History Project.

Looking Ahead

Elizabeth Milne and Mathias Schulze

There is a novel written by Cecelia Ahern, *One Hundred Names*,[342] that tells the story of a journalist being given a list of names, which unknown to her were picked randomly from a telephone book. In searching for and interviewing these people, the novel's protagonist realizes that every person has a life story or an episode of their life that is of interest to others. Everybody has a story worth sharing and worthy to be heard. The interviewers, transcribers, and authors of this book can readily support Cecilia Ahern's hypothesis. We were more fortunate than the journalist in the novel. Our interviewees came to us and generously provided a unique perspective on what Generalkonsul Walter Stechel in the preface called the German-Canadian "transnational belonging." The stories brought laughter and tears, moments of quiet reflection and the recognition of shared experiences to the tellers and the listeners. We heard about the joys and pains of leaving a Heimat and establishing a new home in a different country. We heard about adventures, at once exciting and frightening and about losses and gains. We were entrusted with a wealth of recollections, personal histories, and compelling glimpses into history and cultures from more than one hundred different perspectives.

We estimate that the 124 interview hours have resulted in about one million words in the transcripts. Unfortunately, not everything everybody said could be included in this book. Many of the very interesting stories the interviewees told us could not be retold due to lack of space. However, this book was not created to only recount individual stories. Rather, the authors and editors of this book were tasked with looking for and presenting the themes and patterns within these stories to give readers a glimpse of what it meant and means to be a German-speaking immigrant to Canada. We have attempted, as Katy Funk Wiebe suggested in her memoir, to pass on the values of our storytellers, and provide them the opportunity to give voice to their memories and their hope for the future.[343]

In describing their migration stories, we noticed our storytellers shared virtues of perseverance, optimism, and bravery. Not surprisingly, these traits were often mentioned in response to the final interview question asking for a message they would like to pass on to you, the readers. The value of using your experiences to foster personal growth came up often. Michael Heitmann told us that even though it can be tiring, it feels good when you know that you are learning; "it's the best feeling in the world." His philosophy is that through learning, you become a better person.

---

342 Cecelia Ahern, One Hundred Names (HarperCollins Publishers, 2012).
343 Katie Funk Wiebe, The Storekeeper's Daughter: A Memoir (Scottdale: Herald Press, 1997).

According to Alex Müntz, "Versuch neue Leute, neue Länder, neue Kulturen zu erleben, weil — das erweitert deinen Horizont."[344]

Immigrants can find themselves in an uncomfortable position and are often required to make hard decisions. It is no surprise that many of our interviewees had pragmatic, practical, and down-to-earth advice to pass on. "Get education first of all," is what Brigitte and Karl Schmidt emphasized followed quickly with the admonition to pay attention to "Gesundheit, denn die hat man nur einmal."[345] Waldemar Scholtes was even more specific about education and health: "Learn as many languages as you can and study lots of music because the exercise of the brain transfers to so many other activities."

The interviewees also gave tips on how you might best want to approach living as a newcomer within Canada or any place new to you. As well as being able to laugh at your circumstances, Johann Wolf advises, "be slow to anger and be very forgiving." Michael Heitmann adds, "Be accepting and non-judgemental." Alex Müntz used a metaphor to explain the immigrant experience:

> "…landing in a new culture can feel like jumping into cold water;
> the shock can be great, but as you move around, you become
> warmer, and you can start to swim. Within five years you are
> swimming well."

While the past is not forgotten, our interviewees tend to live very future-focussed lives. Manfred Conrad was explicit about this when he said, "I can't change history…but I certainly can make an impact on the future." Peter Wiese talks about learning languages with the goal of moving out into and becoming a citizen of the world, "because then you can live life to the fullest."

One aim of this project was to make sure that the collective past of German-speaking immigrants to Waterloo Region was not forgotten. We have hundreds of hours of recordings and pages of transcripts to show for our work in preserving the past. We will continue to work with the interview transcripts. Now that they have served as a very useful base for the research by the authors of this book, we will carefully redact each transcript to protect the personal information of our interviewees and them compile them into an archive — linguists call this a text corpus — that will be made available to researchers in linguistics, (oral) history, and cultural studies in the future.

While *Germans of Waterloo Region* may be completed, the work of documenting, researching, and reflecting on the history, culture, and language of German-speaking immigrants to Canada continues to provide new insights.

---

344 Translation: Try to experience new people, new countries, new cultures because this will expand your horizon.
345 Translation: Health, because you only get that once.

Bibliography

Printed Materials

Ahern, Cecelia. *One Hundred Names*. HarperCollins Publishers, 2012.

Alcock, Antony. *A History of the Protection of Regional Cultural Minorities in Europe: From the Edict of Nantes to the Present Day*. London: Macmillan Press, 2000.

Antonsich, Marco, "Searching for Belonging — An Analytical Framework." *Geography Compass* 4, no. 6 (June 1, 2010): 644 – 659. doi:10.1111/j.1749-8198.2009.00317.x.

Auer, Peter. "Bilingual Conversation Revisited." In *Code-switching in Conversation: Language, Interaction, and Identity*, edited by Peter Auer. New York, London: Routledge, 1998.

Ballantyne, Neil. *Century Celebration: 1912-2012: Kitchener Marks 100 Years as a City*. Kitchener: Metroland Media Group, 2012.

Bauder, Harald & John Shields (eds.), *Immigrant Experiences in North America. Understanding Settlement and Integration*. Toronto: Canadian Scholars' Press Inc, 2015.

Bauman, Zygmunt. *Identity*. Cambridge: Polity Press, 2004.

Berglund, Sten, and Frank H. Aarebot. *The Political History of Eastern Europe in the 20th Century: The Struggle Between Democracy and Dictatorship*. Lyme: Edward Elgar Publishing Inc., 1997.

Blaschka-Eick, Simone. *In die Neue Welt! Deutsche Auswanderer in drei Jahrhunderten*. Reinbek: Rowohlt, 2010.

Bundesministerium für Vertriebene, Flüchtlinge und Kriegsgeschädigte. *Das Schicksal der Deutschen in Jugoslawien*. Vol. 5. 5 vols. Dokumentation der Vertreibung der Deutschen aus Ost-Mitteleuropa. Düsseldorf: Oskar Leiner-Druck K.G., 1961.

Canadian history: A Reader's Guide. Toronto: University of Toronto Press, 1994. 2 vols. (Vol. 1: *Beginnings to Confederation*. M. Brook Taylor, ed.; Vol. 2: *Confederation to the Present*. Doug Owram, ed.)

Castro, Vanessa Smith. *Acculturation and Psychological Adaptation*. London: Greenwood Press, 2003.

Clyne, Michael. *Dynamics of Language Contact*. Cambridge: Cambridge University Press, 2003.

Danziger, Kurt. *The Socialization of Immigrant Children Part I*. Toronto: York University, 1971.

Dovidio, John F., ed. *The SAGE Handbook of Prejudice, Stereotyping and Discrimination*. London: SAGE, 2010.

Dowling, William. *Ricoeur on Time and Narrative*. Notre Dame: University of Notre Dame Press, 2011.

Dyck, Cornelius, J. *An Introduction to Mennonite History*. Kitchener-Waterloo: Herald Press, 1993.

Engelmann, Nikolaus. *Heimatbuch der deutschen Gemeinde Schöndorf*. Vöcklabruck: Kroiss & Bichler GmbH, 1989.

English, John and Kenneth McLaughlin. *Kitchener. An illustrated History*. Waterloo: Wilfrid Laurier University Press, 1983.

Epp, M., "Pioneers, refugees, exiles, and transnationals: Gendering diaspora in an ethnoreligious context." *Journal of the Canadian Historical Association*, 12 (2001): 137-153.

Erll, Astrid and Marion Gymnich. *Interkulturelle Kompetenzen: Erfolgreich kommunizieren zwischen den Kulturen.* Stuttgart: Klett, 2013.

Fishman, *Joshua. Language maintenance, language shift, and reversing language shift.* Oxford: Blackwell, 2006.

Fitzgerald, David Scott. "The Sociology of International Migration." In *Migration Theory. Talking Across Disciplines*, edited by Caroline B. Brettell and James F. Hollifield 3rd Ed., New York, London: Routledge, 2015: 115 –147.

Frisse, Ulrich. "Berlin, Ontario, 1800-1916: Historische Identitäten von "Kanadas Deutscher Hauptstadt": *Ein Beitrag zur deutsch-kanadischen Migrations-, Akkulturations- und Perzeptionsgeschichte des 19. und frühen 20. Jahrhunderts*, Wissenschaftliche Reihe, Geschichte Forschungen zur Geschichte Nordamerikas. New Dundee: Trans-Atlantic Publishing, 2003: 39.

Funk Wiebe, Katie. *The Storekeeper's Daughter: A Memoir.* Scottsdale Arizona: Herald Press, 1997.

Goerzen, Jakob Warkentin. "Low German in Canada: A Study of Plautdietsch.*"* Unpublished PhD diss., University of Toronto.

Goethe, Johann Wolfgang von: Faust. Der Tragödie Zweiter Teil. 5. Akt, Bergschluchten, Chor seliger Knaben.

Grigaitis, Danuta. *To Whom It May Concern: Poetry and Autobiography in 2 Parts.* Kitchener: Danuta Grigaitis, 2010.

Hayes, Geoffrey. *Waterloo County: An Illustrated History.* Kitchener: Waterloo Historical Society, 1997: 3.

Hayes, Paul, ed., *Themes in Modern European History, 1890-1945.* London; New York: Routledge, 1992.

Hedetoft, Ulf and Hjort, Mette. *The Postnational Self.* Minneapolis: University of Minnesota Press, 2002.

Hedges, K.L. *"Plautdietsch" and "Huuchdietsch" in Chihuahua: Language literacy and identity among the Old Colony Mennonites in Northern Mexico.* (Unpublished Ph.D. diss.) New Haven: Yale University, 1996.

Heffner, John, and Frisse, Ulrich. *From Hungary to Canada: The Building of My Dream.* Kitchener: Transatlantic Publishing, 2009.

Heidegger, Martin. *Being and Time.* New York: State University of New York Press, 1996.

Held, Joseph. *The Columbia History of Eastern Europe in the Twentieth Century.* New York, Oxford: Columbia University Press, 1992.

Helling, Rudolf A., and Bernd Hamm. *A Socio-Economic History of German-Canadians: They, Too, Founded Canada: A Research Report.* Vierteljahrschrift für Sozial- und Wirtschaftsgeschichte: Beihefte; Nr. 75. Wiesbaden: F. Steiner, 1984.

Hoerder, Dirk. *Geschichte der deutschen Migration vom Mittelalter bis heute.* München: C.H. Beck oHG, 2010.

Hughes, James L. *Canadian History.* Toronto: W.J. Gage, 1881.

Hutfluss, Michael. *Familienbuch Ridjica: Batschka 1804-1943.* Vol. B 475. Schriftenreihe zur donauschwäbischen Herkunftsforschung 155. Plaidt: Cardamina Verlag Susanne Breuel, 2010.

Kampen Robinson, Christine. "Contesting the centre: Low German-speaking Mennonite identity, language, and literacy constructions." Unpublished Ph.D. diss., University of Waterloo, 2017.

Keiner, Stefan. *Gara: Beiträge zur Geschichte einer überwiegend deutschen Grenzgemeinde in der Nordbatschka/Ungarn*. Langenau: Honold GmbH, 1991.

Knoll, Paul W. "The Most Unique Crusader State: The Teutonic Order in the Development of the Political Culture of NorthEastern Europe during the Middle Ages." In *The Germans and the East*, edited by Charles W. Ingrao and Franz A.J. Szabo, 37-48. West Lafayette: Purdue University Press, 2008.

Knowles, Valerie. *Strangers at our Gates: Canadian immigration and immigration policy*. Toronto: Dundurn, 2007.

Koch-Kraft, Andrea. *Deutsche in Kanada – Einwanderung und Adaption: Mit einer Untersuchung zur Situation der Nachkriegsimmigration in Edmonton, Alberta. – Kanada-Studien.* Bd. 7. Bochum: Universitätsverlag Dr. N. Brockmeyer, 1990.

Krahn, Cornelius and H. Leonard Sawatzky. "Old Colony Mennonites." Global Anabaptist Mennonite Encyclopedia Online. 1990. Accessed February 16, 2016, https://gameo.org/index.php?title=Old_Colony_Mennonites&oldid=113570

Krumpholz, Johann, Judy Otto, and Thomas Willand. "Siedlungsgebiete." Kolut in der Batschka. Accessed August 14, 2015, https://kolut.wordpress.com/siedlungsgebiete/

Lavric, Eva, and Carmen Konzett, eds. *Food and Language =: Sprache Und Essen*. InnTrans, Bd. 2. Frankfurt am Main: P. Lang, 2009.

Levitt, Peggy. "Transnational Migration: Taking Stock and Future Directions." *Global Networks* 1, no. 3 (July 1, 2001): 195 – 216. doi:10.1111/1471-0374.00013.

Levitt, Peggy, and B. Nadya Jaworsky. "Transnational Migration Studies: Past Developments and Future Trends." *Annual Review of Sociology* 33, no. 1 (July 18, 2007): 129 – 156. doi:10.1146/annurev.soc.33.040406.131816.

Liebscher and Dailey-O'Cain. *Language, Space, and Identity in Migration* (Palgrave Macmillan: Basingstoke, 2013).

Loewen, R. "The poetics of peoplehood: Mennonite ethnicity and Mennonite faith in Canada." In *Christianity and ethnicity in Canada,* edited by P. Bramadat & D. Seljak. Oxford: Oxford University Press, 2008.

Loewen, R. *Village among nations: "Canadian" Mennonites in a Transnational World, 1916-2006*. Toronto: University of Toronto Press, 2013.

Lovasz, Bastian Bryan. "Animosity, Ambivalence and Co-Operation Manifestations of Heterogeneous German Identities in the Kitchener-Waterloo Area during and after the Second World War." Library and Archives Canada = Bibliothèque et Archives Canada, 2010.

Marcus, Lucy P. "The Carpathian Germans." In *German Minorities in Europe: Ethnic Identity and Cultural Belonging,* edited by Stefan Wolff, 97-108. New York: Berghahn Books, 2000.

Mazeika, Raisa. "An Amicable Enmity: Some Peculiarities in Teutonic-Balt Relations in the Chronicles of the Baltic Crusades." In *The Germans and the East*, edited by Charles W. Ingrao and Franz A.J. Szabo 49-58. West Lafayette, Indiana: Purdue University Press, 2008.

Merten, Ulrich. *Forgotten Voices: The Expulsion of the Germans from Eastern Europe after World War II*. New Brunswick, New Jersey: Transaction Publishers, 2012.

Millet, F.D. "From the Black Forest to the Black Sea." *Harper's New Monthly Magazine*, December 1891.

Moelleken, W.W. "The Development of the Linguistic Repertoire of the Mennonites from Russia." In *Diachronic Studies on the Languages of the Anabaptists*, edited by K. Burridge, W. Enninger 64-93. Bochum: Universitätsverlag Dr. N. Brockmeyer, 1992.

Morson, Gary S. "The Chronotope of Humanness: Bakhtin and Dostoevsky." In *Bakhtin's Theory of the Literary Chronotope*, edited by Nele Bemong and Pieter Borghart. Gent: Academia Press, 2000.

Neustupný, J.V. and Jiří Nekvapil, "Language Management in the Czech Republic", *Current Issues in Language Planning* 4 (2003): 194.

O'Connor, Kevin C. *The History of the Baltic States*. Second Edition. Santa Barbara, California: ABC-CLIO, 2015.

Paetkau, H. "Separation or Integration? The Russian Mennonite Immigrant Community in Ontario, 1924-1945." Unpublished Ph.D. diss., University of Western Ontario, 1986.

Pearce, W. Barnett and Kang, Kyung-Wha. "Conceptual Migrations: Understanding 'Travelers Tales' for Cross-Cultural Adaptation." In *Cross-Cultural Adaptation: Current Approaches*, edited by Kim Gudykunst, 20-41. Los Angeles: Sage Publications, 1988.

Penner, Nikolai. "The High German of Russian Mennonites in Ontario." Unpublished Ph.D. diss., University of Waterloo, 2009.

Plakans, Andrejs. *A Concise History of the Baltic States*. New York: Cambridge University Press, 2011.

Plötzl, Norbert F. and Klaus Wiegrefe. "Die Heimkehr des Krieges." *Der Spiegel*, no.5 (2005): 50-61. Accessed October 12, 2015, https://www.spiegel.de/spiegel/print/d-39178608.html

Primoratz, Igor, and Aleksandar Pavković. *Patriotism Philosophical and Political Perspectives*. Aldershot; Burlington: Ashgate, 2007. https://www.worldcat.org/title/patriotism-philosophical-and-political-perspectives/oclc/230703428

Randi Marselis, "Migrant Life Stories and the Web: The Experience of Having Your Life Story Made Public", *Social Semiotics* 23, no. 3 (2013): 268, doi:10.1080/10350330.2012.738995.

Ricoeur, Paul. *Time and Narrative*. Chicago: The University of Chicago Press, 1985.

Rilke, Rainer Maria. *Es gibt nur – die Liebe*. Compiled by Ulrich Baer. Frankfurt: Insel Verlag, 2006.

Rösler, Dietmar. *Deutsch als Fremdsprache: Eine Einführung*. Stuttgart: Metzler, 2012.

Rowell, Marg. *Welcome to Waterloo: An Illustrated History of Waterloo Ontario in Celebration of Its 125th Anniversary 1857-1982*, 1st ed., Waterloo: Waterloo Printing Co, 1982: 8.

Swiggum, S. & M. Kohli, "The Shiplist", last modified June 22, 2013, https://www.theshipslist.com/ships/descriptions/ShipsB.shtml#beav

Samuel, Richard H. and Thomas Richard Hinton. *Education and Society in Modern Germany*. The Sociology of Education, in 28 volumes; 7. London: Routledge, 1998.

Sauer, Angelika E. "A Matter of Domestic Policy? Canada changed its Immigration Policy and the Admission of Germans, 1945-50." *Canadian Historical Review* 74, no. 2, 1993, 226–263.

Schmalz, Ronald E. *Former Enemies Come to Canada: Ottawa and the Postwar German Immigration Boom, 1951-1957*. Ottawa: National Library of Canada = Bibliothèque Nationale Du Canada, 2001.

Schmalz, Ronald. "Former Enemies Come to Canada: Ottawa and the Post-War German Immigration Boom, 1951-57." Unpublished Ph.D. diss., University of Ottawa, 2000.

Schroeder, David. "Evangelicals Denigrate Conservatives", *Preservings*, 15, 1999, 47-48.

Schullerus, Adolf. "Verein für Siebenbürgische Landeskunde, Deutsche Akademie der Wissenschaften zu Berlin, Academia Republicii Socialiste Românâ, and Academia Românâ." *Siebenbürgisch-sächsisches Wörterbuch: mit Benützung der Sammlungen Johann Wolffs*. Berlin: W. de Gruyter, 1971.

Sedlar, Jean W. *East Central Europe in the Middle Ages, 1000-1500*. Seattle: University of Washington Press, 1994.

Siemsiatycki, M. "Continuity and change in Canadian immigration policy." In *Immigrant Experiences in North America. Understanding Settlement and Integration,* edited by Harald Bauder & John Shields, 93-117. Toronto: Canadian Scholars' Press Inc., 2015.

Smith, C.H. *Smith's Story of the Mennonites* 5th ed., Newton: Faith and Life Press, 1981.

Smith, Sidonie and Julia Watson. *Reading Autobiography: A Guide to Interpreting Life Narratives* 2nd ed., Minneapolis: U of Minnesota P, 2010.

Stead, Robert J.C. "Canada's Immigration Policy", *Annals of the American Academy of Political and Social Science* 107 (May 1, 1923): 59.

Steiner, Sam. *In Search of Promised Lands: A Religious History of Mennonites in Ontario*. Kitchener-Waterloo: Herald Press, 2015.

Stenger Frey, Katherine. *The Danube Swabians: A People with Portable Roots*. Belleville: Mika Publishing Company, 1982.

Sundhaussen, Holm. *Deutsche Geschichte im Osten Europas*. Edited by Günter Schödl. Berlin: Wolf Jobst Siedler Verlag GmbH, 1995.

Suppan, Arnold. "'Germans' in the Habsburg Empire: Language, Imperial Ideology, National Identity, and Assimilation." In *The Germans and the East*, edited by Charles W. Ingrao and Franz A.J. Szabo, 147-190. West Lafayette: Purdue University Press, 2008.

Tschinkel, Walter. *Wörterbuch Der Gottscheer Mundart. Mit Illustr. v. Anni Tschinkel.* Vienna: Verlag der Österreichischen Akademie des Wissens, 1973.

Uttley, W.V. *A History of Kitchener, Ontario.* Waterloo: Wilfrid Laurier University Press, 1975.

Veltman, Calvin. *Language Shift in the United States*. Berlin: Mouton Publishers, 1983.

Wagner, Jonathan. *A History of Migration from Germany to Canada 1850-1939*. Vancouver: UBC Press, 2006.

Werbner, Pnina. "Migration and Culture." In *The Oxford Handbook of the Politics of International Migration*, edited by Marc R. Rosenblum and Daniel J. Tichenor, 215 – 242. Oxford Handbooks. New York: Oxford University Press, 2012.

Yoshikawa, Muneo Jay. "Cross-Cultural Adaptation and Perceptual Development." In *Cross-Cultural Adaptation: Current Approaches*, edited by Kim Gudykunst, 140-149. Los Angeles: Sage Publications, 1988.

Websites

"$20,000 Donation Increases Scope of Oral History Project | Waterloo Centre for German Studies", accessed January 18, 2016, https://uwaterloo.ca/centre-for-german-studies/news/20000-donation-increases-scope-oral-history-project

"About (Kitchener-Waterloo Collegiate & Vocational School)", accessed October 10, 2015, https://kci.wrdsb.ca/about/

"About the Centre", Waterloo Centre for German Studies, accessed December 16, 2015, https://uwaterloo.ca/centre-for-german-studies/about

"Beaverbrae", accessed May 21, 2019, https://www.theshipslist.com/ships/descriptions/ShipsB.shtml#beav

Burkholder, Paul H. and John M. Bender, "Ontario (Canada)", Global Anabaptist Mennonite Encyclopedia Online. 1990. Accessed August 15, 2015, https://gameo.org/index.php?title=Ontario_(Canada)&oldid=114359

Canadian Council for Refugees. "Brief history of Canada's responses to refugees", last modified October 4, 2010, https://ccrweb.ca/sites/ccrweb.ca/files/static-files/canadarefugeeshistory.htm

Citizenship and Immigration Canada Government of Canada. "Forging Our Legacy: Canadian Citizenship and Immigration, 1900-1977 - Archived", last modified July 1, 2006, www.cic.gc.ca/english/resources/publications/legacy/chap-5.asp

"Concordia Club Facts", Concordia Club, accessed December 9, 2015, https://www.concordiaclub.ca/about-the-club/interesting-facts

"Concordia Club History", accessed January 20, 2016, https://www.concordiaclub.ca/index.php?option=com_content&view=article&id=2&Itemid=2

"Deutsche Auswanderer-Datenbank", accessed May 21, 2019, https://www.deutsche-auswanderer-datenbank.de/index.php?id=532

"German Pioneers Day Act, 2000, S.O. 2000, c. 7", accessed May 18, 2019, https://www.ontario.ca/laws/statute/00g07

German-Canadian Business & Professional Association, accessed May 21, 2019, https://www.germancanadianbusiness.com/

"German-Canadian Studies", Waterloo Centre for German Studies, accessed December 17, 2015, https://uwaterloo.ca/centre-for-german-studies/research-activities/wcgs-research-groups/german-canadian-studies

Government of Canada. "Census of Canada, 1911." Library and Archives Canada, accessed May 21, 2019, https://www.bac-lac.gc.ca/eng/census/1911/Pages/about-census.aspx

"History - The Aud", accessed October 18, 2015, https://www.theaud.ca/en/contact-us/history.aspx

"History & Milestones - Toyota Motor Manufacturing Canada Inc.", accessed November 14, 2015, https://tmmc.ca/en/toyota-manufacturing-plants/

"History of Conrad Grebel | Conrad Grebel University College", accessed October 10, 2015, https://uwaterloo.ca/grebel/about-conrad-grebel/history-conrad-grebel

"History of the Gottscheers", Alpine Club, accessed December 8, 2015, https://alpineclub.ca/our-story/history-of-the-gottscheers/

"History", Transylvania Club, accessed December 8, 2015, https://transylvaniaclub.com/about/history/

"Home", German-Canadian Business & Professional Association, accessed December 8, 2015, https://www.germancanadianbusiness.com/

"Kitchener Meets Its Waterloo", Macleans.ca, accessed May 18, 2015, https://www.macleans.ca/news/canada/kitchener-meets-its-waterloo/

Kitchener Schwaben Club, accessed Oct 8, 2020, https://kitchenerschwabenclub.com/?option=com_content&view=article&id=41&Itemid=58

Ministry of Education. "English as a Second Language and English Literacy Development: A Resource Guide." Government of Ontario. 2001. http://www.edu.gov.on.ca/eng/document/curricul/esl18.pdf. "Oktoberfest - Welcome", accessed October 18, 2015, https://www.oktoberfest.ca

"Ontario Academic Credit", accessed Oct 8, 2020, https://en.wikipedia.org/wiki/Ontario_Academic_Credit

"Oral History Project Contributors", Waterloo Centre for German Studies, accessed May 12, 2014, https://uwaterloo.ca/centre-for-german-studies/research-activities/oral-history-project/oral-history-project-contributors

"Oral History Project Info Letter.web - Oral_history_project_info_letter.web_.pdf." accessed January 10, 2016, https://uwaterloo.ca/centre-for-german-studies/research-activities/oral-history-project/participant-information/oral-history-project-information-letter

"Oral History Project", Waterloo Centre for German Studies, accessed December 17, 2015, https://uwaterloo.ca/centre-for-german-studies/research-activities/oral-history-project

"Project Seeks the Untold Stories of German Immigration", Arts, accessed December 17, 2015, https://uwaterloo.ca/arts/news/project-seeks-untold-stories-german-immigration

Region of Waterloo. "2011 Census Bulletin 6: Language." https://www.regionofwaterloo.ca/en/resources/Census/2011_Census_Bulletin_6_Language_singles.pdf

"Research Links Personal and Public Histories of German-Canadians | Waterloo News", accessed January 15, 2016, https://uwaterloo.ca/news/news/research-links-personal-and-public-histories-german

"Sinnspruch", Universität Bremen: Arbeitsgebiet Grundschulpädagogik, accessed September 10, 2015, https://www.grundschulpaedagogik.uni-bremen.de/aktuell/sinnspruch.html

Statistics Canada. "Census of Canada, 1911." Library and Archives Canada, last modified February 28, 2015, https://www.bac-lac.gc.ca/eng/census/1911/Pages/about-census.aspx

"Stats Canada Download of Table A350.xlsx", referenced in "The Pier Goes to War: Halifax's Pier 21 and the Second World War | CMIP 21", n.d., https://www.pier21.ca/blog/steve-schwinghamer/the-pier-goes-to-war-halifax-s-pier-21-and-the-second-world-war

"Stocherkahnrennen", accessed May 21, 2019 https://de.wikipedia.org/wiki/Stocherkahnrennen

"Struwwelpeter", accessed May 18, 2019, https://en.wikipedia.org/wiki/Struwwelpeter

"Table 13.2 Immigrants to Canada, by Country of Last Permanent Residence, 1959/1960 to 2009/2010", accessed November 18, 2015, https://www150.statcan.gc.ca/n1/pub/11-402-x/2011000/chap/imm/tbl/tbl02-eng.htm

"There Are Two Lasting Bequests We Can Give Our Children: Roots and Wings", Quote Investigator: Exploring the Origins of Quotations, accessed September 10, 2015, https://quoteinvestigator.com/2014/08/12/roots-wings/

"Trans-Canada Alliance", Trans-Canada Alliance of German Canadians, accessed December 8, 2015, https://data2.archives.ca/pdf/pdf001/p000000076.pdf

"Transcript Divas Transcription Services Toronto", accessed January 18, 2016, www.transcriptdivas.ca/.
Now called "Transcript Heroes" https://transcriptheroes.ca

"Transcription Guidelines for the Oral History Project", accessed January 12, 2016, https://uwaterloo.ca/centre-for-german-studies/sites/ca.centre-for-german-studies/files/uploads/files/transcription_guidelines_for_the_oral_history_project_final_0.pdf

"Transkription von Interviews u.a. | Günstige Preise", accessed January 18, 2016, http://www.transkribisch.de/cgi-bin/transkribisch/index.html

"Wahl.pdf", 515, accessed October 10, 2015, https://www.cchahistory.ca/journal/CCHA1983-84/Wahl.pdf

"Welcome", Oktoberfest, accessed December 8, 2015, https://www.oktoberfest.ca/#welcome

"Wilfrid Laurier University - The Canadian Encyclopedia", accessed October 11, 2015, https://www.thecanadianencyclopedia.ca/en/article/wilfrid-laurier-university/

"Wolf Dog", accessed Oct 8, 2020, https://www.imdb.com/title/tt0052401/

"Wörterbuch Siebenbürgisch-Deutsch." Kirchberg in Siebenbürgen, 2015, https://kirchberg-siebenbuergen.de.tl/W.oe.rterbuch-siebenbuergisch-_-deutsch.htm

Maple leaves.
Artist: Walther Otto Müller, botanist.
In Otto Wilhelm Thomé: *Flora von Deutschland, Österreich und der Schweiz* (1885). http://www.biolib.de